CORNELL JOURNAL OF ARCHITECTURE

CORNELL JOURNAL OF ARCHITECTURE

ISSUE 12

AFTER

BECOMING AFTER

I imagine students sitting around the table brainstorming a title for the next *Journal*. Imagining an emergence from the global pandemic, a sense of optimism is in the air. Perhaps even a certain euphoria sets in? Coming off of Journal 11's *Fear*, I'm pretty sure the question hanging in the air was: what possibly comes *after Fear*?

After (fear) thus seems an inevitable choice. Unlike 'fear,' which is a thing in and of itself, 'after' is almost always referencing something else, either an event that comes after *something*, or a slightly diminished version of the original, again dependent on the *something*.

'After' is most often used as a prefix (as in afterlife, afterward, afterthought, afternoon, afterbirth, afterglow, aftershock, aftershave, after-party, after-school, after-effect, after-the-fact, after all, after hours, "after you"). Thus, being after something requires a familiarity with that something. For what is afterlife without life? In other words, after is always *relational*—in other words the 'before' becomes the context for the 'after.'

ANDREA SIMITCH

STEPHEN H. WEISS PRESIDENTIAL FELLOW; PROFESSOR & CHAIR, DEPARTMENT OF ARCHITECTURE; B. ARCH. 1979

So today, we are in the process of—one hopes—arriving after *the pandemic*. Might we also be in the process of becoming after *racism*? And after *injustice*? And after *inequality*? And after *environmental degradation*? To do so, perhaps our discipline must hold up a mirror so that the context of these 'afters' is genuinely understood. Thus, the question we face within the academy is how might architectural education engage these 'arriving at after' conversations in meaningful ways? We must develop the tools for deeply engaging a multiplicity of voices and histories, a commitment to culturally, environmentally, and materially sustainable practices, and the right of all to a beautiful and healthy environment.

While indeed challenging, therein resides an optimism that is exhilarating. For what can be more magical than imagining an 'after' with all of its possibilities? The humanity we discovered, the generosity we discovered, and the courage we discovered during this period of global upheaval makes it self-evident that we cannot act alone. We build strength in collaboration.

I challenge us all to imagine that 'after'—but not to just imagine: to act. For it is only through acts of architecture that architecture can begin to heal, to effect change, and to truly embrace the optimism of the 'after.'

AN AFTER WORD

The questions one might most reasonably ask of this Journal are, "After what?" and "After, what?" If the first question asks for a diagnosis, the second, with its understated caesura, pleads for a remedy.

Neither comes easily. This is especially the case in architecture, where the diagnosis of a situation depends on an exhaustive analysis of all relevant contexts (always difficult, if not impossible) and the sensation of a palpable conclusion; and the remedy may depend on tools that are borrowed, invented, improvised, anticipated, or fantasized. The architect must necessarily always "urge the mind to aftersight and foresight," as the Dantesque stranger in T.S. Eliot's "Little Gidding" counsels, because:

> ***. . . Last season's fruit is eaten***
> ***And the fullfed beast shall kick***
> ***the empty pail.***
> ***For last year's words belong to***
> ***last year's language***
> ***And next year's words await***
> ***another voice.***

VAL WARKE

EDITOR-IN-CHIEF
(B.ARCH. 1977)

The authors included in this volume are seeking these other voices. There are essays that ask, "How had architecture been able to move forward in the past?" and others that ask "How should architecture proceed now, as we move further into the third decade of the twenty-first century?" Some suggest where we might find ourselves if voices are ignored. Some attempt to give voice to voices too frequently unheard. And some discover the resonance in echoes.

Eliot began writing "Little Gidding," one of his last poems and the conclusion of his Four Quartets, in the early 1940s during the devastations of the air-raids on Great Britain. In attempting to make some sense of these events and their aftermath (as well as somewhat of an atonement for some of his younger self's politics), Eliot came to realize the precarious reciprocities implicit in 'after.'

We shall not cease from exploration
And the end of all our exploring
Will be to arrive where we started
And know the place for the first time.

One tends to see an afterward as both the conclusion to a completed event and the commencement of a fresh chapter. But such distinctions are rarely so tidy.

EMERGING AFTER

This twelfth installment of the *Journal* speculates on what comes *after*. It confronts our present situation and its connected past, begging us to question where we're headed. We humans tend to find ourselves constantly grasping for an *after*, even as we face futures with a certain degree of apprehension. *After* exists at different scales of time and context. There's after an instant, after a day, after an era. Each after is both an end and a beginning. Every after has a before.

For most individuals, the implications of after can give rise to feelings of fear and unease, even denial, since they mean abandoning the comfort one imagines in the present for the unfamiliarity of what awaits us. However, it seems that architects, by nature a forward-looking group, have been predisposed to evaluate current conditions in anticipation of imminent contingencies. The expectation of an *after* is a given within our design discipline and the promise of a brighter future catalyzes change, creativity, and innovation.

Stretching from the formation of the earth 4.5 billion years ago (Mehra, p.014**), to medieval**

TODD
PETRIE

(B. ARCH. 2020)

monasteries (van Assche, p.044)**, to 1970s Los Angeles** (Büttner Dias, p.238)**, to contemporary events, and finally to a post-pandemic, post-capitalist society** (Jeyifous, p.352)**, the articles in this issue explore the relationship of architecture with the inevitable passage of time. Anticipating a looming after, they provoke us to question our behavior in the face of catastrophe** (Chen, p.134)**, reexamine the architect's practice in the wake of BLM** (Better Barraza, Piermarini, p.094)**, posit how our structures respond to a warmer planet** (Krause, p.300)**, and urge us to consider the built environment's inherent role in material and waste cycles** (Heisel, p.058)**. The many *afters* they depict demonstrate how our past informs our present, and history gives form and meaning to what it precedes.**

***After* is a portal to a future: the possibility to reimagine and reshape our cities and buildings, to proactively respond to the growing needs of a changing world. As architects facing uncertain ecological, social, and political futures, we're obliged to project our work into a hereafter that can be only loosely understood. The articles in this twelfth volume hope that, in the aftermath, the architecture that emerges bears some resemblance to our own best aspirations.**

& THE EDITORS

CONTENTS

014

(-4.5B–2.5B)

AKSHAY
MEHRA

ON GEOLOGIC TIME AND ARCHITECTURE

When James Hutton, a founding member of the field of Geology, first laid eyes on Siccar Point in the North Sea in 1788, he was "gleeful."[1] In the juxtaposition between vertical micaceous schist and horizontal sedimentary rocks, Hutton saw a series of processes that must have taken much longer than the biblically prescribed length of 6000 years to occur. Writing about that moment, John Playfair, one of Hutton's companions, stated, "The mind seemed to grow giddy by looking so far into the abyss of time."[2]

Today, we know that the most ancient objects found on Earth are 4.375 billion years old.[3] We also know that our planet is slightly older than those dateable remnants, as isotope geochemistry on meteorites has enabled researchers to determine that Earth formed roughly 4.55 billion years ago. Looking to the future, we can be certain that our sun will one day begin to fade, and 1.75 to 3.25 billion years from now, Earth will become completely uninhabitable.[4]

How can we even begin to understand what those numbers mean? Consider, for a moment, that the average life expectancy of a human being in 2020 is approximately 72.6 years. From the perspective of an individual, a great deal can happen in 72.6 years. If, for example, one was born in 1900, by their death in 1973 they would have lived through, among other events: two world wars, the rise and fall of colonial empires, the advent of flight, the invention of computer science, and the realization of space travel. And yet, those 72.6 years represent a mere 0.000001604% of Earth's history. Put another way, if all elapsed time on Earth was represented by a 24-hour day, the average human life would be 1.386 milliseconds long—far shorter than the proverbial blink of an eye.

Clearly, applying a moniker of *deep time*[5] to Earth's history is appropriate. *Deepness* explains how, though moving centimeters a year, continents can subduct into Earth's depths or collide and form large mountain ranges. It enables the chemical and physical

All images by Akshay Mehra. This page: Columns made of basalt. (Isle of Staffa, Scotland, May 2018.)

This page: One billion years ago, the features in these rocks incrementally formed on the ocean floor. Mediated by microbes, each lamination precipitated out of seawater, thereby creating a brand-new antecedent topography for the layer to come. Such microbial constructions—the remains of which, on Earth, stretch back 3.5 billion years ago—are proto-architecture. (Great Slave Lake, Northwest Territories, Canada, August 2019.)

processes that, over time, turn rock into soil and erode even the largest forms down to nothing. Deepness elucidates the fact that sediments, accumulating at rates of millimeters per year, can form packages that are kilometers-thick and record the day-to-day histories of several million years. Deepness means that human beings are not Earth's first architects and/or engineers, and likely not its last. Deep time delivers unending evolution, continually transforming the landscapes, organisms, and even the atmosphere, of our planet.

Crucially, on certain temporal and spatial scales, the processes of deep time are imperceptible, a fact which enables people to experience landforms as somewhat static. While mountains are actively wearing down and earthquakes, landslides, and sinkholes are a lived reality for many, all of us will be long gone before tectonics fundamentally reorganize the surfaces of our planet.[6] It is true that humanity's takeover of Earth—the unintended effects of which can be seen in melting glaciers and the presence of plastic in the deepest trenches of the world's oceans—have quickened certain expressions of deep time.[7] The fact remains, however, that we wake up each day in a world that largely hides its ever-changing nature.

This hidden nature can keep from us an inescapable truth: on long enough timescales, nothing is permanent.[8] From the moment of creation, anything built begins to undergo transformation.[9] Though impermanence is universal, ephemerality is unevenly applied. Differential preservation means that it is possible to find finely detailed fossilized remains of 3.5-billion-year-old microbial constructions while other, much more recent structures have all but crumbled away.[10]

Ultimately, sans a *deus ex machina* event, Earth processes will march forward regardless of what preservative or destructive actions humans may take. Even if human beings make Earth completely inhospitable for life, such as Mars appears to be, our planet will still exist, different but whole. Likely, landforms will continue to be raised and then eroded away, ice sheets will go on growing and shrinking, and life may even begin to proliferate once again.[11] Having geologic time to contend with, Earth is indifferent to our behaviors. In effect, humanity's actions are solely to the benefit, or detriment, of ourselves.

These realities raise an important question: How can and/or should architecture engage with notions of deepness? In answering, one must note that the discipline regularly interfaces with deep time and its expressions, though often in conflicting ways. It embraces the seemingly static nature of landforms, building on and shaping earth with a confidence borne from the idea that the ground will always be as it is now. Simultaneously, architecture acknowledges and exploits impermanence by harvesting natural resources and turning them into building materials, usually without any context for an object's long history. What the discipline does not often do is incorporate transformation—the sort of unavoidable physical changes that occur on the scale of geologic time—into its visions for the built environment.[12] Which is all to say that the act of "interfacing" is not always the same thing as "engaging."

True engagement with deep time comes with inherent challenges. First, there is the issue of scale: how can one conceive of values on the order of one million or one billion when numbers of such magnitude are never encountered in daily life? And, supposing that it becomes second nature to think about time as being "deep," how does one grapple with the fact that many Earth processes are both temporally and spatially imperceptible? Finally, there is the problem of impermanence, which certainly can invite a sense of despair. After all, if everything built will one day rejoin Earth, what is the point of making anything last?

There are no easy answers to be found in these questions. That said, there exist at least two parallel paths for architecture to engage with deep time in a constructive manner.[13] These paths can be broadly thought of as "stewardship" and "geologic incorporation." The first concerns itself with sustainability, while the second considers how to fold natural processes into the built environment. Admittedly, neither is a particularly novel strategy, but both are still worth contemplating using the lens of deep time.

The path of stewardship begins with the dual considerations that everything will one day return to the earth and that it is in humanity's best interests to build with sustainability in mind. The realities of deep time ensure the former consideration, as physical processes such as the weathering of rock, movement of tectonic plates, and subduction of crust guarantee that very little remains undisturbed on Earth's surface. Everything that is built will one day be incorporated into geologic workings, with the possibility of reappearing (in a best-case scenario) as disjointed blocks floating in a matrix of rock, much like the remnants of ancient coral reefs. In a reality where everything will eventually be recycled—negating our very worst mistakes, even if we are not around to see the mitigation—it is our interests in self-preservation and harm reduction that beg the latter conceit.

Stewardship is conscious of the fact that we are at the mercy of the health of a world whose functions operate on the scale of deep time. Although we can artificially speed up and/or regulate certain geologic processes, such as in the production of artificial diamonds or the creation of flooding control in the Netherlands, our abilities to do so are in no way all-encompassing. Every time we dredge sand for concrete or use granite as cladding, we are depleting resources whose replenishment will require us to wait for quite some time.[14] To be a steward is to be deliberate about how a construction is sourced, utilized, and, perhaps most importantly, recycled and/or reused, with the express goal of making everything last for as long as is possible. As such, stewardship means critically reevaluating architectural priorities.

If stewardship involves our own preservation, geologic incorporation seeks to make the constant state of imperceptible flux on Earth a part of design thinking.

This page: Though impermanence is ensured, the rock record has a way of preserving the fine details of events that may have taken anywhere from seconds to days to occur. (Great Slave Lake, Northwest Territories, Canada, August 2019.) **Next spread:** Shows mm-scale layers of stromatolites, microbially mediated constructions that grew incrementally, layer by layer over the course of months to years. (Great Slave Lake, Northwest Territories, Canada, August 2019.)

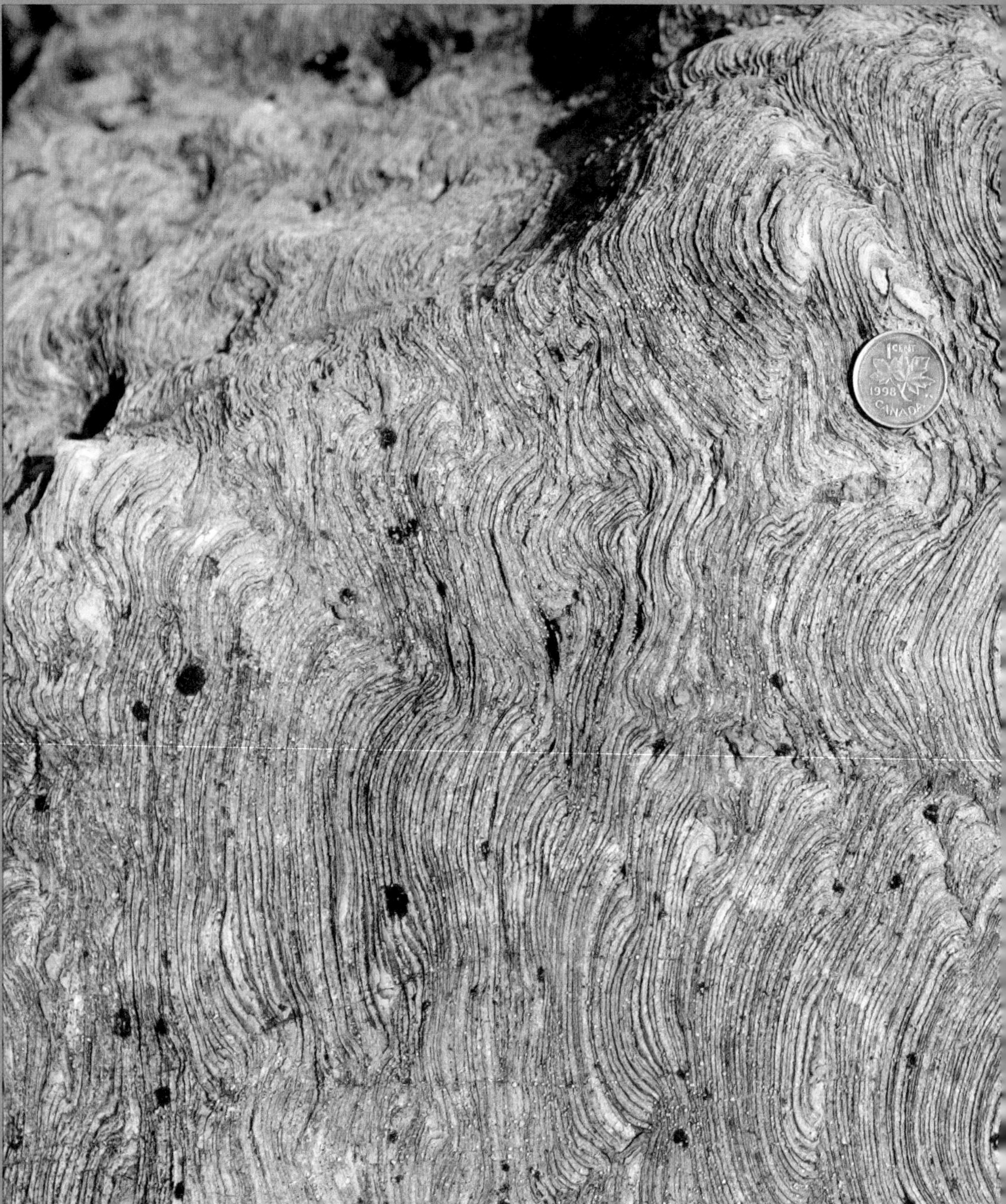
1 CENT
1998
CANADA

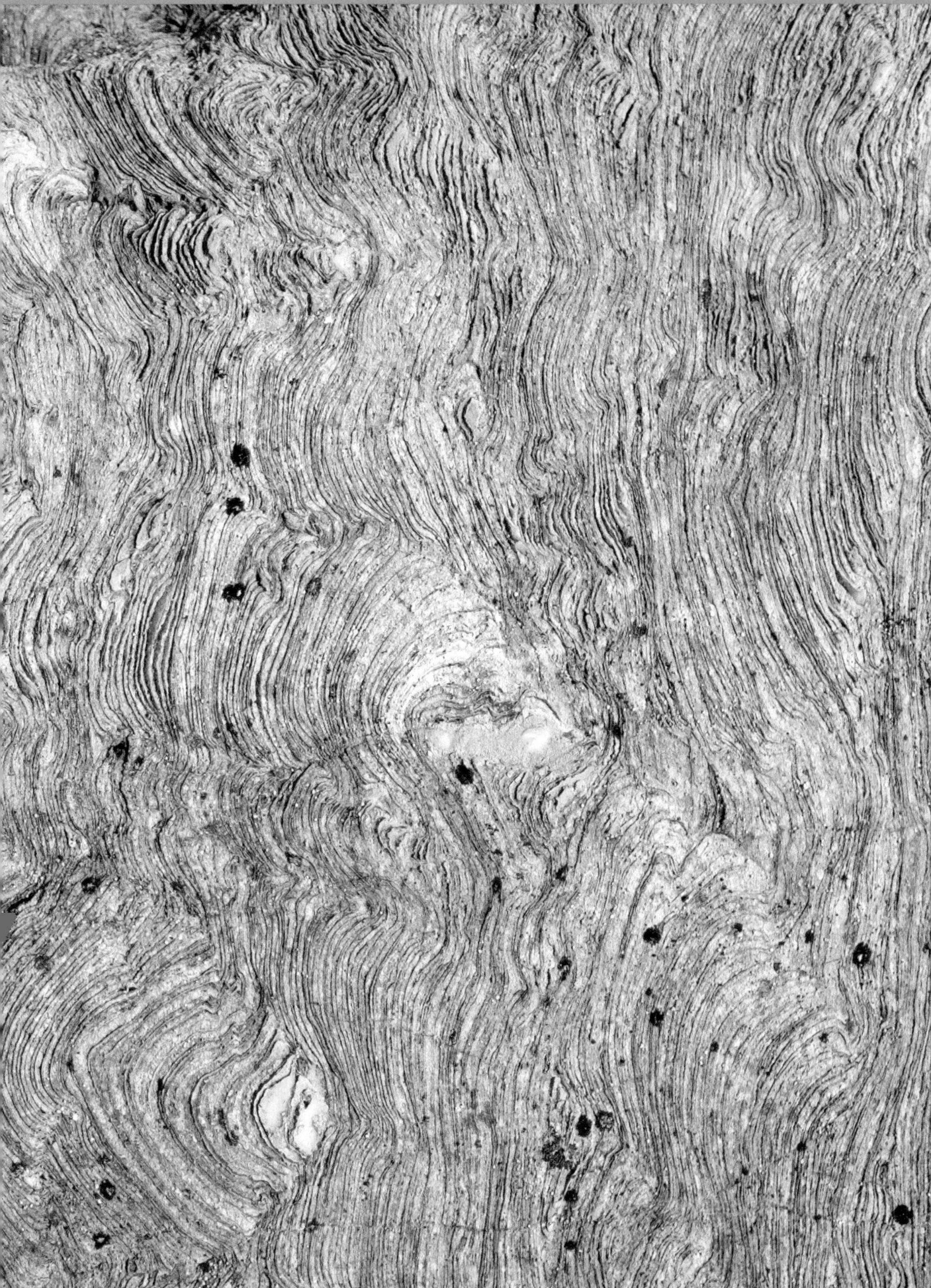

Such thinking cannot be limited to concepts of materiality, siting, and/or analogies—considerations which architecture has embraced since the very advent of the discipline of Geology.[15] Instead, geologic incorporation should seek to make long-term aspects of deep time an integral part of how a construction is conceived, designed, built, and eventually expected to deteriorate. To that end, geologic phenomenon—the anastomosing of rivers, the rise (or fall) of sea level, the rebound of recently deglaciated land, the thinning of crust as it is pulled apart, the collision and deformation of rocks as they are smashed together, and even the relatively staid constant accumulation of sediment in basins, to name a few—might be turned into the central foci of design, as opposed to technical challenges or, arguably worse, aesthetic influences. When combined with stewardship, geologic incorporation may enable the production of deep time constructions, whose transmutations can only be dreamt of by those designing and/or building them. In this way, architecture can actively engage with what Playfair called the "abyss of time" and what we should know as a rich, dynamic physical reality rife with possibility.

This page: Depicts a "breccia," a rock comprised of clasts that were ripped up and redeposited, perhaps by a storm event. (Zebra River Canyon, Namibia, July 2014.) Opposite: This layer-cake of rocks—roughly 200 or so meters tall—covers millions of years of time and includes some of Earth's earliest putative metazoan fossils. Deep time is vast, but its recording can be surprisingly compact. (Zebra River Canyon, Namibia, July 2014.)

1 Jack Repcheck, *The Man Who Found Time: James Hutton and the Discovery of the Earth's Antiquity* (Cambridge, MA: Perseus, 2003). See also James Hutton, "X. Theory of the Earth; or an Investigation of the Laws observable in the Composition, Dissolution, and Restoration of Land upon the Globe," *Earth and Environmental Science Transactions of The Royal Society of Edinburgh* 1, no. 2 (1788): 209–304.

2 Ibid.

3 These objects are crystals of a hardy mineral known as zircon (chemical formula: $ZrSO_4$). Each zircon crystal contains minute amounts of Uranium (U) and its daughter product Lead (Pb). By knowing something about how fast U decays—and assuming that all Pb in an individual zircon grain is the result of U decaying to Pb—scientists can calculate an age for each crystal. Timekeeping has existed on Earth from its very origin.

4 Andrew J. Rushby, Mark W. Claire, Hugh Osborn, and Andrew J. Watson, "Habitable zone lifetimes of exoplanets around main sequence stars," *Astrobiology* 13, no. 9 (2013): 833–849.

5 A term first coined by the writer John McPhee in his book *Basin and Range*.

6 Geoff Manaugh, "Move Over, San Andreas: There's an Ominous New Fault in Town," *Wired*, April 10, 2019, https://www.wired.com/story/walker-lane-move-over-san-andreas-fault/.

7 For example, anthropogenic climate change and the rising oceans.

8 In his 2016 film *Into the Inferno*, Werner Herzog stands on the rim of the volcano Erebus and muses, "It's good that they [volcanoes] are there. And the soil we are walking upon…is not permanent. There is no permanence to what we are doing, no permanence to the efforts of human being, no permanence to art, no permanence to science…"

9 On May 20, 2019, the kilogram was defined in terms of fundamental natural constants. Before that (and since 1889), the definition of "one kilogram" referred to a physical object: A platinum-iridium cylinder, 39 mm in diameter, known as the International Prototype of the Kilogram (IPK). See Ian M. Mills, Peter J. Mohr, Terry J. Quinn, Barry N. Taylor, and Edwin R. Williams, "Redefinition of the kilogram: a decision whose time has come," *Metrologia* 42, no. 2 (2005): 71. The validity of the standard was verified by periodically comparing the IPK (held in the International Bureau of Weights and Measures [BIPM] in Saint-Cloud, France) to its copies (several stored in the BIPM and others held by various countries). Though stored in climate-controlled rooms and handled with the utmost care, over time, the masses of the different copies began to diverge. It turns out that inert pieces of metal, even those stored under multiple nested bell jars, are anything but. For example, the cylinders gained mass by adsorption of atmospheric contaminants (though even after correcting for this problem, the apparent divergence in mass persisted). On Earth, *everything undergoes change.*

10 That said, humanity is very good at affecting preservation, especially with respect to objects of our own creation. Whether it be protecting, re-purposing, recycling or outright destroying, human beings do have some agency to dictate what exists and for how long.

11 Several times in its history, Earth's oceans have been covered from pole to pole in ice. Not only did organisms survive through these so-called "Snowballs," but they diversified, laying the groundwork for all modern life.

12 Which is not to say that no architects or architectural theorists are concerned with transformation that occurs over very long timescales. Leon Alberti, for example, was very concerned about "physical deterioration." See Laurie Schneider, "Leon Battista Alberti: Some biographical implications of the winged eye," *The Art Bulletin* 72, no. 2 (1990): 261–270.

13 The number of paths is not exhaustive. The reader is invited to consider what other sorts of frameworks may exist (e.g., in this essay, little has been said about biology, chemistry, evolution, etc., all of which may have their own deep time implications and relationships with architecture).

14 The world is already facing a shortage of sand because of increased rates of construction. See Vince Beiser, "Why the World Is Running out of Sand," *BBC Future*, November 17, 2019, https://www.bbc.com/future/article/20191108-why-the-world-is-running-out-of-sand. As time passes, it is likely that the depletion of "deep time resources" will force a rethinking of what materials are used in building and how those materials are sourced and valued.

15 See, for example, Edward John Gillin, "Stones of Science: Charles Harriot Smith and the Importance of Geology in Architecture, 1834–64." *Architectural History* 59 (2016): 281–310.

JOSÉ
IBARRA

ARCHITECTURE AFTER THE END: A CALL FOR GEOEMPATHY

024

(-1.8B—A)

Per Max Ernst's *Europe After the Rain II*,[1] biological and geological matter were no longer independent, but instead enmeshed with and indistinguishable from one another. His new Europe is made of distinct parts that are, nonetheless, inextricably connected. The painting shows a series of interconnected landforms composed of a mixture of bones, rocks, tissue, vegetation, and other matter. Several human-like figures seem to have merged with non-human parts, producing new creatures and relationships that might function more like a rhizomatic[2] network than a series of independent beings. These enmeshed beings suggest the establishment of a new form of collective knowledge integrated with the very land that the beings occupy. Meanwhile, a blue and undisturbed sky, which would not seem out of place in any other landscape painting, perhaps serves to emphasize how enmeshed every other entity is with the ground itself. While the atmosphere lies ambivalent and still, the ground is animated and full of modes of existence.

The Anthropocene keeps the human (*Anthropos*) at the forefront while simultaneously demanding an overcoming of that same human and an enmeshing with our larger ecological and geological systems.[3] Ernst's bird-headed figure offers a way to consider what this entanglement might look like. This creature constitutes one of the most identifiable parts in the painting. It appears to have human legs, a bird head, and a mixed torso that blends seamlessly with its own upper and lower extremities, as well as with the landscape. Behind this figure, a thin spear-like object grows and thins out again, only to connect with another extremity in the landscape. That the figure and their spear appear as a type of liminal growth seems on par with post-apocalyptic action. Healing an ecosystem necessitates a process of becoming with the ecosystem itself. Today, the aftermath of the end also involves the dissolution of the edge dividing Life and Nonlife, the biological and the geological.

The world ended in 1784, says Timothy Morton, "when James Watt patented the steam engine" and humanity turned into "a geophysical force on a planetary scale."[4] On its own, the concept of the end seems definitive and inflexible. However, an "end" is defined as an area that lies at the boundary of something, an extreme, and a turn of events.[5] These definitions imply more than a conclusion: they suggest an aftermath, or a new thing to come after another. This moment *after* can be generative and productive, prompting a rethinking and restructuring of anything which was once known. For Morton, the end of the world is linked to *hyperobjects*,[6] which are things, beings, and concepts that are massively distributed in time and space, and which transcend specificity. This essay proposes that architecture in the Anthropocene respond to massive scales and temporalities, remodeling itself after geological processes and considering living and nonliving beings on our planet (rocks, plants, animals, and people) to be a hyperobject. The essay makes a call for *geoempathy*, a new term used to describe the design of processes, rather than forms, through which architecture can extend for centuries and its constituents can become more than human.

Architecture has, for too long, modeled itself after biological beings and their behavior,[7] which has narrowed the discipline and centered its efforts on the image of "man." This has contributed to an exclusionary outlook that has marginalized people from conversations that have shaped the world, literally and figuratively. It is no surprise that animals, plants, grounds, and atmospheres have never stood a chance in joining these conversations either. Just like living beings, buildings have a lifespan and a time of expiration. What is perhaps surprising is that, as technology and capital advance at unprecedented rates, humans live longer and buildings die faster and sooner. Meanwhile, the ecological disaster to which this wasteful practice has contributed also harms to a greater extent those which it has excluded.

In 2011, several architects looked at geology in an attempt to slow the field down and to substitute the vertical for the horizontal.[8] Landform Building[9] arose as a series of provocations that looked at architecture, landscape, and urbanism in order to synthesize buildings with nature by swapping the biological for the geological.[10] However, the promise of this turn to landscape has been limited by a predominant focus on artifice and form. Even when buildings began to perform more like landscape (as was the case with FOA's Yokohama Port Terminal or Weiss/Manfredi's Olympic Sculpture

Previous spread: Max Ernst, *Europe After the Rain II*, 1940–1942, oil on canvas.

Park), a clear disconnect still existed between the architecture's exploitation of site, its degree of completion, and its ability to endure (or change) through time. As Esther Choi points out, "the crux of the problem not only with 'green architecture,' but the cognitive dissonance of architecture's sustainability discourse as a whole: sustainability is interested, by definition, in maintaining the status quo."[11]

Today, architecture requires large systemic changes to stay relevant in a changing world. Arguing for balance, *geoempathy* can help the field mend its human and non-human transgressions. This new term encompasses geontological empathy, a process through which all Life and Nonlife become constituents in the design of the world. In *Geontologies: A Requiem to Late Liberalism*, Elizabeth Povinelli highlights the biontological enclosures of existence and reminds the reader that from a geological stance, planet Earth began without Life. In other words, all sorts of Life inherited a world animated and produced by Nonlife.[12] Povinelli seeks a new model of shared governance in the world between Life and Nonlife. The anthropologist uses the term "geontology"—which contrasts *geos*, or Nonlife, with *ontology*, or being—to scrutinize the power of and over Nonlife beings. She explains that "Nonlife is affect without intention and is affected without the intentional agency to affect." This is to say that Nonlife does not fail, die, or cease to be because it does not have an intention toward itself. Instead, Nonlife is affected by forces to which it can only respond with inertia.[13] Entangled into this understanding of Life and Nonlife is Robert Vischer's theory of feeling into objects, which he called aesthetic sympathy or *empathy*. For Vischer, objects bridged a gap between "the perception of exterior limits to a form [which] can combine in some obscure way with the sensation of [one's] own physical boundaries."[14]

In this sense, *geoempathy* is a design of process, which yields new objects that respond to and interact with other things in the world. This mode of designing does not quite exist yet, but it shares many of the concerns of ecological work in architecture for which the well-being of other organisms is equated against an object. A fundamental difference that geoempathy offers is embedding obsolescence into architecture, which in turn welcomes changes in the form, function, performance, and users of the very objects that arise from this process. Seen in this light, architects could plan their buildings to last for hundreds, if not thousands, of years by engaging in an inclusionary process where there is power in difference. This temporal change becomes an imperative as we welcome other beings to participate in the design of our shared planet.

If biological beings and processes have shaped our discipline, an important shift for geoempathy is to use geological knowledge to guide the work of our generation. Geological processes work in a continuum, involving the reuse and recycle of the same geological matter that concocts them, along with other accumulated substances. Rocks, for instance, have the capacity to self-organize. They came into existence at some point, when the gaseous Earth began to cool down and condense into hard matter.[15] As perhaps the earliest form of power and culture in the universe, rocks have the ability to develop and reconstruct territories. They have done so both during the deep geological history of the Earth, when slow and gradual shifts formed mountain ranges and oceans, and during the Anthropocene, when movements are caused by human forces. This is to say that geological change is both very slow and very drastic: it is an act of power that reorganizes Life and Nonlife through a gradual process of transformation.

An early example of this is the Vishnu schist, which is the oldest exposure of Precambrian rocks in the Grand Canyon system. This 12,000 ft. thick stretch of crystalline basement rocks has seen innumerable formal, programmatic, and performative configurations throughout its long history of folding and metamorphism. First, millenia-old gases solidified and created mountain ranges in the region, after which the rock formations eroded until reaching an almost perfectly level surface. This peneplain was followed by a major subsidence event in which the area was intermittently covered by an inland sea.

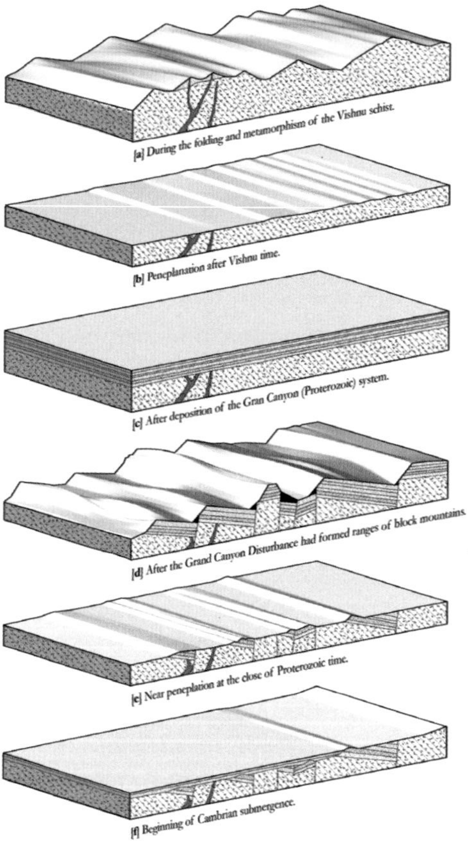

Six stages in the Precambrian history of the Grand Canyon Region, drawing after Schuchert and Dunbar's history of the Grand Canyon region in *Outlines of Historical Geology* (New York, NY: John Wiley & Sons, 1941). Drawn by José Ibarra, 2021.

For the next several million years, the region was uplifted, folded, and broken by a fault that created mountains that then eroded.[16] The same geological formation has seen hundreds of different states and has been a medium for hundreds of different forms of existence. Sometimes an ocean, other times a mountain, and today a steep-sided gorge, humanity has only been part of a tiny fraction in a series of events that make up the impressive Grand Canyon.

Consider instead how fixed architecture's intentions tend to be, or how unambiguous architects' disregard for the ground is. Buildings are usually understood first as isolated objects and then as objects on a site, objects with users, and so on. Moving away from architecture's fixed and static formal explorations and thinking through the design of processes can have important consequences in our discipline and practice. However, buildings that encompass multiple configurations, states, users, and uses might not just be an idea for the future, but a necessity for our present survival.

Geological formations are productive for their lessons on process, but they can also be generative in their approach to form-making. Consider the process of fossilization. Fossils are "any recognizable organic remains or impressions of the same, preserved from the geologic past by burial in the Earth's crust."[17] Typically, fossils occur when organic matter hardens into stone, whereby the organisms themselves tend to get dissolved and their absence leaves behind a spatial trail akin to a mold. In these devices, Life and Nonlife share physical space. The establishment of such a relationship in which Nonlife accepts the living as a constituent in its own formal logic and spatial composition is an important departure from the typical process of architectural production. Here, a shared mode of spatial governance arises in which Life and Nonlife coexist in harmony after the end times. In this sense, what earlier or more primordial form of architecture might there exist than this one?

The formal lesson from geology is that form, itself, adapts to and is adapted by its contexts and users; in other words, there is no fossil without fossilization. Importantly, this formal change occurs accidentally: the organisms themselves never intended to be fossilized. Thus, on the one hand, an inherent logic of an organism's shape dictates the formal qualities of a first mold. On the other hand, the disturbances of the ground and other geological processes (such as erosion, crustal movements, and so on) can modify the formal qualities of a negative (the mold) until it becomes unrecognizable from its original positive (the organism). Put differently, the accident does not dictate the fossil, but it does certainly modify it. For this reason, fossilization reminds us of Bernard Tschumi's provocation that there is no architecture without event.[18] Architecture cannot merely be abstracted to its physical manifestation: it comprises form and performance, object and operation, organism and mold.

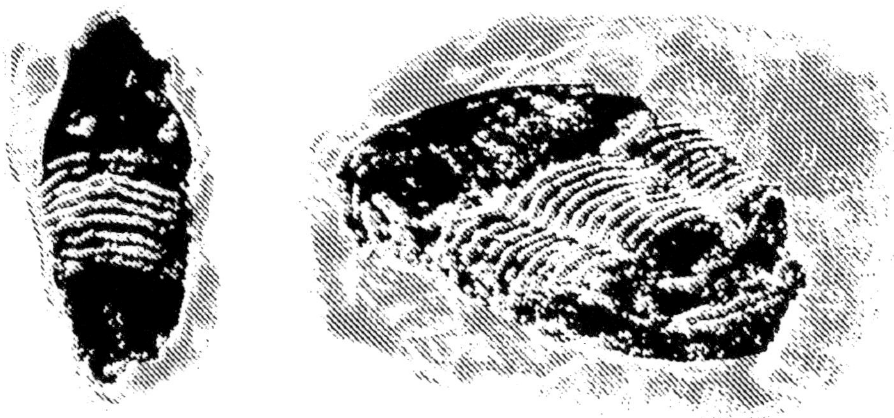

Comparison of a well-preserved trilobite (left) with one deformed by the formation of the late Paleozoic mountains in France (right), drawing after Schuchert and Dunbar's photographs of two fossils held at the Yale Peabody Museum in *Outlines of Historical Geology* (New York, NY: John Wiley & Sons, 1937). Drawn by José Ibarra, 2021.

Although we are used to discussing the accident as a fertile means of artistic production (consider the innumerable possible variations as Ernst's paint traveled the space between one surface and the canvas of his paintings[19]), it took a long time for this to arrive at architecture through Tschumi's theory of the event. Perhaps architects already expect contingency in their work as they deal with volatile clients, contractors, and even material or structural failure. Nonetheless, an event or accident can still renew the heart of architectural practice as uncertainty and unpredictability become embedded in the apparatus that compose it. This could involve the structural and formal makeup of the architecture itself, as well as its possible functions. The question is how can we design (and design for) contingency and volatility? The answer might be to design processes rather than objects.

The London-based duo Cooking Sections have developed an investigation that asks, "how do we eat as humans change climates?"[20] *CLIMAVORE: On Tidal Zones* is a prime example of ecological design making use of process. In this case, the architecture allows multiple biological systems to meet as shared constituents in the design of the planet. The installation is located on the intertidal zone of the Isle of Skye, Scotland, and consists of a "multispecies table" for eating, breathing, cleaning, growing, harvesting, and more. A series of cages, fabricated with steel rods and wires, house oysters, scallops, clams, mussels, seaweeds, and bivalves. During high tide, the table is completely underwater. Its dwellers filter the shore, conducting the remediation of a heavily damaged water ecosystem through respiratory functions. During low tide, the table rises above the water surface and becomes accessible to humans by foot. The structure is then used as a chair and a table. There, humans enjoy eating some of the mollusks and seaweeds that were just submerged, all the while they discuss climate action. In an article addressing this very project, the anthropologist Anna Lowenhaupt Tsing explains, "Eating each other does not destroy the tidal zone, in this conception; instead, it reaffirms the necessity of living together. Eating with becomes a practice to be contrasted to eating against. In the latter, the planetary environment suffers every time we take a bite. In the former, we reaffirm our residence in a common zone of more-than-human liveability. Eating oysters and seaweed immerses our senses in the tidal zone, reminding us where we are and what we have to lose."[21]

Cooking Sections, *CLIMAVORE: On Tidal Zones*, 2017. Photograph by Nick Middleton.

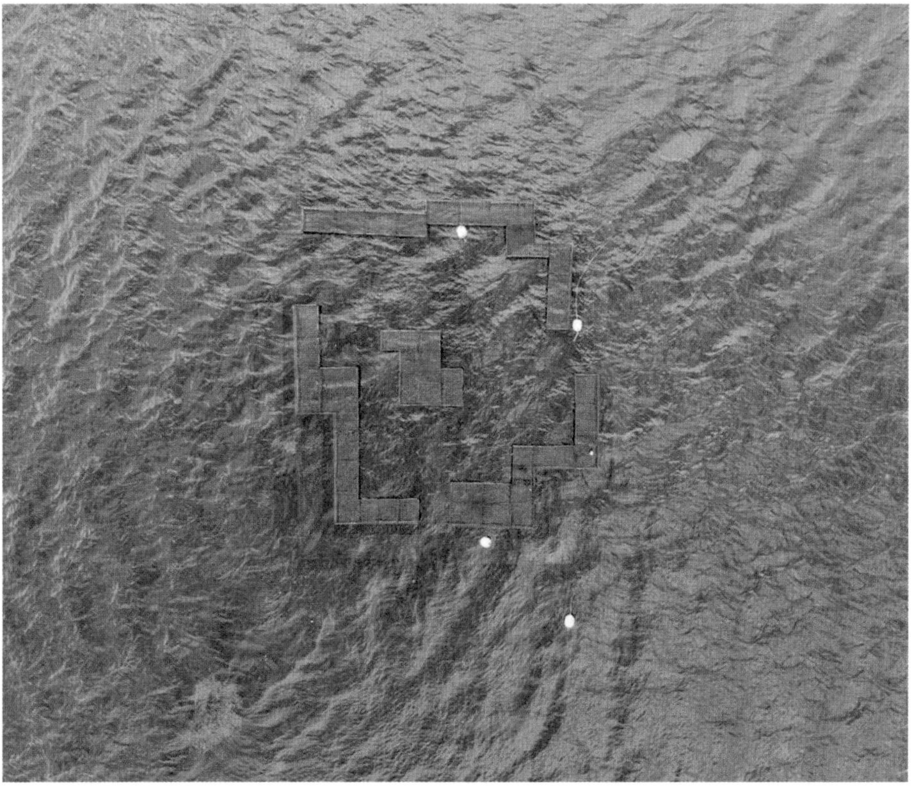

Cooking Sections, *CLIMAVORE: On Tidal Zones*, 2017. Photograph by Nick Middleton.

CLIMAVORE seeks a return to a cleaner, perhaps more primal stage of the Earth as a precedent for a brighter future. The project uses knowledge from science and technology to address an ecological crisis with (and for) organisms. It is clear that *CLIMAVORE* is a small-scale investigation that cannot be retrofitted into many other circumstances, nor can it become a model for cities and buildings. Yet, the lesson from it is twofold: on the one hand, the project learns from existing site processes and capitalizes on the crisis of a damaged water ecosystem to make space, time, and culture. On the other hand, the project addresses its human and non-human constituents, promoting a response that restates our shared duties and responsibilities with and to other forms of existence, which includes other humans. This response is instructive in paving a way for *geoempathy*, where (and when) the ground relationship would inevitably need to change. What involving the ground as another constituent can begin to do is embed a capacity for change in deep time, giving productive obsolescence to buildings that, in turn, exerts climate action.

Our ecological and geological entanglement already exists as an interconnected network in which hierarchical models lie in negligible vacuums. Should our practice's codes and our buildings' boundaries begin to blend with each other and with nature, we might find ourselves in an agile field that operates for humans and non-humans for thousands of years to come. Today, we need not fear the end of the world, for the end has already happened. This moment after requires reflection and prompts us to look beyond the biological boundaries of existence. If geological models tell us anything about ourselves it is that we have been enmeshed with Life and Nonlife since the beginning of time.§

1 The title of this essay pays homage to Anthony Vidler's course, "Architecture After the Rain." Taught at Princeton University and several other architecture schools, it was in this context that I first encountered Ernst's *Europe After the Rain II*. Years later, while thinking about the geological, I remembered this work and saw it in a new light.

2 In *A Thousand Plateaus: Capitalism and Schizophrenia* (Minneapolis, MN: University of Minnesota Press, 1987), Gilles Deleuze and Félix Guattari developed the idea of a rhizome (or rhizomatic network) to describe non-hierarchical modes of representation and knowledge that are multiplicitous. The authors explain, "A rhizome has no beginning or end; it is always in the middle, between things, interbeing, *intermezzo*. The tree is filiation, but the rhizome is alliance, uniquely alliance. The tree imposes the verb "to be," but the fabric of the rhizome is the conjunction, "and... and...and..." (p. 25).

3 Donna Haraway's work was instrumental in my own understanding of the human as the center of a geological epoch that merited that very human's displacement. See Donna J. Haraway, *Staying with the Trouble: Making Kin in the Chthulucene* (Durham, NC: Duke University Press, 2016).

4 Timothy Morton, "A Quake in Being," in *Hyperobjects: Philosophy and Ecology After the End of the World* (Minneapolis, MN: University of Minnesota Press, 2013), p. 7.

5 See definitions 1a, 6, and 7 of the noun "end" in *Merriam-Webster's Dictionary*: https://www.merriam-webster.com/dictionary/end.

6 Aside from offering the term hyperobjects, Morton's text promoted many of the ideas that ignited this research. This includes the understanding of the moment after the end through the notion that the world has, in fact, already ended. See Timothy Morton's *Hyperobjects: Philosophy and Ecology after the End of the World*.

7 Consider Vitruvius's *Ten Books of Architecture*, where the order of buildings is modeled after "a well-shaped man." More recently, other human analogies have included Ernst Neufert's *Man as Measure and Goal*, Frederick Kiesler's *Biotechnique Man*, and Le Corbusier's *Modulor*. New critical understandings of architecture-as-organism have been developed by many after, but two illuminating sources for me are Caroline O'Donnell's *Niche Tactics: Generative Relationships between Architecture and Site* and Beatriz Colomina & Mark Wigley's *are we human?*

8 Stan Allen, "From the Biological to the Geological," in *Landform Building: Architecture's New Terrain*, ed. Stan Allen and Marc McQuade (Baden, Switzerland: Lars Müller Publishers, 2011), p. 23.

9 Landform Building started as a conference held in 2009 at the Princeton University School of Architecture. "The agenda was to learn from the recent past by surveying contemporary production, while at the same time mapping out a new project," says Stan Allen in "From the Biological to the Geological."

10 See note 14.

11 Esther Choi, *Sustainability's Image Problem* (Oslo, Norway: Library Stack, 2019), p. 12.

12 Elizabeth A. Povinelli, "The Three Figures of Geontology," in *Geontologies: A Requiem to Late Liberalism* (Durham, NC: Duke University Press, 2016), p. 11.

13 Ibid., p. 45.

14 Robert Vischer, "On the Optical Sense of Form: A Contribution to Aesthetics" in *Empathy, Form, and Space: Problems in German Aesthetics, 1873–1893*, pp. 98–99.

15 Charles Schuchert and Carl O. Dunbar, "Before the Cambrian," in *Outlines of Historical Geology*, 4th ed. (New York, NY: John Wiley & Sons, 1955), pp. 58–59.

16 Ibid., pp. 63–64.

17 Charles Schuchert and Carl O. Dunbar, "A Living Record of the Dead," in *Outlines of Historical Geology*, 4th ed. (New York, NY: John Wiley & Sons, 1955), p. 39.

18 Bernard Tschumi, "Architecture and Violence," in *Architecture and Disjunction* (Cambridge, MA: MIT Press, 1994), p. 121.

19 Ernst's "Europe After the Rain II" was painted using a technique known as *decalcomania*. This painting technique was adopted by Surrealist artists, including Ernst, to create imagery by chance rather than through conscious control. Decalcomania is the process of transferring designs from prepared paper onto another surface, ranging from sheets of paper, to canvas, glass, and even porcelain.

20 Cooking Sections, "About," Climavore, 2017, https://www.climavore.org/about/.

21 Anna L. Tsing, "Climavore: On Tidal Zones," visibleproject, 2019, https://www.visibleproject.org/blog/text/climavore-on-tidal-zones/.

§ Thanks to Spyros Papapetros for bringing Elizabeth Povinelli and Schuchart & Dunbar's work to my attention, and for the many conversations about the ground—inorganic and organic, inanimate and animate.

ISIDORO
MICHAN-GUINDI

TORRE AVENIDA CHAPULTEPEC

036

(-2000—A)

ARCHITECT: **ISIDORO MICHAN-GUINDI**
ARCHITECT COLLABORATOR: **SINA OZBUDUN**
TEAM: **ENRIQUE GARCÍA, ANGÉLICA SARMIENTO, EMMANUEL DURÁN, LUIS MÉNDEZ**
ENGINEERING: **CESAR MÉNDEZ FRANCO S. C.**
LOCATION: **AV. CHAPULTEPEC NO. 495-500, ROMA NORTE, 06700, CIUDAD DE MÉXICO**

**All beauty, resonance, integrity,
Exist by deprivation or logic
Of strange position.**

—John Ashbery, "Le livre est sur la table," *Some Trees*, 1956.

Torre Avenida Chapultepec **navigates between architectural history and an ongoing movement of re-interpretation to find moments within these narratives in which future possibilities lie.**

The 26-level tower is half building and half creature. The former is constituted by a banal grid embedded within the Mexico City skyline, whereas the latter paradoxically contrasts with the urban streetscape to touch the ground in an idiosyncratic gesture on four legs shaped as inverted pyramids. The building's porousness toward the ground allows the city to flow through, blurring the boundaries between the building and its immediate context. The tower's pigmented concrete exoskeleton serves as both façade and structure.

The form of the tower resonates with the archaic context of Mexican regionalism obsessed with the cliché of its formal archetype: the pre-Hispanic pyramid. Throughout the history of Mexican architecture, there has been a continuous lineage of monumental buildings that reinterpret the pyramid, spanning from the mid-nineteenth century to date. Although the function of the pyramid has shifted, it has remained a constant in Mexican architecture, establishing a formal dialogue between past, present, and future.

Alluding to an inverted pyramid, ***Torre Avenida Chapultepec*** **seeks to join this familiar dialogue with Mexican history and the city's monumental buildings. On the other hand, its specific autonomy enables conversations in unfamiliar territories with architectures still to come.**

All images by Isidoro Michan-Guindi. P.37: Square ornaments and steel human limbs, eyes, ears, mouths, and noses are attached to the lower part of the tower. (*Torre Chapultepec 1:100 Model (detail)*, 2020, pigmented concrete, aggregates, marble dust, acrylic, and silver.) **Previous page:** *Torre Chapultepec 1:100 Model*, 2020, pigmented concrete, aggregates, marble dust, acrylic, and silver. **This page left:** *Torre Chapultepec 1:200 Model and Sun Pyramid*, Teotihuacan, Mexico, March 2019. **Right:** *Torre Chapultepec Transversal Section*, 2020, ink on paper.

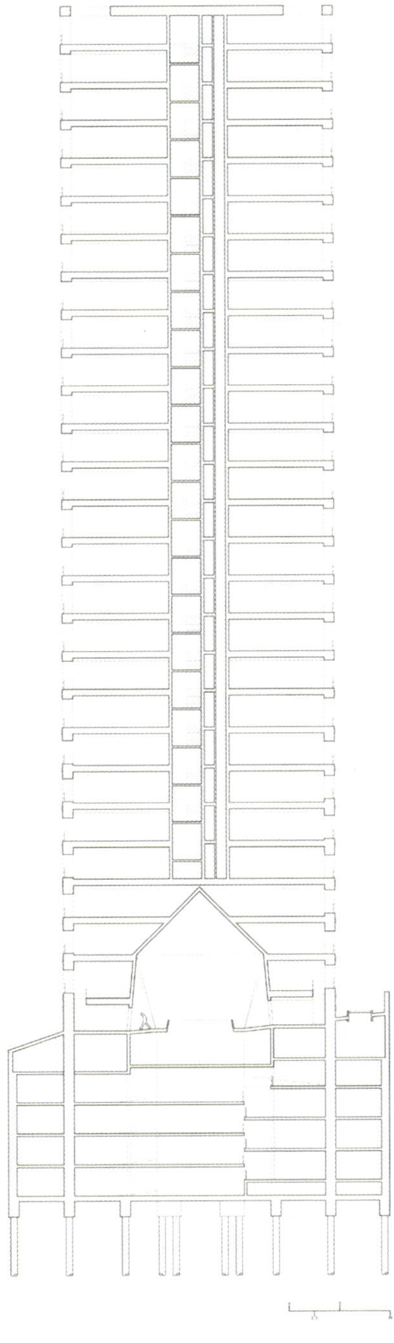

ISIDORO
MICHAN-GUINDI

TORRE AVENIDA
CHAPULTEPEC

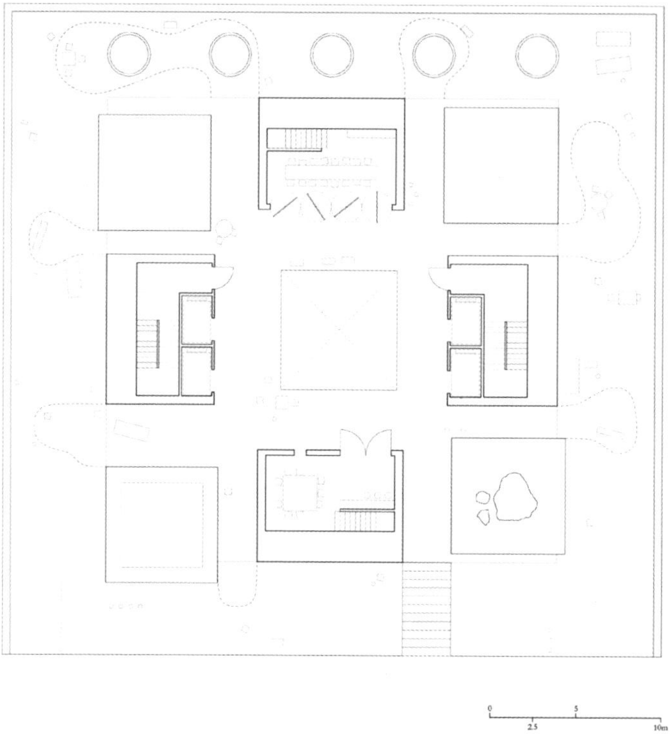

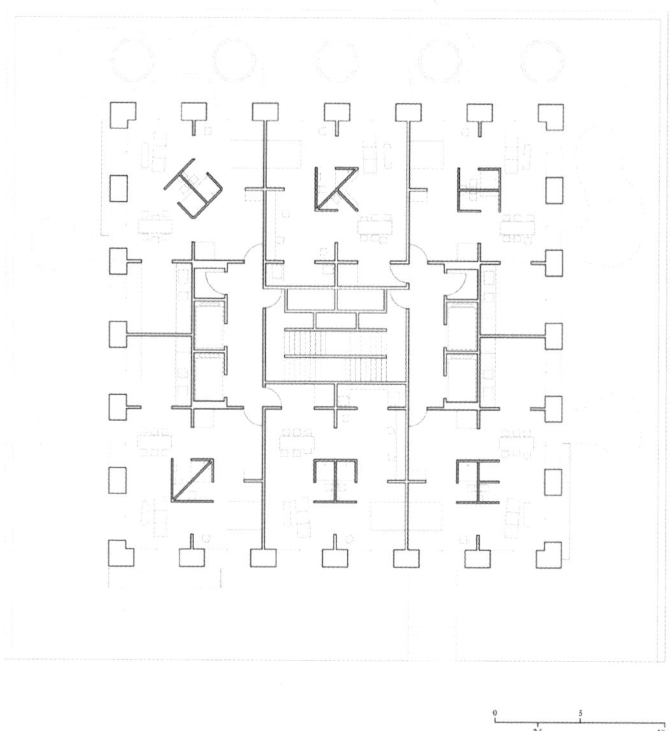

Top: *Torre Chapultepec Ground Floor Plan*, 2020, ink on paper. **Bottom**: *Torre Chapultepec Level 20 Plan*, 2020, ink on paper. **Opposite**: *Torre Chapultepec 1:200 Model and Context*, 2020, pigmented concrete, aggregates, marble dust, acrylic, and MDF.

ISIDORO
MICHAN-GUINDI

TORRE AVENIDA
CHAPULTEPEC

044

(-1000—A)

PETER
VAN ASSCHE

ARCHITECTURE AGAINST TIME

The French philosopher Roland Barthes once wrote: “The essence of an object has something to do with the way it turns into trash.”[1] The society in which we live loves to produce trash, but the essence thereof usually reveals little beauty. The waste that we produce leads to inconvenience, pollution and would appear to be an irrevocable hindrance to us in the long term. The demolition of buildings contributes to the production of waste to a substantial extent.[2] That has not always been the case. Pulling down buildings to produce waste is a method that would have been unthinkable about 150 years ago.

The history of three monasteries shows how buildings survive in times that are—by their very nature—inconceivable. They teach us that the use and reuse of material and space can be part of the essence of a building, even if this goes far beyond the original intention of its architecture. However, since the beginning of modernism, progress has been associated with "clearing up and starting afresh." Consciously or unconsciously, demolition ideologically underpins our idea of the future. Replacing an ideology of demolition with an ideology of transformation reduces the production of waste, but above all offers opportunities for a more interesting architecture with a greater impact.

The story of the first monastery starts in 1906, when the French banker Éduard Aynard buys an old abbey next to the stream of Fontenay. The abbey was seized during the French Revolution and soon after bought by the Montgolfiers, Éduard's in-laws, who turned the complex into a paper mill. Aynard saw something which nobody had seen up until then: the enormous cultural significance of the abbey complex. The poorly maintained buildings he bought stood in sharp contrast to what the Cistercian Abbey of Fontenay had once been: one of the most important religious centers of the Middle Ages. The beautifully restored complex, still owned by the Aynard family today, is now one of the most complete and best-preserved Medieval monasteries in Europe and is a UNESCO World Heritage Site.

The forge at the time of its use as paper mill, *Abbey of Fontenay*, Marmagne, Côte-d'Or, France. Reprinted from Lucien Bégule, *L'abbaye de Fontenay et l'architecture cistercienne* (Lyon: A. Rey, 1912), 80.

The history of the Abbey of Fontenay is a simple example of the fact that buildings can, in the course of their history, be used in a way that goes far beyond the original intent. The architect of the Romanesque church of Fontenay could not have predicted his design would be used as a church, as depot for paper, as well as a museum, nor would he have suspected that his forge, on the other side of the site next to the stream, was ideal for manufacturing paper. History proved that the austerely designed monastery was well suited to use and reuse over the course of eight centuries—and still is.

The second monastery in our story is the spiritual predecessor of the Fontenay Abbey: the Benedict headquarters in the nearby Cluny. The all-powerful Benedictines governed monastic life throughout Europe from here. The abbey must have been of overwhelming grandeur and beauty in the eleventh century but was, like Fontenay, not able to escape the violence of the French Revolution. In 1793, the monastery was destroyed by the revolutionaries. Over the course of twenty years, what was left of the building was disassembled stone by stone and reused as building material in the town. Only a transept is left over from the original church, a pale shadow of what the church once was.

The Abbey of Fontenay appears to have been treated better by history than Cluny Abbey. The reuse of the buildings of Fontenay still provides us with an impressive glimpse into history, even after eight centuries. We can read and admire the craftsmanship of the construction, the precision in terms of the siting of the buildings and the organization of the day-to-day life. We see that the design of space, incidence of light and logistics lends the plain architecture a significance that is in keeping with the specific way of life of the monks. What is left over of Cluny Abbey does not provide us with all these insights, but history also demonstrates meaningful transformation and reuse here. Almost all the buildings that were made in the town of Cluny in the early nineteenth century must contain building material that comes from the abbey. The abbey served as the town's DIY material depot until 1823. The stones from Cluny Abbey were designated for reuse in new houses, schools, and workshops, where people still live, learn, and work today. The Cluny Abbey, although scattered throughout the city, has never stopped being part of the lives of the inhabitants of the little village.

Both Fontenay and Cluny underwent their most dramatic transformation during the French Revolution. The period marks the transition from one social system to the other, in this case: from monarchy to republic. A lot of religious heritage perished or was

Church Interior, Abbey of Fontenay, Marmagne, Côte-d'Or, France. Reprinted from Lucien Bégule, *L'abbaye de Fontenay et l'architecture cistercienne* (Lyon: A. Rey, 1912), 17.

defaced in the maelstrom of violence. The French Revolution is not alone in this; it seems that all major social upheavals must go hand in hand with chaos and violence, destruction, and reconstruction. However, demolition is not only a byproduct of violent revolutions. Twentieth century history teaches us that demolition is an ideologically motivated method for the creation of a better world. About a century ago demolition was not the by-product of the fury of a revolution, but an inevitable necessary and planned part of realizing a new, better world.

The construction of a metro line in Amsterdam demonstrates the almost casual inescapability of this method of demolition before new construction. In 1968, the city decided to construct a metro network to connect the city's districts with each other. The construction of the metro was part of a bigger story: growth of the city was to be facilitated by separating living and working, and ensuring superior accessibility by public transport and car. In addition to the four metro lines, the American traffic engineer David Jokinen devised ten so called "city streets," which would connect the city center, designated as working areas, like radials with the residential areas at the edges of the inner city.[3] To be able to build these traffic arteries, the plan made provisions for the demolition of large sections of the old city. The so-called "suburbanization" came to a halt with the demolition of the Nieuwmarktbuurt, a working-class neighborhood on the border of the Medieval part of the Amsterdam. In 1975, the residents revolted against the demolition of their homes, which were in good condition, in favor of the construction of a metro tunnel. The protest could not prevent the metro tube from being built, but from then on the rest of the plans were scrapped. The compromise meant that a section of the old working-class neighborhood would nevertheless be demolished. The photo from 1975 shows what this meant. It is almost inconceivable in our time that so many good intentions could justify so much demolition fury.

The story of the Amsterdam Nieuwmarkt neighborhood is not, of course, an isolated case. In the wake of the CIAM (*Congres Internationaux d'Architecture Moderne*) ideal of separation of functions, many old city centers were demolished with a great sense of belief and optimism, in order to make way for something newer, better, and more modern. Demolishing buildings was motivated by the conviction that beginning with a blank slate is always better than elaborating on what was already there. Methodical demolition was part of a conceptual model that aimed to help shape a better world as effectively as possible. But in contrast to the reuse of Fontenay and Cluny the ideology of the CIAM did not envisage a reuse-strategy of buildings, material, or function. The demolished houses of the Nieuwmarkt neighborhood became waste. Nobody knows where they are.

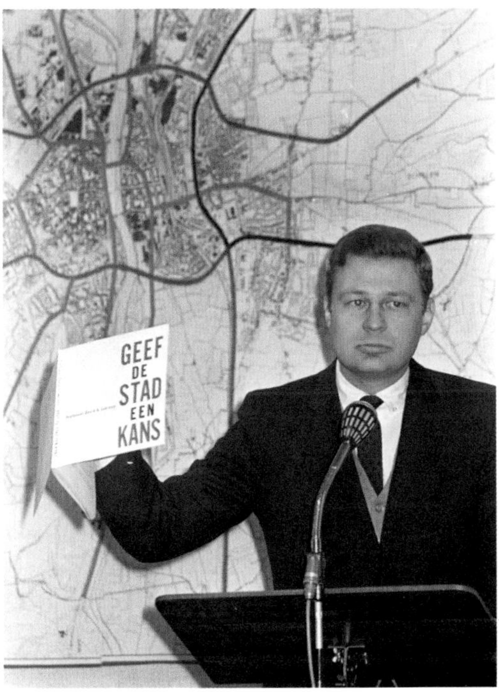

David A. Jokinen, portrait holding his book *Give the City a Chance*, December 7, 1967. Photo by Ron Kroon.

Demolition as prelude to a better world is still deeply ingrained in our system. In 2020, the government of the United Kingdom announced a measure that encourages the demolition of vacant buildings. Office buildings built before 1990 can be demolished without a demolition permit, provided that they are replaced by a new

Demolition of Nieuwmarkt neighborhood to make way for the East Line tunnel of the Amsterdam metro, August 1975. Photo by Gerhard Jaeger. Reprinted from Fred Feddes, *A Millennium Of Amsterdam: Spatial History of a Marvellous City* (Bussum: Uitgeverij Thoth, 2012).

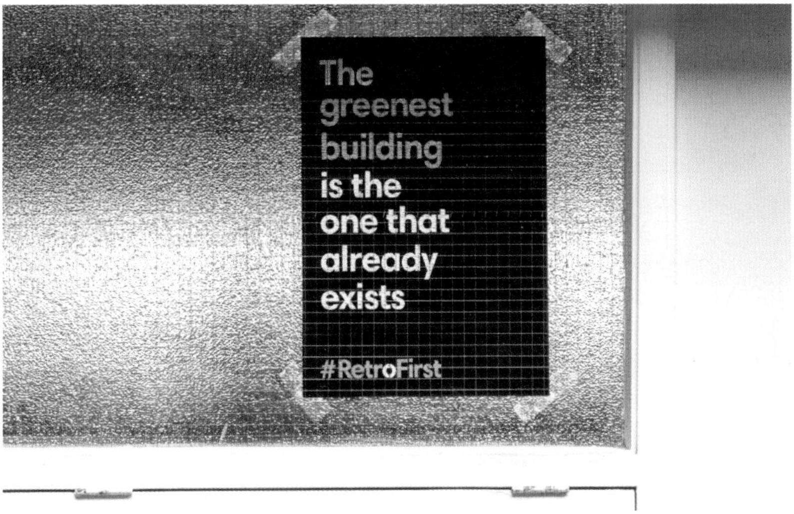

RetroFirst poster, *Architects' Journal*, February 28, 2020.

residential building—for which not even a building permit is required.[4] Good news for architects, it would seem: finally relieved of time-consuming red tape. However, it is actually British architects who are resisting their own government's predilection for demolition. An initiative by the name of RetroFirst launched by the *Architects' Journal* last year aimed at making reuse more attractive than demolition/construction has now been signed by three quarters of all architectural firms in the United Kingdom, including fourteen winners of the Stirling Prize, such as Caruso St John, Norman Foster, David Chipperfield and WilkinsonEyre. Their motivation? Climate change. *Architects' Journal* managing editor Will Hurst said: "It's crazy that the government actually incentivises practices that create more carbon emissions."[5] The motto of RetroFirst is: "The greenest building is the one that already exists."[6]

Transforming these existing buildings is, however, a tough job. The floor plan is no-good, the structural features are minimal, and the building insulation qualities are most probably dramatic. A quick look at our built environment shows that it is predominantly motivated by short-term thinking: speed and money. Good for a while, but poorly equipped for the long term. "For a while" in the property world is equivalent to thirty years. That is not only the customary financial depreciation period; the structural, functional and overall building qualities are worn out after thirty years. And then? Transforming an unsaleable building is complicated, time consuming, and expensive. With its impressive collection of problematic real estate, society has inflicted harm on itself.

The lack of a proper reuse strategy as part of the design means that the likelihood of demolition becomes an inherent feature of a building. With a different design strategy, intelligent reuse may be more self-evident. But how do you do that? Which tools do architects have to ensure that their creations are not a problem, but a blessing in thirty years' time?

A third monastery, also in the same region as Cluny and Fontenay, may provide an answer. The Dominican monastery Sainte Marie de La Tourette would be Le Corbusier's final work. It was not so much a future-proof building that his client Father Couturier wanted, but rather a building for the future. His choice of atheist Le Corbusier as architect was carefully considered. It was not that he believed that atheists were better architects, but that he saw few progressive religious architects: "It is safer to work with geniuses without faith, than believers without talent."[7] In La Tourette, a highly specific program and a highly specific architectural concept converged. Father Couturier drew the sequence of the various functions of the future monastery for Le Corbusier. "Like this and no different," said the drawing. Le Corbusier placed his *Plan Libre* (Free Plan) alongside it. The result was an open floorplan for a unique function. The Sainte Marie de La Tourette monastery can in no way be called a generic building: church, chapterhouse, library, and bedrooms are extremely explicitly articulated.

The *Plan Libre* was certainly not devised by Le Corbusier as a strategy for reuse. It gave him complete freedom, unhindered by load-bearing internal walls, to design interior and exterior independently of each other in an uncompromising way. Nevertheless, an opportunity for effective transformation is ingrained in the design methodology. In retrospect, the *Plan Libre* could function as a design strategy that provides a "typological anticipation" due to the possibility of creating new floorplans. Whether that is truly the case may soon become clear. La Tourette can accommodate sixty-four monks, but despite the efforts of Couturier and Le Corbusier, the community only consists of eight Dominicans today. The hope for a renaissance of faith has not yet been abandoned by the monks, but it may well be that the demand for reuse arises soon. We can then see how Sainte Marie de La Tourette will cope with a transformation, just like Fontenay and Cluny did.

In addition to developing a new architectural vocabulary to facilitate transformation—in whatever way—a fundamental re-evaluation of the relationship with our existing built environment is necessary. We must revise our idea of progress. The alarm bells sounded by RetroFirst regarding the consequences of our way of building on the climate are genuine but overlook the fact that the addiction to demolition is deeply ingrained ideologically.

Our historical failings can only be re-addressed with a disruptive strategy, so it seems: we create the better world by destroying that which lies behind us and building that which is new and fresh. Strangely enough, that better world is always just about to emerge, but never to be reached. Just like the monks in Fontenay could not have anticipated a French Revolution, the future always takes us unawares. Time and time again, we start working on that better world afresh—for real now!—and begin first by destroying that which lies behind us. In the story of the Nieuwmarkt neighborhood in Amsterdam, the damage from demolition is manageable, but the stakes are ever higher with our technical achievements. In the meantime, we are risking the quality of life for humanity on earth, as argued by the British RetroFirst in its manifesto. If that fails, we still have in some scenarios the planet Mars as a back-up.[8] The childish fantasies about a new opportunity on another planet are amusing but become dangerous if we seriously think we can fall back on a plan B as an alternative to human existence on earth.

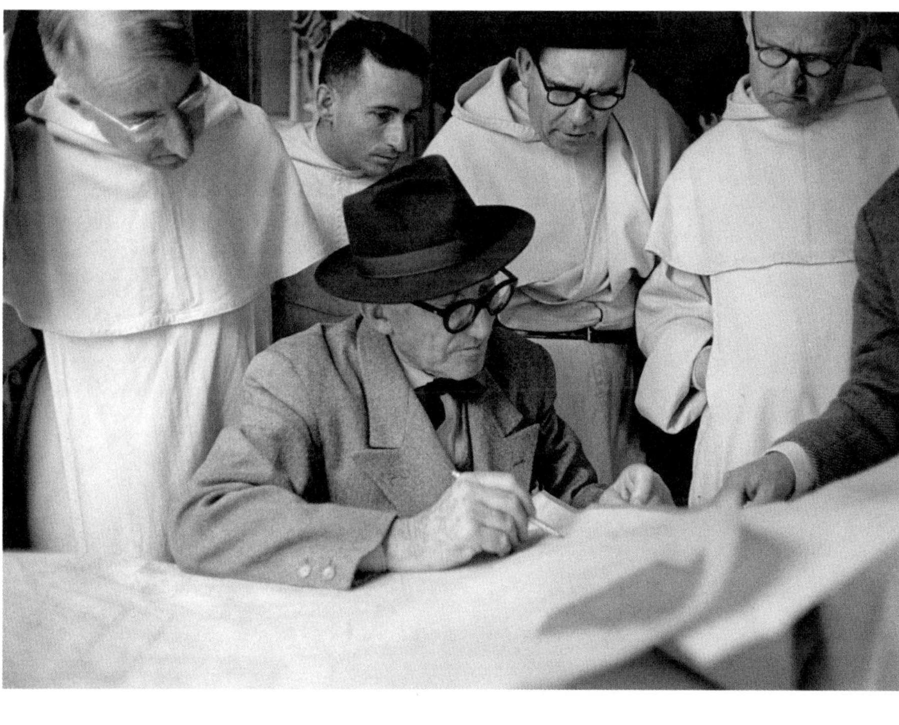

Le Corbusier shows his building plans to the Dominican Fathers of the *La Tourette* monastery, Eveux-sur-Arbresle, France, 1959. Photo by René Burri.

Le Corbusier inspecting the *La Tourette* building site with Dominican monks, Eveux-sur-Arbresle, France, 1959. Photo by René Burri.

In contrast to the self-evident ideology of demolition-before-new-construction, there should be an equally self-evident ideology of use/reuse. That is a relatively new phenomenon for our construction industry. This ideology, or to avoid too much pretension: a collection of design strategies, should offer more than just an ecological benefit. In the best-case scenario, it offers a perspective on more interesting, typologically stronger, and more pleasant buildings. If we—without Le Corbusier's permission—view the *Plan Libre* that was applied in the de La Tourette monastery as a circular strategy, a strategy in which reuse is assured, then the exceptional spatial quality of the monastery is attributable to precisely this way of thinking. In other words: the typological innovation that the reuse strategy entails leads to more interesting buildings.

In the past, design strategies have been devised that deploy reuse for objectives that go beyond practical considerations. The use of spolia provides a good example. The strategy for the use of spolia, popular in late antiquity, strives for an intelligent processing of the heritage from the past. Spolia (etymologically related to the word "spoil") is the collective name for reused materials from old buildings. The general perception is that this was mainly due to practical considerations: the demolished buildings consist of usable building material, so why would you pass up on this? The sixteenth-century artist and historian Giorgio Vasari even saw the use of spolia as an admission of weakness, simply demonstrating "a lack of good artists."[9] Examples of spolia show, however, that the application goes further than just recycling or artistic indolence. The use of spolia has a spiritual dimension: by incorporating something from history—in a carefully controlled setting—into the design, the power of the old building was used for personal gain. In this way, the new design was glorified and the old building visibly disparaged. This contrasts the 'clean slate' ideology in which the new was always better than the old. With spolia, an architect or artist can be deemed as great through interpretation, change or inclusion of the past. In our society, the use of spolia is virtually unheard of. The classification of our heritage is schizophrenic: an existing building is either a monument, and you should stay away from changing it, or it is of no value—and then it becomes waste. Up until two hundred years ago, both viewpoints would have been deemed ridiculous.

The use of new design strategies makes the transition to a circular economy more than a hygienic assignment, a necessary clean-up operation in order to save human existence

Pretty Plastic cladding tiles are entirely made of recycled PVC construction waste. Photo by Jeroen van der Wielen.

on earth. It provides opportunities that contribute to the improvement of the quality of our lives. With new strategies, reuse is not a necessary evil, but a qualitative improvement. The second life of the building—in whatever way—should be better than the first life. The paper mill in the Abbey of Fontenay was the best mill in the country in a spectacular setting. The houses, schools, and workshops in Cluny gain a spiritual dimension through the visible use of the large stones from the monastery. Hospital wings become beautiful homes, plastic waste becomes sexy facade material.[10] Devising new buildings is also imbued with a sense of optimism through the use of circular design strategies. Just as Le Corbusier used typological innovation in his final work for the renaissance of a religious experience, circular design strategies—more than traditional design methods—can offer new perspectives on the problems of this world.

1 Roland Barthes, "Non Multa Sed Multum," in *Cy Twombly: Catalogue raisonné des oeuvres sur papier Volume VI 1973–1976*, ed. Yvon Lambert (Milan: Multhipla Edizioni, 1976).

2 Statistisches Bundesamt, *Abfallbilanz 2016*, 30.

3 David A. Jokinen, *Geef de stad een kans* [Give the city a chance] (Roosendaal: Stichting Weg, 1968).

4 Ella Jessel, "Permitted development rights expanded to allow demolition without permission," *The Architects' Journal*, March 13, 2020, https://www.architectsjournal.co.uk/news/permitted-development-rights-expanded-to-allow-demolition-without-permission.

5 Roger Harrabin, "Don't demolish old buildings, urge architects," *BBC News*, August 4, 2020, https://www.bbc.com/news/business-53642581.

6 "RetroFirst," *The Architects' Journal*, https://www.architectsjournal.co.uk/news/retrofirst.

7 Le Corbusier, Sérgio Ferro, Chérif Kebbal, Philippe Potié, and Cyrille Simonnet, *Le Couvent de la Tourette, Monographies d'architecture* (Marseille: Éditions Parenthèses, 2006), 12. Original quote: "Il est plus sûr de s'adresser à des génies sans la foi qu'à des croyants sans talent."

8 Elon Musk: "You want to wake up in the morning and think the future is going to be great—and that's what being a spacefaring civilization is all about. It's about believing in the future and thinking that the future will be better than the past. And I can't think of anything more exciting than going out there and being among the stars." In "Mars and Beyond: The Road to Making Humanity Multiplanetary," SpaceX, https://www.spacex.com/human-spaceflight/mars/.

9 Maria Fabricius Hansen, *The Eloquence of Appropriation: Prolegomena to an Understanding of Spolia in Early Christian Rome*, Analecta Romana Instituti Danici 33 (Rome: L'Erma di Bretschneider, 2003), 11.

10 "Pretty Plastic–Upcycled Tiles," Pretty Plastic, https://www.prettyplastic.nl.

058

(-700—A)

FELIX
HEISEL

AFTER CONSTRUCTION, INEVITABLY COMES DE-CONSTRUCTION

"I propose to build for eternity."[1] This ambition was formulated by Italian mathematician, engineer, and builder Filippo Brunelleschi (1377–1446), who is remembered as the founding father of the Renaissance style in architecture, as well as the inventor of the one-point linear perspective in drawing and painting. Brunelleschi's most famous construction is the dome of the Cathedral of Santa Maria del Fiore in Florence, which significantly changed the engineering and construction technology of the time and was the largest dome in the world for almost five hundred years after its construction in 1441. Until today, the dome fulfills the ambition of its creator.

In (too) many cases and much more humble settings, the vector of the architectural design process still points towards eternity. It is not necessarily because architects actively aim to design their buildings to last forever—after all, we are all painfully aware of declining material durability, increasing pressures on land resources, and the effects of the climate crisis. Rather, building designs represent unique, carefully crafted propositions to specific sets of challenges and tasks, set out in the brief and influenced by aspects such as the site, society, technology, and many others. Often, the framing of these aspects is the current situation in the here and now—either assuming these conditions remain constant or negating their change over time.

However, there is no static here and now. The world is constantly evolving, and with it are the specific sets of conditions and requirements an architectural solution aims to respond to. Contradictory to our ambitions (and common sense), the life span of buildings has been on a constant decline over the past few centuries and increasingly so over the past decades. While historic buildings (for example conventional wood or masonry constructions) reach an average life span of 120 years before needing major renovation, buildings of the modernist area only last half that long.[2] In a recent study, the Council on Tall Buildings and Urban Habitat found that the world's one hundred tallest buildings demolished so far only reached an average age of 41 years.[3] Chinese researchers estimate that while the country is designing its buildings for a technical service life of (only) 50 years, the average life expectancy is actually closer to 35 years—with most buildings being demolished after 20 years of service.[4]

AFTER-LIFE?

There are many reasons for this global trend: rising real estate prices, cheap and low-quality building materials, a decline in construction quality, or the monopoly of reinforced concrete to name just a few. The result, however, is devastating: Globally, the construction industry is the biggest consumer of energy and materials. Over the full life cycle, building construction and operation account for 36% of energy use and 39% of energy and process-related greenhouse gas emissions,[5] as well as over half of all raw material extraction and solid waste production.[6] Since 1970, the global consumption of non-renewable resources, particularly industrial and construction minerals, has increased by 376%[7] and—driven by decreasing building life spans coupled with an increasing demand for shelter and infrastructure by a growing population with rising expectations and wealth—the global construction market is expected to further increase from 84 billion metric tons of raw materials entering the economic system in 2015 to 170–184 billion metric tons in 2050.[8]

These numbers present a potentially catastrophic scenario for the environment, our society's equality and equity, and even (although counter-intuitive) the economy. The fundamental problem lies in the prevailing linear economic system of raw material consumption based on a take-make-throw pattern. Products are being manufactured using harvested or extracted materials and are disposed of once broken, old, or simply out of fashion—destroying not only all of the material resources but also the embodied energy, work, and knowledge of these products. As long as we stay within this linear economic model, we may only be able to postpone the system's collapse through technological development; the end, however, seems inevitable. What we need instead is a systemic paradigm shift: a shift from a linear towards a circular economy, one that will radically change our economic and ecologic understanding.

CIRCULAR CONSTRUCTION

Inevitably, any building will reach the end of its use phase at some point in time—be it after a day or 3000 years. Paradoxically, this aspect often does not represent an essential design parameter in a structure's conception, nor does the consequent demolition, deconstruction, or renovation. However, acknowledging and embracing the "after" of a building's timeline can lead to a radical shift in how we design and manage our buildings[9] while mitigating the industry's negative environmental, social, and cultural effects.

Following this logic, the Circular Construction Lab[10] (CCL) at Cornell AAP understands the built environment as a material depot. The careful and meticulous documentation[11] of all components, materials, and substances within the depot allows for their continuous and value-preserving reuse and recycling. As a precondition, a circular built environment requires an appropriate handling of its stock, which manifests itself above all in the development and application of reversible joining techniques, the selection of pure-fraction and toxin-free building materials, the introduction of design for disassembly strategies, and a radically new understanding of the roles of all actors in the construction industry. Embedded into the systemic change of the circular economy, these strategies go far beyond waste management and treatment. Instead of closing material cycles at the end of a building's life span, a circular economy aims to prevent the generation of waste through innovation and design right at the beginning of a material's or building's use phase. The circular economy in this respect is restorative and regenerative by design. It maintains the highest possible utility, monetary, and embodied values of its materials and components in closed technical and biological cycles.[12]

ACTIVATING THE URBAN MINE

The enormous material and energy wastage of today's architecture makes it painfully obvious that the current built environment is not yet designed or constructed as a material depot. Many building components are connected in ways that prevent their easy and non-destructive separation, and common composite materials inhibit high-quality recycling. The contamination of materials and components with toxic substances further prohibits their reintroduction into new material cycles. Many such examples today are landfilled or incinerated, which amounts to the destruction of both raw materials and embodied values.

On the other hand, the quantitative potential of the built environment as a material reserve is enormous. In fact, the anthropogenic (man-made) stocks of various metals and minerals accumulated in the built environment over the years have already outgrown their respective naturally occurring reserves in the Earth's crust,[13] calling for the exploration of a new type of mine—the urban mine. The challenge will be the development of new technologies that transform this unfit material reserve into a new generation of sustainable (i.e. ecologically non-harmful, technically pure, endlessly usable, and economically advantageous) building materials. Looking at the bigger picture, urban mining plays the role of an intermediate technology, re-activating materials which were neither intended nor designed to be reused or recycled. Due to this fact, urban mining—just like conventional mining—produces by-products of inferior quality and materials that do not meet the criteria of the circular economy. However, once buildings are designed for circular construction within a material depot, urban mining will no longer be necessary, as materials will be able to be reassembled cleanly and waste-free from one building to the next.

The 2015 No-Waste-Vault by the ETH Zurich Professorships of Dirk E. Hebel and Philippe Block reactivated wasted beverage cartons as a structural building material for an outdoor event space. (Photo by Albert Vecerka/Esto.)

The following projects aim to showcase that it is already possible to build with materials from the urban mine and to assemble them in ways that allow for their continuous future use within a built material depot. In 2015, the New Museum commissioned a temporary pavilion as a venue for seminars, lectures, and exhibitions at the *Ideas City Festival* in New York City. Following the festival's theme of the "Invisible City," our project aimed to show the immense potential of often invisible or suppressed waste streams for architectural applications by using discarded beverage cartons as a building material. In 2013, an estimated 178 billion beverage cartons were consumed worldwide[14] and although global recycling rates are increasing, the US landfilled around 430,000 metric tons of beverage cartons in 2010 alone.[15] These packages are usually made of different laminated material layers. In theory, the individual raw materials (cardboard 74%, polyethylene 22%, and aluminum 4%) can be separated from each other, but the process unfortunately and paradoxically requires special machines and large amounts of water and energy. As an alternative, US company ReWall Solutions suggested shredding and repressing these beverage cartons into panels as a replacement to plasterboards. Neither water nor adhesives or additives were required in this process, and the panel material mixture could still be recycled completely after their use.

The *No-Waste Vault* was the first load-bearing, outdoor application of this product. Since the relatively soft panels easily deform when subjected to tension or bending forces, our team optimized the geometry of the structure to meet these characteristics.

Close up, the material reveals its history: orange color from juice boxes, blue from milk cartons, and black from wine canisters. (Photo by Albert Vecerka/Esto.)

The result was a 90 m^2 compression-only vault, consisting of 34 individual pre-stressed arches. In order to achieve sufficient room height, the arches of the pavilion were supported on borrowed industrial pallets. All connections were made by tension straps—without any adhesives or even screws and nails—allowing for a quick, sorted, efficient, as well as waste-free construction and deconstruction. After the event, the ReWall material was recycled into new panels and the pallets were returned to their owner. All materials were simply borrowed from their economic and material cycles and were returned a few days later.

MEHR.WERT.PAVILLON

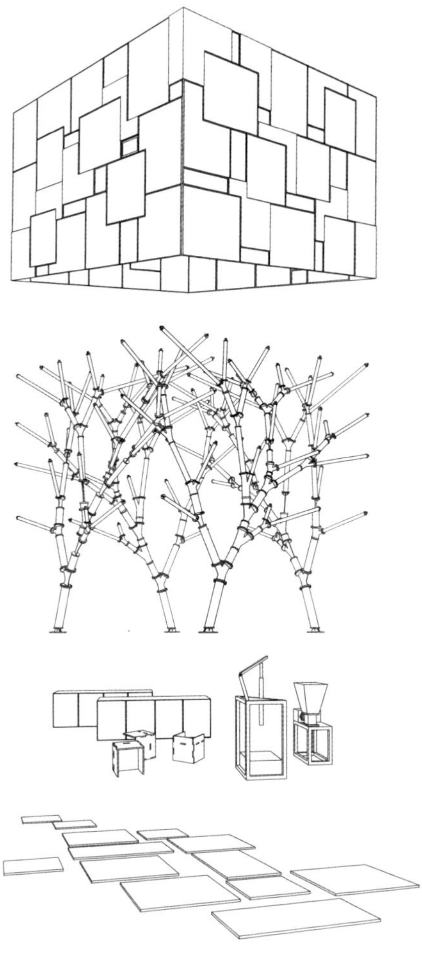

The pavilion activates four different waste streams: recycled industrial and bottle glass, reused structural steel, recycled plastic household waste, and reused and recycled mineral demolition waste. The materials bring their very unique aesthetic qualities into the project. (Illustration by Katna Wiese and Felix Heisel.)

In the context of the 2019 German Federal Garden Exhibition (BUGA) in Heilbronn, the BUGA management, the City of Heilbronn, its recycling companies, and Baden-Württemberg's Ministry of the Environment, Climate Protection and the Energy Sector commissioned a pavilion to initiate a new way of thinking about the consumption of resources in the building industry. All the materials we used for the construction of the *Mehr.WERT. Pavillon* (translation: *Added.VALUE. Pavilion*) had already gone through at least one use cycle and were either reused or recycled. Constructed circular, the pavilion further served as a material depot, to be made available for future constructions at the end of the exhibition. However, the building was so convincing that the City of Heilbronn decided in a first step to reuse the whole structure (instead of accessing its material components). Since it was planned for disassembly, also the relocation of the complete pavilion (including foundations) to a new location was a feasible option.

The pavilion was assembled from four different material categories: glass, steel, plastic, and mineral demolition waste. The façade and roof were made of glass panels from recycled industrial glass while the load-bearing structure consisted mainly of directly reused steel from a decommissioned coal-fired power plant. The furniture was assembled from recycled HDPE plastic waste, and the chairs were 3D-printed from plastic household waste; the pavilion floor and the landscaping of the garden were designed with various reused and recycled products from mineral demolition waste. Finally, the pavilion rested on reusable Lego-like concrete foundation blocks with a recycling aggregate content of 100%.

The direct reuse of structural steel is currently practiced only to a very limited extent. In addition to the careful removal of elements during deconstruction, detailed knowledge of material qualities and the previous use history are required for the successful reintegration of steel elements according to building codes and safety regulations. It must be determined which defects and damages are present on the disassembled element, and what type and frequency of previous stress situations may be relevant. With no available data, the steel elements for the *Mehr.WERT.Pavillon* were examined for tensile strength, elasticity, notched impact strength, and chemical composition through laboratory tests. The steel quality corresponded to that of standard structural steel, which allowed its reuse without compromise. The exercise, however, clearly enforced the importance of detailed documentation of the built material depot as a prerequisite for a successful and economically viable circular economy.[16]

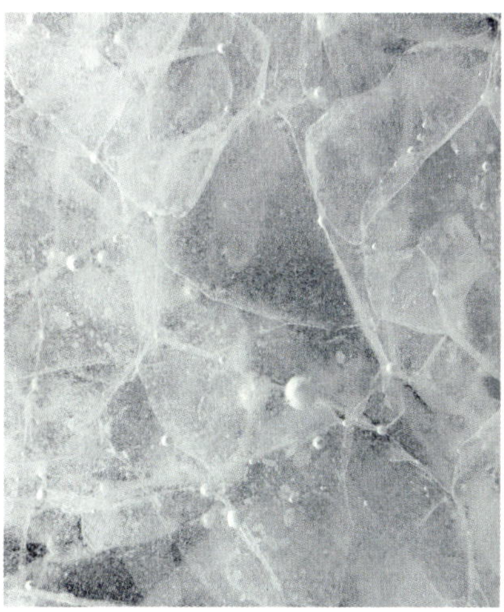

Opposite: The Mehr.WERT.Pavillon by 2hs Architekten und Ingenieur PartGmbB and KIT Karlsruhe is designed for disassembly from recycled and reused materials only. (Photo by Zooey Braun, Stuttgart.) This page left: The shards of the waste glass are still visible in the final product, giving Magna Glaskeramik its unique and compelling aesthetic while transporting its story. (Photo by Felix Heisel.) This page right: Through extensive testing, directly reused steel from a former coal-fired power plant could be utilized to assemble the tree-like structure of the pavilion. (Photo by Zooey Braun, Stuttgart.)

While the first two examples focus on the activation of the urban mine, the last example concentrates on circular construction techniques and building materials. In 2018, we completed the *Urban Mining and Recycling* (UMAR) unit as part of the Empa NEST[17] in Dübendorf, Switzerland. UMAR was designed as a living and research module for two graduate students. At the same time, the unit is open for public tours and events and attracts an average of several hundred visitors per month. In this dual role as a living laboratory and showcase, UMAR aims to validate the principles of the circular economy and convey its advantages, effects, technical details, and aesthetics to visitors, interested parties, and specialists.

Top: The seven modules of UMAR are standing on railings and can be rolled into (and out of) the building easily for assembly and disassembly. (Photo by Wojciech Zawarski.)
Bottom: WasteBricks come in a variety of colors and forms ranging from Salami to Nougat to Aubergine to Wasabi. The names describe the different waste mixtures, e.g. Salami contains mostly clay roof shingles with white ceramic spots. (Photo by Felix Heisel.)

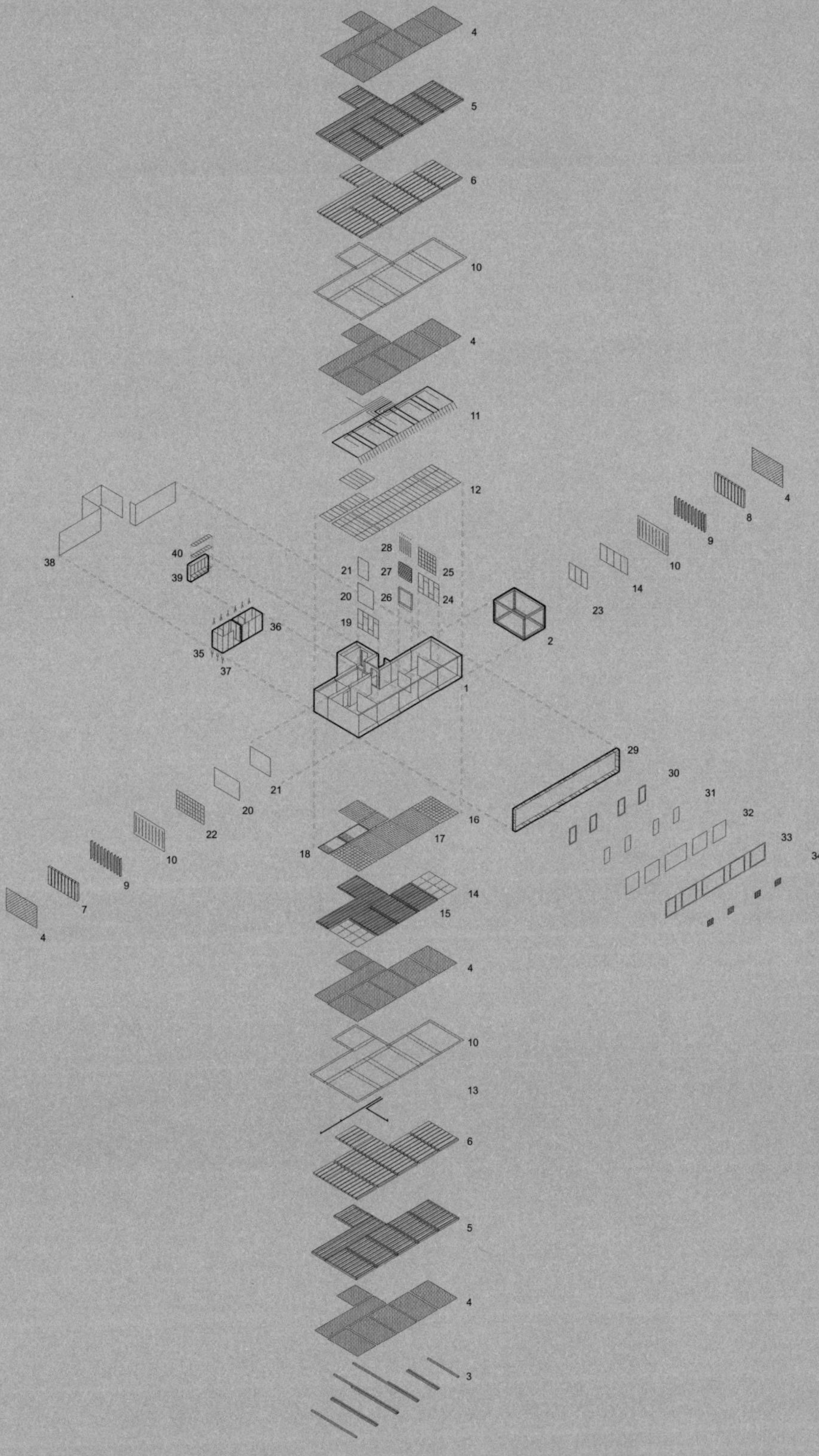

The unit is designed for disassembly so that all products and components can be reintroduced into pure-type material cycles for reuse or high-value recycling. (Illustration by Sara Schäfer and Felix Heisel.)

Previous spread: The Urban Mining and Recycling (UMAR) Unit by Werner Sobek with Dirk E. Hebel and Felix Heisel is designed and constructed as a material depot for future constructions. (Photo by Zooey Braun, Stuttgart.) **This page:** There are no glues, wet sealants, or foams used in the building. Instead, the bathroom is constructed from large panels of recycled HDPE kitchen cutting boards and dry gaskets. (Photo by Zooey Braun, Stuttgart.)

Following the basic understanding that "cycles have no beginning and no end,"[18] UMAR applies materials, components, and joining techniques from various states and positions within their respective material cycles: from newly grown biological raw materials to recycled or reused products and components. Every material decision and every detail had to be examined for its principles, and often rethought: from the overall connection of prefabricated modules on site, to the exclusive use of dry gaskets, to the reengineering of existing products in cooperation with manufacturers (i.e. heating/cooling ceiling panels designed for disassembly) to the development of new products (i.e. mono-material 3D-printed faucets). Additionally, all hybrid materials or products—mixtures of technical and/or biological nutrients that cannot be separated at the end of their use phase—were dispensed with. This principle was more difficult to follow than it may appear at first glance. Today there is an alarmingly large variety of biological/technical hybrid materials on the construction market, including many standard products such as the common OSB board, fiberboard, or wooden elements coated with fungicides and flame-retardant salts or plastics.

In total, the unit was assembled on site from seven prefabricated and fully equipped modules. After their final positioning, the individual modules were connected to each other structurally and infrastructurally via plug connections and coupling devices. There are no glues or adhesive tapes in the entire building (with the exception of one fully biodegradable product for bonding wood to wood in furniture construction). All connections are reversible by screw, plug, clamp or interlocking mechanisms, easily accessible and well documented in preparation for the unit's disassembly.

PLANNING FOR THE "AFTER"

In the early 1990s, British architect Frank Duffy and American writer Steward Brand introduced the concept of "shearing layers"[19] into the architectural debate, describing a building as a set of layers that evolve in different timescales. Brand later quoted Duffy with the words that there is "no such thing as a building,"[20] but rather a compilation of several layers of longevity of built components. While the structure might be designed for fifty or more years, the interior partitions have a use phase of five years and the furniture arrangement might only stay the same for several days. However, as Columbia professors Jeffrey Inaba and Benedict Clouette remark: "From the moment a building is 'completed,' the synchronicity of these lifecycles begins to break apart."[21] Seen over the whole life cycle, the greatest investment in a building is interestingly not the structure itself, but rather the constantly changing internal space plan. Consequently, remodeling accounts for about half of demolition waste in the United States.[22]

While there is certainly nothing wrong with change—change might be one of the only few constants—the problem lies in the lack of its acceptance as a given design parameter. Why does changing the interior space plan still create waste, when its expected use phase is only five years? Why do we still demolish rather than deconstruct, when so much material resources, energy, and knowledge could be diverted from landfills? And why do we still not plan for the reapplication of resources after their initial use phase ends? Circular construction aims to build a holistic system—where material stocks and flows on all scales (from the material to the urban) and across timelines—are part of a dynamic whole. The concept is based on nature's closed and waste-free cycles, where at the end of life, everything turns into building blocks for a new life. Durability, as one of the current sustainability goals,[23] thus applies to the materials themselves, not their configuration within a building, structure, or piece of furniture. Circular design concentrates on the easy adaptation and recovery of materials, energy, and knowledge. Filippo Brunelleschi's vector towards eternity thus can and should be applied towards the level of the biological and technical building blocks that comprise and re-comprise all our materials, products and components, and eventually buildings. At Cornell, we are now working towards the necessary paradigm shift in how we design and manage such a circular built environment.

1 “Filippo Brunelleschi Quotes,” BrainyQuote.com, BrainyMedia Inc, accessed July 20, 2020, https://www.brainyquote.com/quotes/filippo_brunelleschi_737848.

2 Witold Rybczynski, “Short Life,” *On Culture and Architecture* (blog), July 22, 2015, https://www.witoldrybczynski.com/architecture/short-life/.

3 Council on Tall Buildings and Urban Habitat (CTBUH), “Tall Buildings in Numbers: World's Tallest Demolished Buildings,” *CTBUH Journal* 2 (April 2018).

4 China Economic Review, “How Will a Slowing China Cope with Rapidly Aging Buildings?,” June 28, 2013, *China Economic Review*, https://chinaeconomicreview.com/unstable-foundations-part-2/, accessed July 20, 2020; Qian Yanfeng, “‘Most Homes’ to Be Demolished in 20 Years,” *China Daily*, August 7, 2010, sec. Society, http://www.chinadaily.com.cn/china/2010-08/07/content_11113982.htm, accessed July 20, 2020.

5 International Energy Agency and the United Environment Programme, *2018 Global Status Report: Towards a zero-emission, efficient and resilient buildings and construction sector*, December 2018, 11.

6 Transparency *Market Research, Construction Waste Market - Global Industry Analysis, Size, Share, Growth, Trends, and Forecast 2017 – 2025* (Albany, NY: Pre-Book Report, 2020).

7 Materialflows.net, “Global trends of material use,” 2018, http://www.materialflows.net/global-trends-of-material-use/, accessed 25 January 2019.

8 Circle Economy, *The Circularity Gap Report: Closing the Circularity Gap in a 9% World* (Amsterdam, Netherlands: Circle Economy, January 2019); Ellen MacArthur Foundation, *Towards the Circular Economy: Economic and Business Rationale for an Accelerated Transition* (London, UK: Ellen MacArthur Foundation, 2013), 1; Betts M, Robinson G, Burton C, Leonard J, Sharda A, and Whittington T, *Global Construction 2030: A Global Forecast for the Construction Industry to 2030* (London, UK: Global Construction Perspectives and Oxford Economics, November 2015).

9 Dirk E Hebel, Marta H. Wisniewska, and Felix Heisel, eds., *Building from Waste, Recovered Materials in Architecture and Construction* (Berlin, Germany: Birkhäuser, 2014).

10 The Circular Construction Lab at Cornell AAP is directed by Felix Heisel. http://ccl.aap.cornell.edu.

11 Felix Heisel and Sabine Rau-Oberhuber, “Calculation and Evaluation of Circularity Indicators for the Built Environment Using the Case Studies of UMAR and Madaster,” *Journal of Cleaner Production* 243 (2020): 118482, https://doi.org/10.1016/j.jclepro.2019.118482.

12 Ellen MacArthur Foundation, *Towards the Circular Economy: Business Rationale for an Accelerated Transition* (London, UK: Ellen MacArthur Foundation, 2015), 4.

13 Takashi Nakamura and Kohmei Halada, “Potential of Urban Mine,” in *Urban Mining Systems* (Tokyo, Japan: Springer Briefs in Applied Sciences and Technology, 2015), 7–29.

14 Tetra Laval, *The Tetra Laval Annual Report: Ensuring Food Protection* (Pully, Switzerland: Tetra Laval, 2014).

15 Chaz Miller, “Profiles in Garbage: Aseptic Boxes & Cartons,” *Waste 360*, March 28, 2013, https://www.waste360.com/research-and-statistics/profiles-garbage-aseptic-boxes-cartons.

16 Felix Heisel, Karsten Schlesier, and Dirk E. Hebel, “Prototypology for a Circular Building Industry: The Potential of Re-Used and Recycled Building Materials,” *IOP Conference Series: Earth and Environmental Science* 323 (2019): 012023, https://doi.org/10.1088/1755-1315/323/1/012023.

17 “Introducing NEST,” Empa, accessed September 7, 2018, https://www.empa.ch/web/nest/aboutnest.

18 Walter R. Stahel, “The Functional Economy: Cultural and Organizational Change,” in *The Industrial Green Game: Implications for Environmental Design and Management* (Washington, DC: National Academy Press, 1997), 91–100.

19 Frank Duffy, *The Changing Workplace* (London, UK: Phaidon Press, 1992).

20 Stewart Brand, *How Buildings Learn: What Happens After They're Built* (New York, NY: Viking, 1994).

21 Jeffrey Inaba and Benedict Clouette, “The Life of Buildings: Design for Adaptation in Tokyo” (syllabus, Advanced Architecture Studio V, Columbia University, Fall 2014), http://www.columbia.edu/cu/arch/courses/facsyl/20143/67796_014_2014_3_140902_Tokyo%20Design%20Studio.pdf.

22 US Environmental Protection Agency (EPA), *Estimating 2003 Building-Related Construction and Demolition Material Amounts*, March 2009.

23 Jennifer O'Connor, “Survey on Actual Service Lives for North American Buildings” (paper, Woodframe Housing Durability and Disaster Issues Conference, Las Vegas, NV, October 2004), https://cwc.ca/wp-content/uploads/2013/12/DurabilityService_Life_E.pdf.

076

(-400—A)

DAVID
SALOMON

AFTER TIME: NOTES AROUND THE EVER-AFTER

CORNELL JOURNAL OF ARCHITECTURE
ISSUE 12
AFTER

Let's start with time.
After seconds and minutes: hours and days and weeks.
After weeks: months and years and decades.
After decades: centuries and millennia and eons.
After eons: eternity.
After time: the ever-after.

Let's start again.
Let's start with the Anthropocene.
It assembles the biologic, geologic, and atmospheric.
It mixes the miniscule with the monumental.
It recombines the modern with the religious.
After the Anthropocene: modernity.

Let's start again.
Let's start with modernity.
It is the age of biology, of capitalism, of machines.
It is measured in human life spans, 30-year mortgages, planned obsolesce.
It is disruptive.
After modernity: architecture.

Let's start again.
Let's start with architecture.
It fuses the moving and the still.
It merges the living with the non-living.
It mediates the social and the meteorological.
After architecture: culture.

Let's start again.
Let's start with culture.
Cultures lasts for centuries, millennia even.
Cultures are consistent yet fluid.
Cultures "construct humans, divinities and nonhumans."
After culture: geology.

Let's start again.
Let's start with geology.
With things that never lived.
With rocks and water and air.
It is measured in eons, eras, periods, and ages.
After geology: religion.
Let's start again.

Let's start with religion.
Religion goes beyond life.
Perpetual paradises, infinite
returns, nothingness.
Every ever-after is forever.
After religion: Acoma.

Let's start again.
Let's start with Acoma.
Anthropology says it has been
occupied for 1,000 years.
Oral history say it is much much older.
History says its buildings
are 350 years old.
After Acoma: San Estévan.

Let's pause.
Let's pause at the San Estévan del
Rey Mission Church of Acoma.
It was begun in 1629, and again in 1706,
and 1924, and 1934, and 1980, and 2000.
It is made of ancient earth from close by.
It is made of sacred pines from far away.
After San Estévan: return.

Let's go back.
Let's go back to Acoma.
Acoma endures.
It belongs to those not yet born.
It is of its place.
After Acoma: religion.

Let's go back.
Let's go back to religion.
Religion returns.
It belongs to the infinite.
It is of no place.
After religion: geology.

Let's go back.
Let's go back to geology.
Geology endures.
It belongs to Earth.
It is of the cosmos.
After geology: culture.

All images by Ansel Adams. P.77: *Church, Acoma Pueblo*, side wall and tower with cross, Acoma Pueblo, New Mexico, 1941–42. P.79: *Church, Acoma Pueblo*, corner view showing mostly left wall, 1941–42. P.80: *Acoma Pueblo*, looking across street toward houses, 1941–42. This page: *Acoma Pueblo*, full side view of adobe house with water in foreground, 1941–42.

Let's go back.
Let's go back to culture.
Culture persists.
It belongs to those no longer alive.
It is of the past.
After culture: architecture.

Let's go back.
Let's go back to architecture.
Architecture is a capsule.
It belongs to many.
It is of a people.
After architecture: modernity.

Let's go back.
Let's go back to modernity.
Modernity is fleeting.
It belongs to the future.
It is of the now.
After modernity: the Anthropocene.

Let's go back.
Let's go back to the Anthropocene.
The Anthropocene will not go away.
It belongs to all.
It is of us.
After the Anthropocene: time.

Let's end.
Let's end with time.
Time is multiple.
It belongs to none.
It is of the unbounded.
After time: the ever-after.

DUNCAN
STEELE

DRAWN TO THE GUTTER

084

(-400—P)

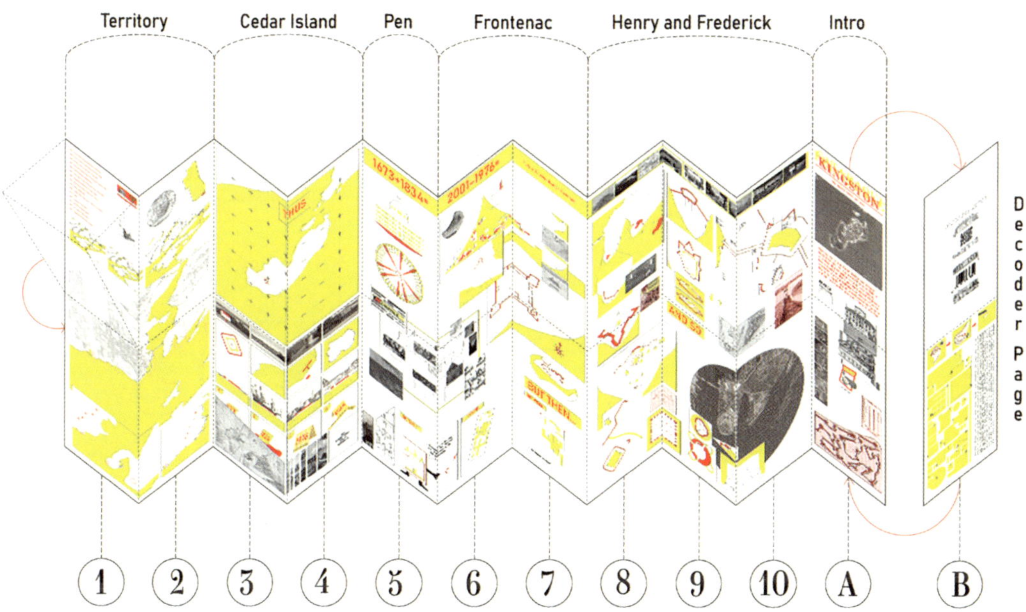
Territory
Cedar Island
Pen
Frontenac
Henry and Frederick
Intro
Decoder Page
1
2
3
4
5
6
7
8
9
10
A
B

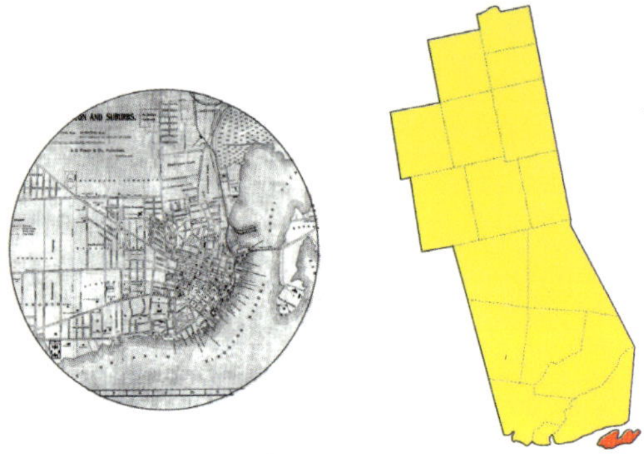

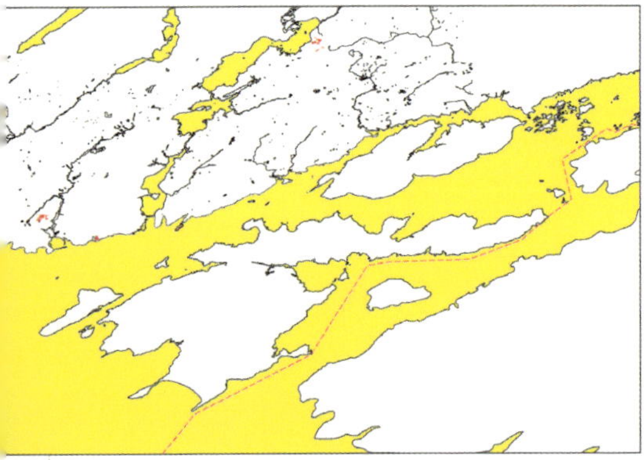

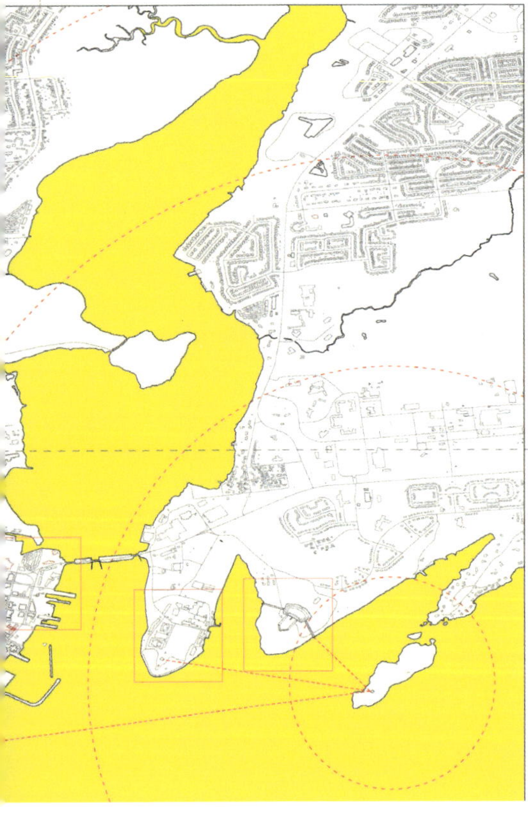

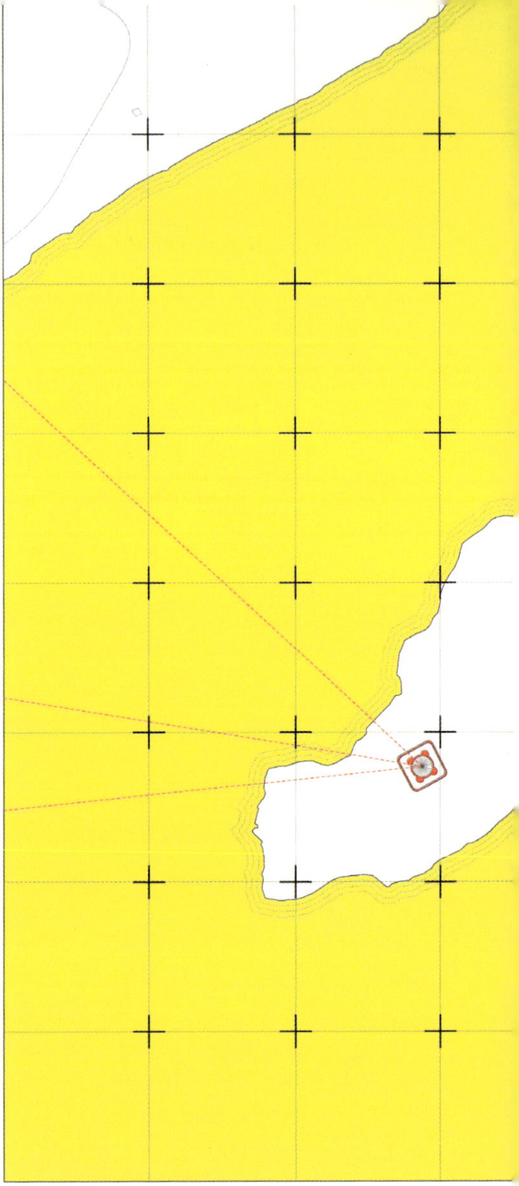

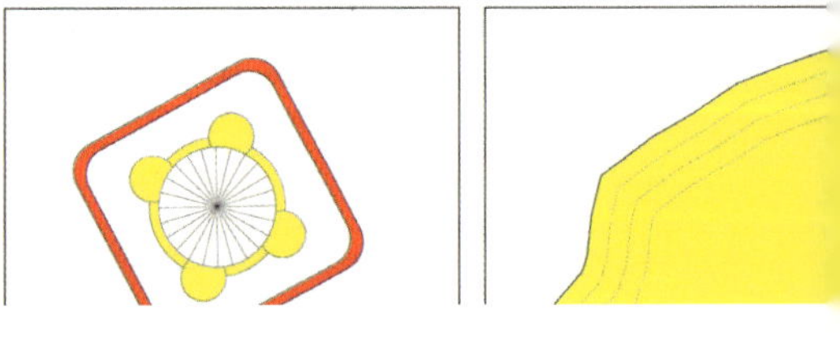

HUS
1673+1834=
IT BEGAN ABOUT A YEAR AGO!
FOUR MINUTES PASSED...FIVE MINUTES...
THE NEXT WEEK,
BUT THAT NIGHT,
SUDDENLY...
MEANWHILE...
SEVERAL YEARS PASSED...
IT WAS AFTER TWELVE
MEANWHILE,

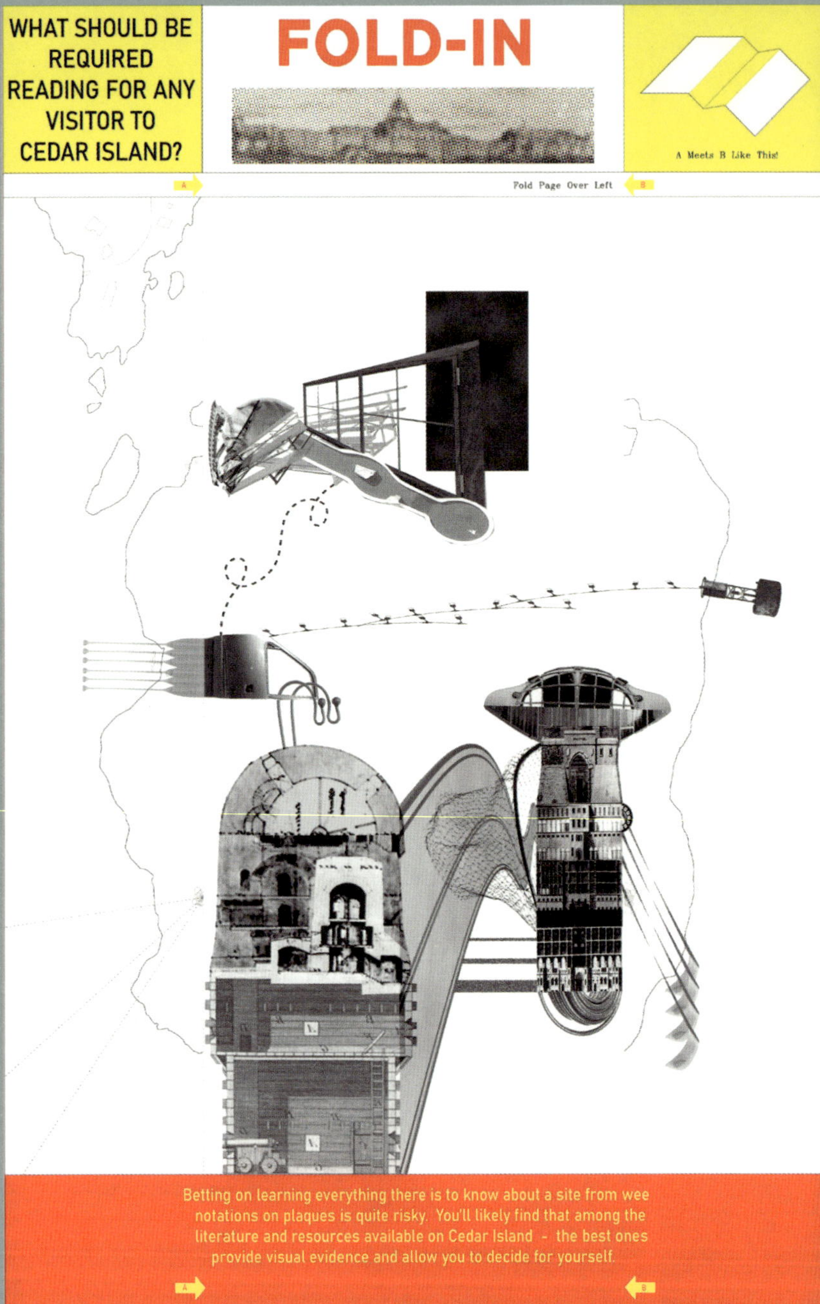

All images by Duncan Steele, 2020. **P.85:** *Guide to the Fold-Out Map*. **Previous spread:** Visualizing how a deep chronology collapses in space between territorial and individual scales and narrative registers—the hyperframe of the page operates to produce misreadings through folding and cut-aways, highlighting how the viewer's participation in reading architectural drawings can make visual evidence and narrative unreliable and flexible. (*Fold-Out Map with Decoder Page.*) **This page:** Inspired by Al Jaffee's *Mad* magazine fold-ins of the 1950s, I investigated how the operation of the page itself can confound a reading of text and space. How can a site too small to contain a multitude of narratives begin to expand its legibility through a process of expansive unfolding? (*Fold-In Site Collage.*)

In his 1943 *Cézanne's Composition*, American painter Erle Loran famously diagrammed the construction of an image as it defined a sequence of reading or visual syntax.[1] Inversely, this project examines how the very operation of picture-reading constructs space, and unfolds the process by which an individual drawing becomes synecdoche for a broader virtual image or diegesis. The gutter (a channel for managing runoff, a sordid environment, or a space between facing images) allows comics to be uniquely fluid in mediating between spaces and moments through projective lapses in sequence—how might architectural drawing better emulate this quality? Moreover, at what point in a sequence of drawings does narrative space begin to emerge?

Reading architectural drawings seems to rely on the same naïve assumption that make comics accessible: that images relate to each other in an earnest way and that, by their juxtaposition, transposition, or by the global structure of their ordering they produce meaningful diegetic space, one image after the other. In *The System of Comics*, Thierry Groensteen defines the *blanc* (gutter) as "That-which-is-not-represented-but-which-the-reader-cannot-help-but-to-infer."[2] More than a blank space, the super-frame of the page is a structured surface against which missing images in an imagined continuity are projected. Like arthrology, analysis of multiple architectural images is the study of joints and articulations at meeting points. When we frame drawings in a set, we design discontinuity and incongruity, the pregnant pause that allows the joke to land and the floating section to be read. The inter-iconic gutter comes to stand in for a series of subjective processes of recombination and mediation between images that seem to be distinctly architectural.

The reader of an architectural drawing anticipates a sufficiently coherent diegesis, consistent space and the object permanence of a project, but rarely demands substantive evidence. The contingency of the detail is rarely audited, not because the observer is passive, but out of an eagerness to link fragments, materials, and divergent chronotopes together. By the definition of a genre of representation, socially agreed-upon conventions dictate our expectations for the relationship between one drawing and the next such that we often cease to be critical of the reliability of the architect as a visual narrator.

Visual incongruities in sequence, between drawings, panels, or even slides in a digital presentation help develop architectural imaginaries that infill gaps constructed by conventions of representation. These maps are an attempt to redraw a contested site such that the many *after's*, *and-so's*, and *but-then's* that inform its historical legibility are made mutable by the process of reading. Conceptualizing the architectural drawing as an operable document, folds, excisions, and gutters start to enable new misreadings of a site-in-time. How might the pliability of the drawing-set-artifact enable novel reconfigurations of our spaces and stories outside of the static image?

1 Erle Loran, *Cézanne's Composition: Analysis of His Form, with Diagrams and Photographs of His Motifs* (Berkeley: UC Press, 1943).

2 Thierry Groensteen, *The System of Comics* (Paris: Presses Universitaires, 1999), 131.

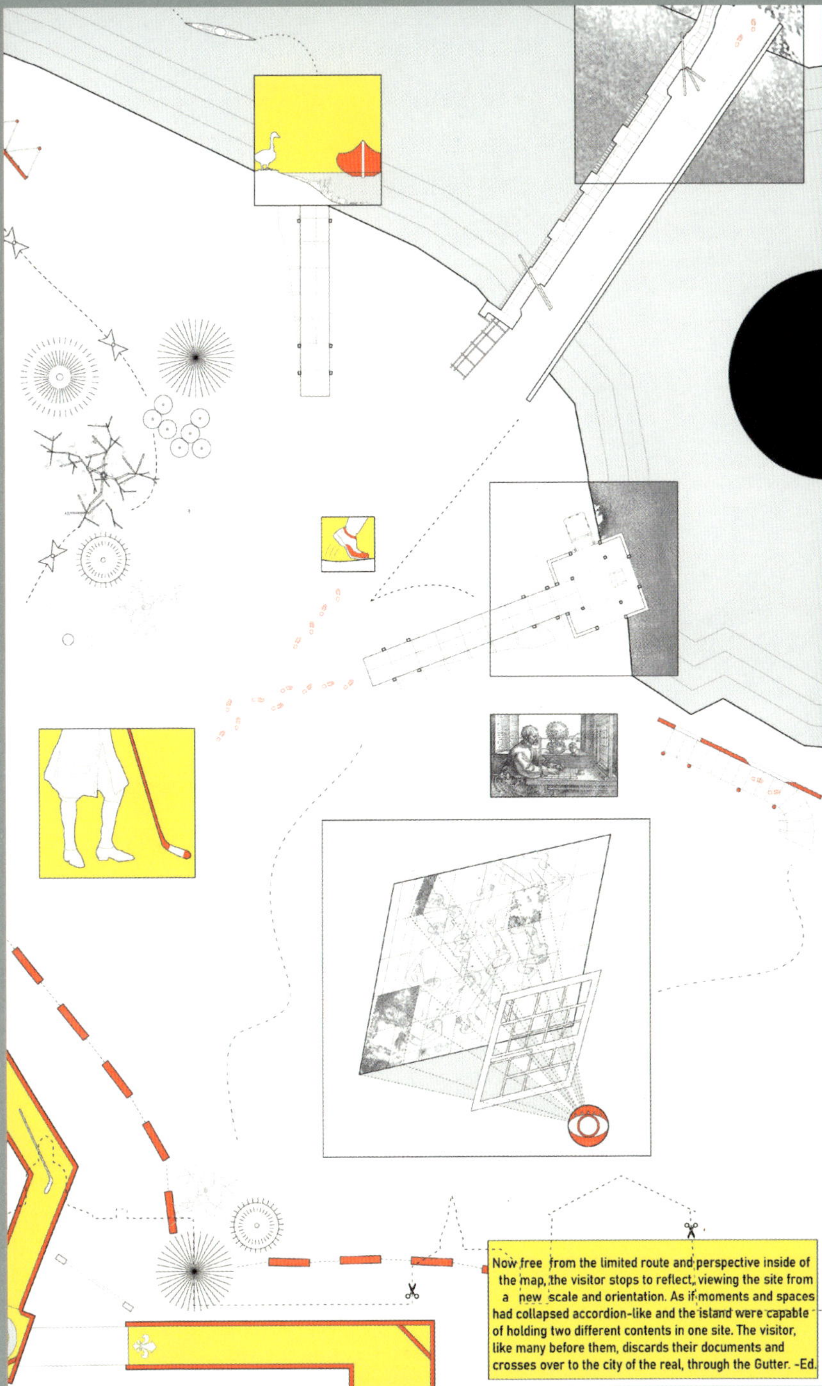

This page: The discovery of this space, and the map's reconfiguration, are uniquely enabled by cutting away at the document. The voids in the page become guides for orienting the visitor towards the gutter (in this case a channel in a body of water) through which they will enter Kingston. The visitor's destructive operation on the document reveals a hidden compartment. (*Plan of the Gutter and Blinds.*) **Next spread:** The guide, as it is unfolded, cut, flipped through, and taken apart—simultaneously becomes a map of the site and obscures a linear reading of it as a visitor tries to navigate through the document and into the city. (*Unfolded Scorecard and Cut-Away Site Map.*)

suddenly some-thing hap-pened
WHACK
AND SO
1845
1982
Les Mauges
Pull!
View of Cedar Island 2020

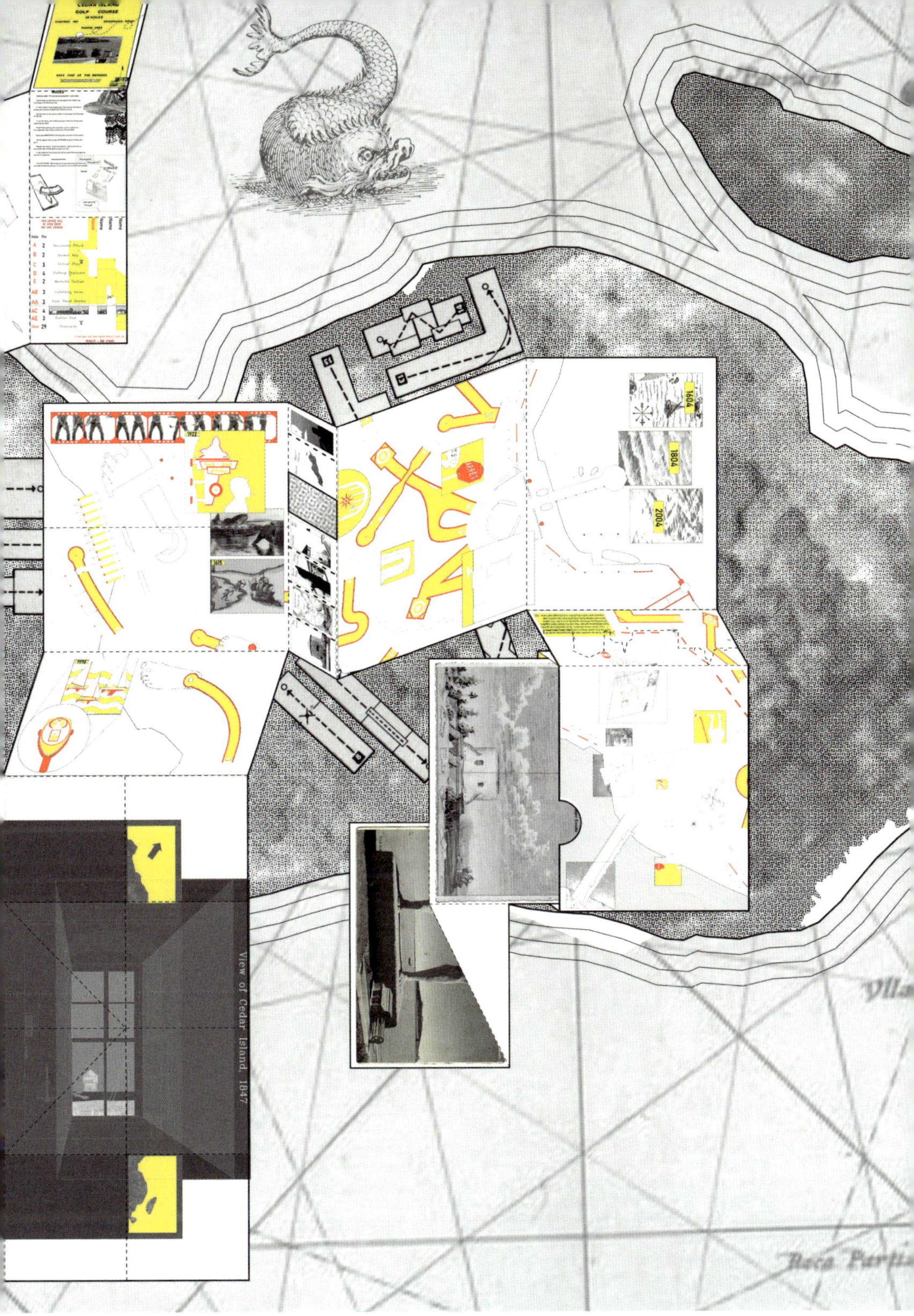
CEDAR ISLAND
GOLF COURSE
1604
1804
2004
View of Cedar Island, 1847

094

(-400—P)

HANSY BETTER BARRAZA

ANTHONY J. PIERMARINI

WORK TO DO

A dialogue on our responsibility in dismantling anti-Black design curricula and spaces in architectural education. The idea for this dialogue occurred after observing that the responsibility and appeals to respond to the institutional racial inequities and discrimination experienced by Black students in the academy disproportionally fell on one of us, who identifies as a person of color. By sharing our identity and perspective as a person who identifies as Latinx or white cisgender male in the same writing space, we're establishing a framework for conversations that acknowledge privilege in parallel to those that have been historically marginalized. To have a conversation on curricular changes towards equity, we advocate that it must happen in dialogue with those groups that are in constant threat of erasure.

AP We are in a moment of significant historical change. At the moment, the pandemic is raging, and we are actively participating in the BLM movement here in the USA. You identify as an anti-racist Latinx architect (among many other layers of identity—mother, daughter, niece, spouse, citizen, advocate, mentor, activist, friend, educator, colleague, and so on). All these facets construct and define your personal identity, they also inform how you approach practicing and teaching. One's values may reside at the intersection of personal identity, moral imperatives, cultural beliefs, and what one discerns as being good for our society. How do you identify and/or define your values with the architectural projects you initiate or take on?

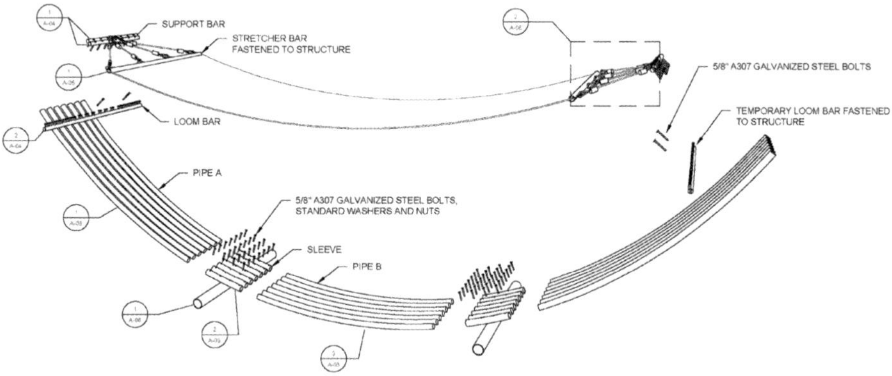

HBB I'm Colombian, a descendant of three different races: black, indigenous, and white. In the United States, I identify as an immigrant Latinx. When I want to emphasize gender, I say I am Latina. I live in two worlds, between Colombia and the USA. I'm connected to these two places through the internet. In practice, I try to link the global to the local where culture, identity, ethnicity, and race could be explored, enhanced, or even celebrated. Our cultural experiences and our identity shape how we think and produce architecture. This is our mission and the value we bring to every architectural project we take on at Studio Luz. For example, in The Big Hammock, sited on the Greenway in Boston, the object provided a space in the city that challenged boundaries, avoided classification of national identity, and created community. The Big Hammock intrinsically takes the form of its occupants—their bodies, their postures, their actions and interactions—its ever-changing form was the result of shared

Opposite: A detail of the woven mesh of the hammock with the colorful patterns. (Hansy Better Barraza, *The Big Hammock*, 2010. Photo by John Horner.) **This page:** A drawing depicting the assembly sequence for installation of *The Big Hammock*. (Hansy Better Barraza, *The Big Hammock*, 2010.) **Next spread:** The hammock was used by up to thirty people at a time. (Hansy Better Barraza, *The Big Hammock*, 2010. Photo by John Horner.)

INDEPENDENCE
WHARF
FOR LEASE

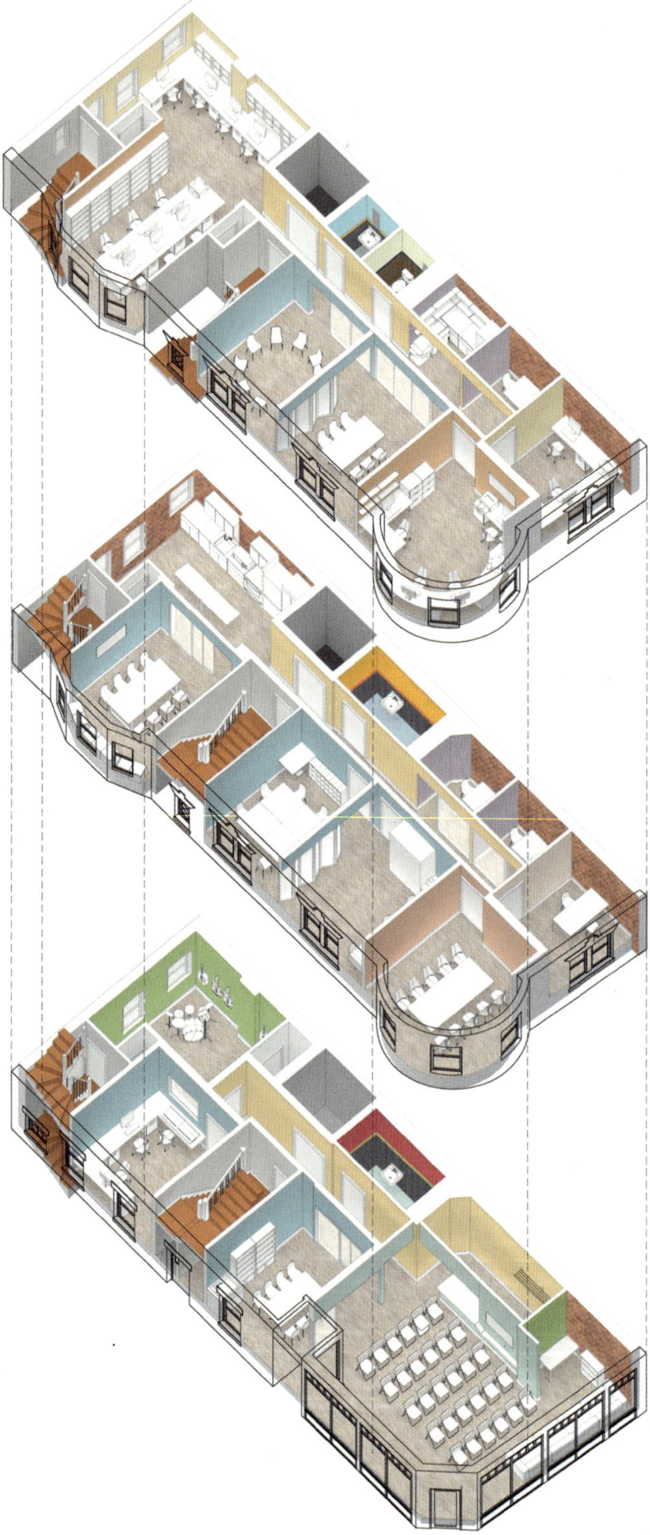

This page: Exploded axonometric drawing showing the new uses of this former multifamily residence, including culinary, fine arts, music, maker spaces, seminar, and performance areas. (Studio Luz Architects, *Sociedad Latina*, Roxbury, Massachusetts, 2016–2020.) **Next spread:** View of renovated outdoor terrace and social lounge. (Studio Luz Architects, *Terrace, Acorns House*, Wellesley, Massachusetts, 2016. Photo by John Horner.)

experiences. As people occupy the hammock's surface, they negotiate positions and balance the forces in the hammock. People are required to engage, to maintain balance or gently swing the structure with a few choregraphed moves, we were excited to see that many conversations were started. The Big Hammock was a woven structure that used rope manufactured from recycled milk bottles, the colors of the rope were selected to imbue the surface with multiple associations, such that people with various cultural heritages may relate to the woven surface. For example, Colombians thought the hammock was representing the flag of their country, Americans thought the American flag was projected, but looking closely at the color sequence, it doesn't fit either category. It was in-between sites that reflected the spaces I've occupied being Colombian raised in America. Shared experiences form common references.

As a white cisgender male, how will you undo the white supremacy that has dominated design pedagogy?

AP I strive to illuminate my personal "blind spots" and root them out of the course content. I strive to create learning experiences for students that reflect their own values, sense of personal identity, and discuss how their specific viewpoints inform decision making. This rooting out must be expanded to include all aspects of the architectural curriculum, as well as the design studio programs. New, anti-racist forms of knowledge must be created that fundamentally inform the discipline of architecture. As a white male, I recognize my privileged position; I am very conscious of the words and images used in the way I teach. To even begin to undo white supremacy, we must acknowledge that it exists and that racism is informing architecture today. We must strive to understand how the past informs the present, and that white supremacy has eclipsed the histories of Black people in the built environment through policy, processes, and cultural expression. I am not ignoring the many other cultures and identities suppressed through white supremacist structures. At this historical moment, it is important to frame this conversation in the context of BLM. This is how change begins to come about. We must strive to include the work of Black architects into all coursework. Learning from the history and contributions of Black people to the culture, spaces, and traditions of place making in the United States is a critical first step. This step will allow for other narratives to emerge, as we must strive to expand the frame

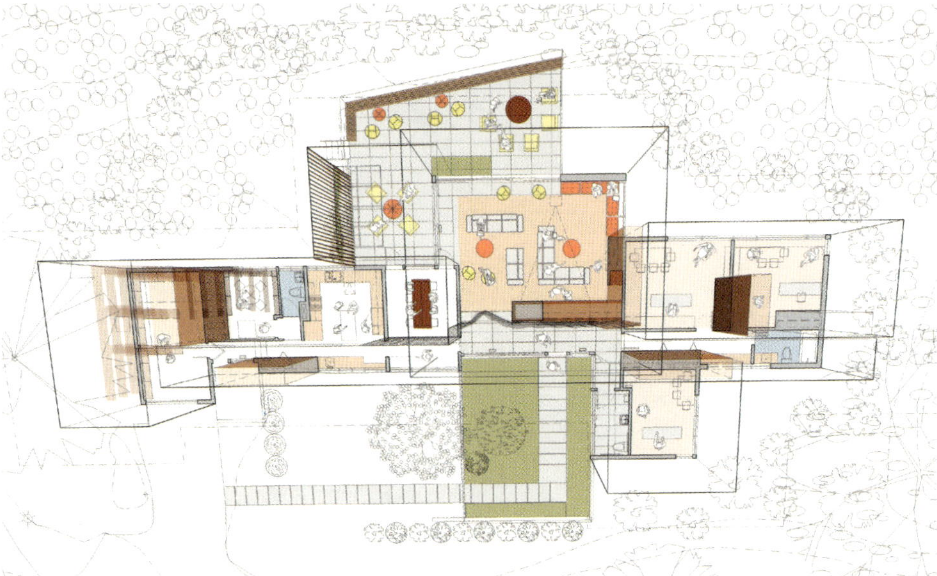

of reference. There must be an amplification of Black voices within the academic environment as a whole. I have a moral and ethical responsibility to provide students with examples that resonate with their lived experiences and expand upon their knowledge.

Design is a process, a process informed by decision-making. The factors that influence decisions must be projected through an anti-racist lens. Design processes must include more Black voices to influence decisions if we want to produce changes in power. As a white educator and architect, as I just stated, I will strive to amplify the Black voices of those that have been silenced and overlooked through the process of design. There needs to be a paradigm shift in design decision-making that strives for equity and resilience. Academically, we must continue to seed our syllabi, discussions, workshops, and assignments with the work of Black people. The contributions of Black people in informing the built environment must become core knowledge to promote activism. I say this in consideration of Ibram X. Kendi's words "Critiquing racism is not activism. Changing minds is not activism. An activist produces power and policy change, not mental change. If a person has no record of power or policy change, then that person is not an activist."[1]

In professional practice, as a white male, I need to know when to step aside and how to build awareness. In our practice, Hansy, as a Latinx woman, it is important that you are the lead for much of what we do, for providing direction for the firm. In the Big Hammock project, you had a clear objective to create a public work that amplifies the social implications of objects in space. We currently have a partnership with a Black artist, Marlon Forrester, designing artworks for a playground. In this project I serve as a trusted collaborator. My voice will be part of the chorus on that project as well. Stepping aside can be an act of social justice.

HBB Architecture is an instrument of power. The profession has had a role in translating abstract ideas into commodities (buildings) that create monetary value. In a capitalist system, this is the goal. Can architecture take on the role in establishing new power structures that deliver equity to communities of color and provide opportunities for wealth creation?

AP I think we need to ask who wields architecture's social and political power, how do we frame architecture as a cultural product over a commodity? It is often not the architects. We also need to ask who benefits from the architectural endeavor as a process and a construct. Who is excluded from the process and the construct? With the exception of very few, I am not convinced that architects have much power over who gets to build what; it is often driven by forces external to the profession itself. We are entrusted with the health and safety of those who inhabit the buildings we design. For architecture to establish new power structures, there needs to be radical new ways of creating opportunity. If architects can engage in local government, serve on community boards, lead community driven projects, innovate new models of design/build practices, and be better at educating developers on the value of and future impacts of the buildings being produced, then I think they can start to wield the power of architecture as a cultural endeavor.

What do you intend to do more of in to order to develop and promote the power of architecture as a cultural endeavor in your work?

HBB "What's needed today is a paradigm shift from valuing objects as an economic investment to a new moral design capitalism that serves society."[2] This quote was relayed to me by Ted Landsmark, the former President of the Boston Architectural College and has stuck in my mind. The architecture that emerges from a shared experience and exchange has motivated our office in finding modes of practice that are alternative to the traditional model. To serve a diverse society and to do creative work, we've had to take on the

Perspective overview showing the new spatial overlaps and uses. (Studio Luz Architects, *Acorns House*, Wellesley, Massachusetts, 2016.)

Various layers of the entry hall can be moved to reveal or conceal the meetings areas. (Studio Luz Architects, *Entry Hall, Acorns House*, Wellesley, Massachusetts, 2016. Photo by John Horner.)

role of initiator, fundraiser, implementer, and at times operator to see the project through its concept phase to construction. Alternatively, projects that have emerged from a moral design capital begin from a bottom's up approach. We need more of this. The renovation of Acorns House, a historic building on Wellesley College's campus, was the result of a student driven initiative—a demand to house Asian, Latinx, and LGBTQ Advising within the Office of Intercultural Education. The Acorns House is a political project. It was part of a larger mission from the institution to create a network of multicultural centers that included the existing Harambee House, focused on students of African descent, and the Slater House, which caters to the international student population. The primary challenge for Studio Luz was to design a space that could accommodate multiple cultures, a multi-cultural center that reflected multiple, intersecting identities. The Acorns project is an example of a project driven by a political will that valued a world that was interconnected and multidimensional, bringing together people with different histories and cultural backgrounds.

What I would like to see more is an inversion of the traditional client and architect power relationship by envisioning the client as part of the end user group and the architect as initiator of a project, so that we might ultimately have control in creatively finding solutions to the needs of a community. Working with Sociedad Latina—a nonprofit organization founded in 1968 that caters to at-risk Latino youth in Roxbury and whose mission is to end the destructive cycle of poverty—has been an eye-opening experience in that our firm has given agency to an organization by providing them with a feasibility study and design services so that they might own their building and resist the pressures of gentrification. The client was driven by a moral imperative of stabilizing the organization for the next fifty years. In addition to the paradigm shift of the developer model of profit-driven projects, I will continue to advocate for design commissions that go directly to support BIPOC-led firms. This is key to the survival and longevity of these firms in the re-imagination of the equitable city we long for.

1 Ibram X. Kendi, *How to Be an Antiracist* (New York: Random House, 2019), 209.

2 James P. Cramer, *Practice is Learning Through Experience*. I heard this quote from Ted Landsmark, Past President of the Boston Architectural College, as he discussed what's needed today for the professional practice and education of architects.

LUCITO

A RAKE'S PROGRESS AND THE MONUMENT AGAINST TIME

108

(-300—P)

This tale, part of an ongoing work-in-progress, is an interpretation of themes underlying the original works suggestive of the title. *A Rake's Progress* is a series of eighteenth-century paintings and etchings consisting of eight plates by the English artist William Hogarth. As a satirical moral allegory, the plates depict the rise and fall of the life of the spendthrift Tom Rakewell, starting from Tom's effortless acquisition of a great family fortune, through living his new life lavishly, to finally settling in Bedlam, the "madhouse." Throughout his journey, Tom lives with reckless abandon and forgoes life's lessons and forgivenesses.

Here, LUCITO's version presents a series of aerial satellite images of the American landscape. A monolithic specter looks upon each scene curiously. Its cast shadow reveals its presence and bears witness to events below. The specific scenes correlate to subject matter within the original. Although portrayed in a non-consecutive historical manner, cues to these leitmotifs linger throughout the imagery and accompanying captions depicting principles, events, and entities of America. In this retelling, historical narrative and ongoing events fuse, and open the way to a projective fiction that corresponds to the unfinished *Plates VII*, *Prison* and *VIII*, *Bedlam*. History folds within itself while producing an endless loop of inevitable fate.

PLATE I: THE HEIR
HULL RUST MINE, HIBBING, MN
[47°34' N, 92°31' W]

The life of this giant is limited and knowingly so, with the eventuality of its own exhaustion and death by mid-Century marking an instance of this historical object. This passing is but a mere transformation of its figure comprising only an appearance within its recent past. A three-way scar in its belly stands as a totem, which has witnessed the birth of ores bearing riches for flying machines and wars alike.

PLATE II: THE LEVÉE
SOUTHAMPTON, NY
[40°54' N, 72°27' W]

Invitees congregate for morning teatime and swing talk on the manicured links. With tailored suits fit for any occasion, the companies kept on these well-heeled lawns take stock in knowing they are united in being amongst the best; in a word, these are citizens about whom there is no question. Beware of the spit jack that is kept locked away, for hospitality a stranger will not find.

PLATE III: THE ORGY
LAS VEGAS, NV
[36°09' N, 115°22' W]

Beyond the flashing lights and buzzing black flies of the nocturnal Strip, modern day alchemists turn silica to gold. Facing vast sandy tracts and little red rocks, cul-de-sac communities with gabled horizons line endlessly patterned streets like the beads of a broken necklace. Yet dreams of homesteading for dear Fannie and Freddie are hardly complete.

All images by LUCITO, 2020.

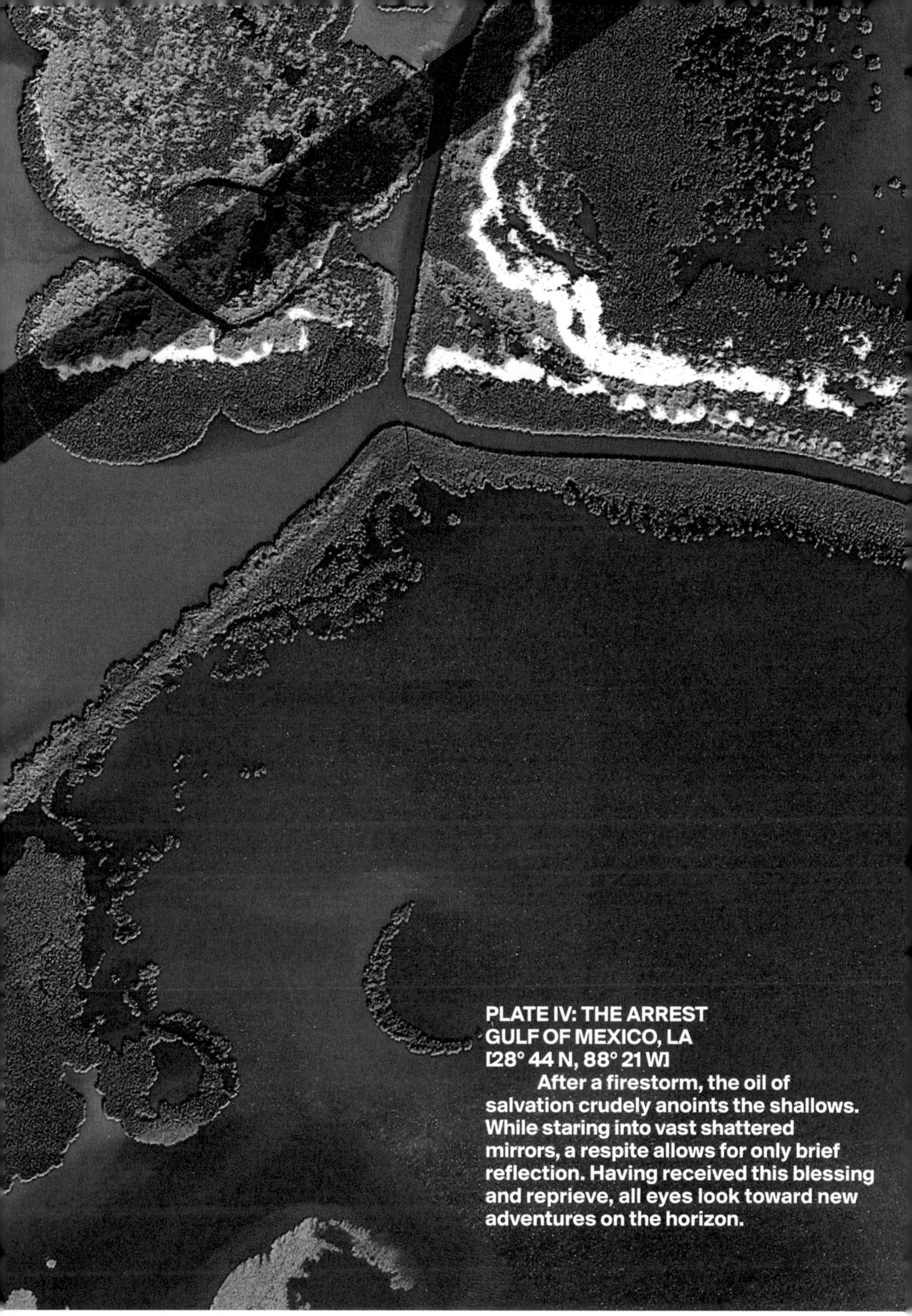

PLATE IV: THE ARREST
GULF OF MEXICO, LA
[28° 44 N, 88° 21 W]

After a firestorm, the oil of salvation crudely anoints the shallows. While staring into vast shattered mirrors, a respite allows for only brief reflection. Having received this blessing and reprieve, all eyes look toward new adventures on the horizon.

(-300–P)

PLATE V: THE MARRIAGE
ARLINGTON, VA
[38°52' N, 77°03' W]

A one-eyed cockerel filled with intelligence and sight stands hand-in-hand with those willing to fight, for now their wings rested and ready for flight. Their arrangement, though clandestine it may be, abounds with endless opportunities built on a taconite dowry.

PLATE VI: THE GAMING HOUSE
NEW YORK CITY, NY
[40°42' N, 74°00' W]

Intercourse and interchange, conflicts and crises, excess and exchange—all are resolved through the unbridled market. Heaven forbids one to question its ethics, and so it goes on making ingots from ashes. As black bears bark toward smoking towers, keep the dice rolling and do not forget to go shopping.

(-300—P)

120

(-300—P)

KATIE MACDONALD

KYLE SCHUMANN

AFTER STANDARDS

Consider for a moment the various productions of Charles and Ray Eames, a design team whose work is inseparable from methods of material, technological, and cultural production. Their oeuvre conjures images of wood formed perfectly to the curves of the spine, furniture profiles that elevate plastics and fiberglass to the halls of cultural institutions, objects which draw from near and far vernaculars, and playful multimedia productions equally suited to the museum and the classroom—each work a realization of their motto "the best for the most for the least." Such designs required intensive material processing and invention, spawning the advent of machines to process material in new ways; for instance, they developed the MacGyvered Kazam! Machine to prototype molded plywood furniture such as the Lounge Chair Wood (LCW).

And yet, a sharp contrast arises between the material and cultural assumptions of the Eames' furniture and their architecture. Their 1949 Case Study House No. 8 (more commonly, the Eames House) was a composition of sometimes novel but commercially available products supplied by manufacturers such as the Truscon Steel Company, the Swedlow Plastics Company, The Celotex Corporation, and others.[1] The home was an elegant assemblage of low cost, accessible materials, in keeping with the requirements set by Arts & Architecture's case study house program for affordable postwar housing prototypes.[2]

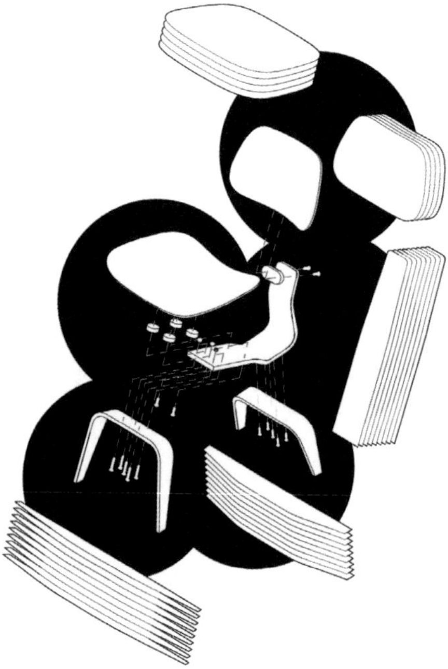

Like the LCW, the Eames House was born of postwar production, but the role of the designer in authoring material was wholly different: invention versus specification. If the Eames eagerly developed entirely new methods of industrial production for their home furnishings, then one questions why they would settle for their own home to be made of standardized products defined and manufactured by others. Couldn't the Eames' industrial processes be scaled and reimagined in the production of architectural components? What would their house be if it were designed with the same materially inventive approach as the Eames Lounge?

All images by Katie MacDonald and Kyle Schumann. **This page and opposite:** The Eames Lounge Chair Wood (LCW) was fabricated from custom parts whereas the Eames House was assembled from existing products. (2020, digital.)

MATERIAL ENTANGLEMENTS

Architectural movements are birthed by the generally agreeable but sometimes contentious pairing of technology and culture. Stereotomy and religion are to the Gothic and Renaissance as industrialization and standardization are to modernism; lineage, linguistics, and plastic commercialism are to postmodernism; high-fidelity computational customization and technocentric optimism to parametricism; and technological self-reflection and a low-fidelity translation of the digital to the post-digital. This is not to mention troves of vernacular architectures that are driven entirely by

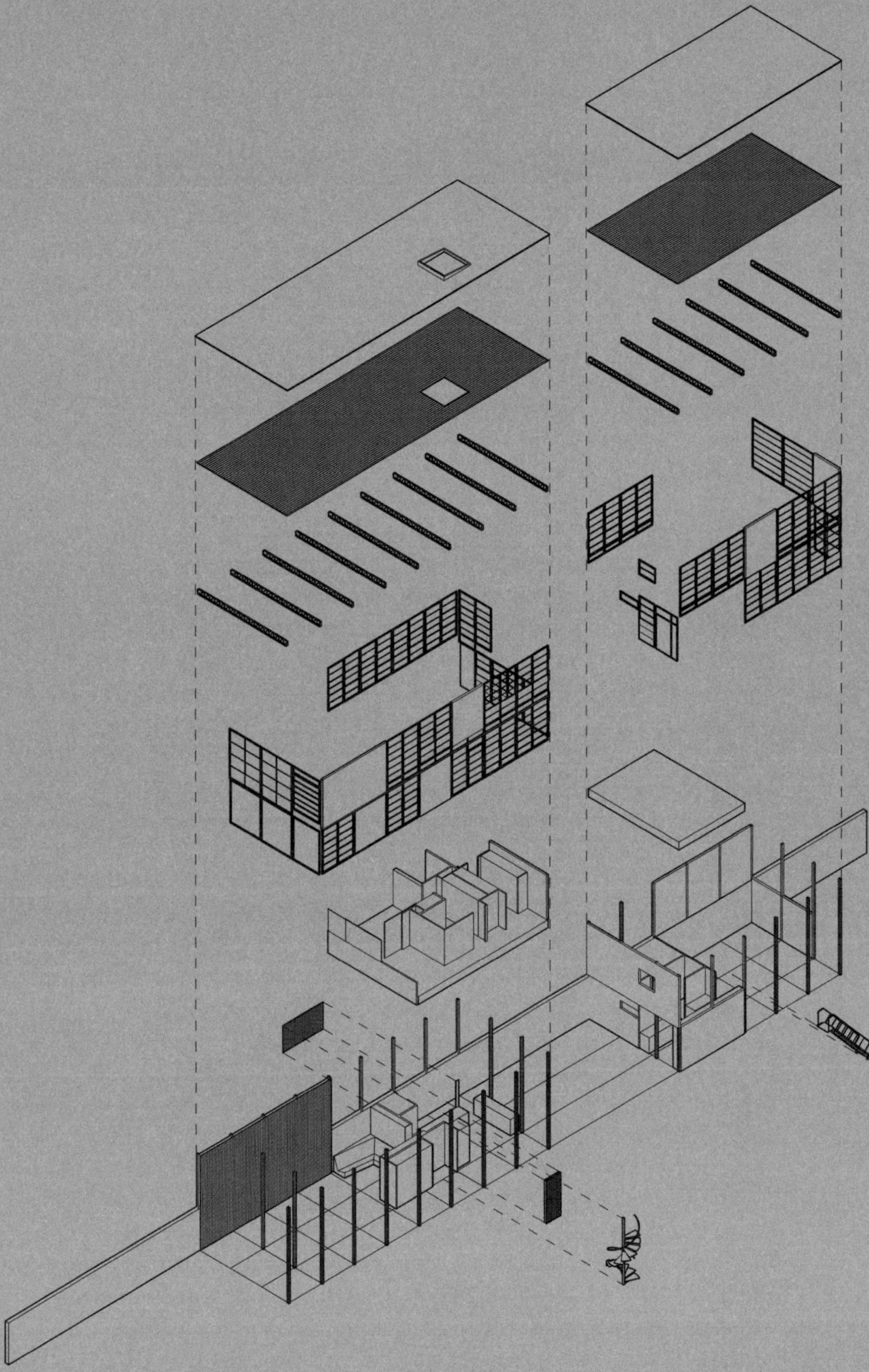

available materials and local cultural practices, but in many cases, are erased in the developing world by modernizing forces.[3] More plainly put, material practices in architecture provide a cultural and ethical portrait of their users.

Let us use modernism, the definer of canon, as the case study of this intertwining and examine its underlying causes, first and foremost of which is the Industrial Revolution. If the Industrial Revolution was primarily technological, it was necessarily also cultural; it fundamentally transformed daily life and societal expectations in the production of a developed world. Modernism, with its emergence at the end of the nineteenth century, became the physical and cultural incarnation of this new order. Otto Wagner's Austrian Postal Savings Bank (1906) and Peter Behrens' AEG Turbine Factory (1909) were among the first applications of industrial and standardized materials in novel building applications—early examples of European modernism.

Standardization was a long time in the making. In its earliest days, industrial production birthed standards, because mass production demanded uniform modes of manufacture regardless of geography. Even before mechanization, this involved "the sequencing and standardization of the artisanal gesture," particularly in the mass production of food for both military and consumer markets.[4] Driven by anthropometric data collected on army recruits, the manufacture of Civil War uniforms gave birth to the modern sizing of clothing, while the Springfield gauge established a national manufacturing standard through a set of physical artifacts, not unlike the physical Kilogram, which served as a global standard unit of measure until 2019.[5] Once physical or measurable standards were established, a number of inventions paved the way for standardization in the building industry: wood screws (1760), the hydraulic press (1795), portland cement (1824), corrugated iron (1829), plywood (1865), the automatic glue spreader (1907), phenol formaldehyde (1909), and masonite (1926), to name a few. Other uniform conventions of architectural production also soon took shape: *Architectural Graphic Standards* (first published in 1932), standards of care, and construction standards all transformed the practice of building.

The rush of new materials appealed to twentieth century designers, who, through their development before, between, and in the aftermath of the two world wars, became accustomed to the heroism of industry. The protagonists of modernist houses were often their newly available industrial materials: Le Corbusier's

Villa Savoye (1929) paired reinforced concrete with masonry blocks, allowing for the infamous free facade and ribbon windows; Pierre Chareau's Maison du Verre (1932) arranged glass block to shield inhabitants and visiting patients from the public eye; Philip Johnson's less discrete Glass House (1949) was in fact as novel for the residential application of steel as its expansive glass. And so, the tropes of modernism became entangled with a standardized material world.

UBIQUITOUS LUMBER

Perhaps nowhere was the relationship between modernism and standardized building products made more overt than in the 1931 exhibition *The Dwelling of Our Time* by Lilly Reich and Mies van der Rohe at the German Building Exhibition in Berlin.[6] The exhibition took place in a large hall and displayed full-scale prototype modern homes on the ground floor. The peripheral mezzanine was populated by an array of materials and products from which the houses were produced. One section devoted to wood, for instance, displayed the systematic processing of a massive tree into small dimension lumber, establishing a clear lineage from industrial sawmilling technology to uniform and predictable lumber. The presentation within the World's Fair-esque context of the German Building Exhibition embodied the cultural ambitions of the project and its blatant association of industrial materials with modern design—a message neatly packaged for a public audience.

By midcentury, a postwar construction boom was shaped by ease, speed, and cheapness. And there is no building product quite so easy, cheap—and therefore, ubiquitous—in American buildings than the humble two-by-four. A two-by-four is a dumbed down tree—reduced in performance and material efficiency so that it may be optimized for human labor. It is sized for the height of an average ceiling, the depth of a wall assembly, and the grasp of a contractor's hand (much like a brick, but with filleted edges and lighter so that more may be carried, and capable of achieving height far more quickly).[7] The two-by-four is advantageous certainly from an economic perspective, but also a technical one—the grading of the lumber marks its structural performance and further enables its use in predictable design assemblies. The dimensions of this single component quickly expand to encompass an entire range of sequential construction practices and building products sized to 3½" deep, 16" on-center studs: batt insulation, 4' × 8' plywood, electrical wall boxes, etc.[8] All of these products—vastly different in function, material, location, and method of manufacture—must fit neatly together on site without specialized labor and meet the prevailing cultural tastes of the day. The two-by-four and other standard (read: specifiable) building components comfort purchasers in their practicality and their machined precision, often building confidence in consumers and tradespeople regardless of skill level.

The two-by-four generates a network of standards that proliferate the building industry. (2020, digital.)

OPERATING ON STANDARDS

If Mies' brand of modernism was an intricately detailed, elevated use of industrial materials, his legacy has since undergone several major transformations that have left contemporary modernism in a very different place. The first was the transition to corporate modernism, which was explored in Rem Koolhaas' exhibition on Wallace Harrison at the Institute for Architecture and Urban Studies.[9] This new modernism highlighted by Koolhaas mandated a more economical use of material than Mies' perfectionistic and often costly expectations (epitomized by his demand for contractors to align screwheads on skyscrapers). Instead, corporate modernism's focus toward cheaper and more efficient methods of construction (economies of scale) established the shift toward standard applications of standardized materials, producing the now widespread curtain wall tower. A second transformation—the effects of which are still evolving—cemented standard wall assemblies by grounding their place in architectural production through practices of specification and BIM modeling software. These practices effectively allow building product manufacturers to dictate how and when their products should be used and feed this information to architects through big data under the guise of improving efficiency in construction management.

Since its emergence, standardization has influenced the agency of the architect. Contending with standards, designers have been alternately enabled by their practicality, confined by their limitations, and at odds with their austerity. Modernism's successors have drawn equal power from their design prowess as from their standardized material palettes, though in applications aimed more at the bespoke than the replicable: Frank Gehry's house (1978) literally and metaphorically elevates chain link fence and corrugated steel, wrapping a traditional home; Ensamble Studio's Truffle House (2010) redefines cast-in-place concrete through a formwork of earth and straw, revealed by the munching of a hungry cow; and Jennifer Bonner's Haus Gables (2018) leverages the precise machining of large cross-laminated timber panels to produce custom vaults free of beams and cross-bracing. In *Complexity and Contradiction in Architecture*, Robert Venturi writes, "is it not standardization that is without circumstantial accommodation and without a creative use of context that is to be feared more than standardization itself? The ideas of order and circumstance, convention and context—of employing standardization in an unstandard way—apply to our continuing problem of standardization versus variety."[10]

More recently, standardization has been critiqued using approaches of misinterpretation, misuse, intervention, and hybridization. These critical approaches often project the irregular onto standards and standards onto the irregular. With echoes of postmodernism and deconstructivism, the linguistics of construction see renewed interest in the structural insulated panel (SIP) dolmens of Anna Neimark, the stud wall ellipses of Erin Besler, the kit-of-parts assemblies of Laida Aguirre, and the drywall choreography of Michelle Chang. In these works, the material is the message.

MECHANICAL SAVIORISM

Le Corbusier writes extensively, as Reyner Banham does a half century later, on how the latest technological devices influence architecture.[11] For Banham, the American love affair with standardization in fact extends from a national fascination with machines: "the most fundamental American response to dreams is to purchase a piece of equipment to make them come true."[12]

Banham unpacks the ramifications of such a national obsession via the Evinrude outboard motor, which trades traditional craftsmanship, highly specialized knowledge, and an integrated, holistic design ideology for a convenient and attainable product that can be implemented by anyone, regardless of skill level—the "back-porch technologist."[13] This combination of American DIY chutzpah and the immediacy of the capitalist industrial complex continues to produce an expanding array of devices that can be added to architecture ad infinitum.

If technology and culture together define the prevailing trends in architecture, then today surely these come up against an ethical turn aimed at confronting the global climate crisis. Sustainability in architecture has taken many forms as it has moved from a fringe hippie movement to an (almost) mainstream ideal.

Tract housing under construction in Anywhere, USA. (2019, photograph.)

The aughts saw LEED and other green certifications proliferate, often propagating either formulaic space-making models related to solar orientation or, on the other hand, a quintessentially American response to the climate crisis: the invention and adoption of a plethora of "savior devices" such as solar panels, wind turbines, shading devices, Energy Star appliances, Nest thermostats, and Teslas. Like Banham's outboard motor, these fixes are more often than not a retrofitting of technology rather than a fundamental rethinking of cultural behavior. As architectural historian Daniel Barber argues: "Buildings must be conceptualized, designed, and built differently. We have to reconsider and renegotiate the terms of comfort and of productivity, equity, quality, and culture."[14] Technology in and of itself (as a perpetual retrofitted upgrade) cannot be the solution—it must be paired with a commensurate cultural response.

Perhaps then what separates the Eames' furniture from their architecture is a postwar sensibility of the house as a machine made of an aggregation of products—technologies to be obtained, owned, and conveniently used—that are (often literally) plugged in and expected to work together. The fundamental difference between the Eames House and the average American postwar suburban dwelling is that the former has the ambition to expose and celebrate the novelty, efficiency, and performance of mass-produced, standardized parts, while the latter settles for mimicking older building styles and hides the very standardized materials that enabled its production.

LOOKING BACK, MOVING FORWARD

In the absence of a critical appraisal of standardization, it is impossible for architecture to change its footing. And yet, in fragments, we as a profession have begun this evaluation. New ethics shed light on standardization's shortcomings. We are beginning to grapple with the realization that standards, in their uniform predictability, are complicit in a culture of othering. Standards conform and institutionalize their authority. They assume the existence of an ideal: one correct way. They reject other points of view, other ethics, and other cultures of production. They do not provide for deviation.

The long ignored ecological conservation warnings which emerged early in the Industrial Revolution have finally become more widely accepted, gaining attention as the climate emergency enters dire territory. We are primed to question materials that

fulfill cultural desires and societal expectations of permanence, durability, cleanliness, and precision—realizing now that these components will long outlast us as we throw ourselves into the fire. New value sets warrant a revisiting of bygone techniques, with the possibility and hope that such developments might even be extended through contemporary and emerging technologies. There may be at last an understanding that there is value in destroying less, to produce fewer, more intelligent parts. Architects, instead of designing buildings as assemblies of products, can design holistic systems and processes, working in concert with other disciplines to author methods of architectural production.

At the same time, the computational design community is unraveling similar questions; novel research utilizes technological advancements including 3D scanning and machine learning to work with irregular raw materials. The Architectural Association Hooke Park's Tree Fork Truss (2016) scans a forest of beech trees to construct a natural irregular truss while Matter Design's Cyclopean Cannibalism (2017) recycles, transforms, and optimizes concrete debris. From such approaches emerge new methods for working with labor-intensive but rapidly renewable non-traditional forest products and other biomaterials, or, as Mario Carpo puts it: "a nimbler exploitation of organic building materials like timber or stone, which may be structurally unpredictable due to natural variations."[15] Maybe architecture's answer to the capitalist model of infinite consumption is to turn material suppliers into technologists who can leverage digital readings of natural and otherwise irregular materials—for building supply chains to enter the frontier of big data, as construction management practices already have.

Banham describes technological devices that together are a kind of catchall, capable of achieving almost any imaginable outcome: "The whole gizmo bit revolves around such unique and discrete objects, named after the specific functions they serve, and this indeed is the prime utility of the whole approach: whatever you want to do, the precise gadget is in the catalogue."[16] In the case of standardized building products, the opposite is true. They force a move toward predictable, specifiable, and codified architectural assemblage. Buildings are reduced to a collection of kitbashed components.

Today's gizmo is not a catchall in the highly specific sense that it was for Banham. The new gizmo is equally acquirable but more fundamental—the Arduino, the Raspberry Pi, the Grasshopper script, an array of sensors, actuators, and visioning devices, the

Biomaterials and growing processes posit nonstandard futures. (*Homegrown*, 2020.)

smartphone that prepackages so many of these components, and the open-source software to make them all work together. These gizmos are empowering not in rendering specialized tasks convenient, but by enabling architects and designers to invent and build working methods and means of manufacture. The "back-porch technologist" is again enabled by technological products, but these are now building blocks that are infinitely more customizable and ultimately empowering to the designer and the architect who, if desired, can reclaim authorship of the components with which buildings are ultimately made.

In the wake of recent technological and cultural shifts, architecture is again at a precipice. Societal ambition to address the climate crisis allows widespread acceptance of new materials and methods that progress toward such ends. Rapid technological advancement—specifically computer visioning and machine learning—are making it possible to understand non-standard parts and simulate their performance in ways that will approach the knowability of the two-by-four. Simply put, the economies of labor, materials, and technology have transformed radically in ways that no longer justify the default specification of standardized buildings products. The conditions are right for the Eames of today to have their Kazam! House tomorrow.

1 Sheridan Burke, et al., "Eames House Conservation Management Plan," (Los Angeles: The Getty Conservation Institute, 2018); Charles Eames, "Case Study House for 1949," *Arts & Architecture* 66, no. 12 (December 1949): 26–39, in Charles and Ray Eames, *An Eames Anthology*, ed. Daniel Ostroff (New Haven: Yale University Press, 2015), 39–56; Kelsey Rose Williams, "The Materials of the Eames House," Eames Foundation, 2020, https://eamesfoundation.org/news/the-materials-of-the-eames-house/.

2 Elizabeth A.T. Smith, *Case Study Houses: The Complete CSH Program* (Cologne: Taschen, 2019).

3 For more on vernacular architecture relative to culture and technology, see: Bernard Rudofsky, *Architecture Without Architects* (New York: Doubleday, 1964); Julia Watson, *Lo-TEK: Design by Radical Indigenism* (Cologne: Taschen, 2020).

4 Mario Carpo, *The Alphabet and The Algorithm* (Cambridge: The MIT Press, 2011), 95.

5 The International Prototype of the Kilogram, or IPK, served as the standard measure of mass in the metric system from 1889–2019. See: Matt Reynolds, "This is why physicists just completely redefined the kilogram," *Wired*, November 16, 2018, https://www.wired.co.uk/article/how-many-grams-in-a-kilogram-weight-change-planck-constant.

6 Wallis Miller, "Tangible Ideas: Architecture and the Public at the 1931 German Building Exhibition in Berlin," PhD diss., (Princeton University, 1999).

7 The lighter weight also influenced the sizing standards of dimensional lumber due to the savings of transporting scant allowance over rough sawn lumber. See: U.S. Department of Agriculture, Forest Service, Forest Products Laboratory, *History of Yard Lumber Size Standards*, by L.W. Smith and L.W. Wood (Madison, Wisconsin, 1964), 2–4.

8 Jason Griffiths, Manifest Destiny: A *Guide to the Essential Indifference of American Suburban Housing* (London: AA Publications, 2011), 60.

9 Belmont Freeman, "'The moment for something to happen,'" *Places Journal*, January 2014.

10 Robert Venturi, *The Museum of Modern Art Papers on Architecture: Complexity and Contradiction in Architecture* (New York: The Museum of Modern Art, 1966), 52.

11 Le Corbusier, *Toward an Architecture*, trans. J. Goodman (Los Angeles: Getty Research Institute, 2007), 145–192.

12 Reyner Banham, "The Great Gizmo," in *Design By Choice* (London: Academy Editions, 1981), 114.

13 Ibid, 110.

14 Daniel Barber, "After Comfort," *Log* 47, (2019): 45–50.

15 Mario Carpo, *The Alphabet and The Algorithm*, 105.

16 Reyner Banham, "The Great Gizmo," 114.

134

(-250—P)

KATE
CHEN

COLLAPSING THE CLIMATE INWARDS: THE BALENCIAGA BLACK BOX

During the first week of March in 2020—amidst the global unease that was rising in response to the COVID-19 pandemic—the spectacle of Paris Fashion Week blithely runs its course. Ten days before sweeping lockdowns across the EU, Balenciaga presents an ominous vision of fashion after climate apocalypse.

The Balenciaga Fall-Winter 2020 show, staged at Cité du Cinéma in Paris, is flooded with several centimeters of water, "submerging" the coveted front-row seats.[1] Suspended from the ceiling is an immense LED screen that projects imagery of thunderstorms, floods, and blood-orange fires. The moving images and bodies are distorted in the murky waters below. Through the set design, Balenciaga reconstructs the phenomena of extreme weather within the black box of an interior space. The severe models and catastrophic visuals elicit a theatrical sense of doom—if only for the duration of the show. In appropriating the visuality of climate crisis, the Balenciaga black box offers a discursive model to examine slippages between interior and exterior within enclosed, opaque systems.

The concept of "climate interiorization" has a substantial, though fragmented, history within architecture. Before delving into the narrative of the black box, it's useful to consider a few precedents of interiorized climates. In particular, the concept is often encapsulated within speculative, avant-garde architecture. Two instances: Étienne-Louis Boullée's *Cenotaph for Newton* (1784) and Buckminster Fuller's Dome Over Manhattan (1960) both embody "climate interiorization" through their radical form, aesthetics, and operations. In these proposals, the interior is an immense, omni-directional Globe that obfuscates and renegotiates its relationship to the exterior. For Boullée, the formal qualities of the Globe are essential in constructing a space that is devoid of edges or boundaries. The vastness and smoothness of this type of interior collapses a body's relation to scale and directionality, allowing for immersion within a virtual "night" or "day."[2] Fuller, on the other hand, proposes a two-mile diameter geodesic dome that would geo-engineer the Manhattan "interior" into a temperate, subtropical microclimate.[3] While Boullée's monument reaches towards an architectural sublime, Fuller's techno-utopian plan grounds itself in its supposed energy efficiency. Regardless of functionality, these proposals both center around the figure of the Globe as a strategy for interiorizing climate. It's also worth noting that these proposals, likely due to technological or financial limitations, were never built.

The 1950–70s foster a new cultural fixation on "climate interiorization" through an understanding of the entirety of Earth as an enclosed interior. Bucky Fuller's "Spaceship Earth" theory embodies this attitude towards humanity.[5] It is not without irony that cybernetics and artificial satellites are the sensing tools that elicit a shift towards climate and ecological awareness. A critical moment

Previous: Balenciaga Fall-Winter 2020 Ready-to-wear, Paris Fashion Week. The scenography, designed by Berlin-based architecture studio sub, shares a visual language with planetariums and sci-fi cinema in its immersive aestheticization of climate. (La Mode en Images, "Balenciaga Fall-Winter 2020 Women's Ready-to-Wear in Paris," 2020, photograph.)
Opposite top: Boullée proposes a mausoleum dedicated to the "sublime mind" of Sir Isaac Newton who "defined the shape of the Earth." In his writings, Boullée expresses disappointment in not being able to reproduce the "magnificence" of nature through the architectural design.[4] (Étienne-Louis Boullée, *Cenotaph for Newton*, 1784, drawing.)
Opposite bottom: Buckminster Fuller and Shoji Sadao propose a two-mile diameter geodesic dome that would create an artificial temperate microclimate. This is one of many of Fuller's projects that reflects his theories on the sustainability of a global interior. (R. Buckminster Fuller and Shoji Sadao, *Dome Over Manhattan*, c. 1960, drawing.)

The Blue Marble is perhaps one of the most reproduced images in history. This image, along with other cultural artifacts from the postwar era of space exploration, contributes to a "universalist" understanding of Earth as a global interior.[8] (NASA/Apollo 17 crew, taken by either Harrison Schmitt or Ron Evans, *The Blue Marble*, December 7, 1972, photograph.)

occurred when the photograph *The Blue Marble* (1972, NASA) as seen from Apollo 17 was released into the public domain.[6] This image accomplishes "the modernist project of interiorization of the whole. It is this sudden feeling that at the very moment we have reached outer space physically, we have lost any meaningful sense of the real outside."[7] *The Blue Marble* is perhaps historically one of the most holistic yet reductive visual artifacts of an "interior" system. As this image saturates mass media, another strange shift happens: the figure of the Globe goes out of fashion. Reconstructing the *spatiality* of Earth is redundant when satellite images contain infinitesimally more detail. Images act as high-resolution proxies to reality and require a different form of architecture: flat planes as projection surfaces and digital screens. Soon, the black box supersedes the Globe as a spatial typology that mediates the vast distance between body and climate.

The Balenciaga Fall-Winter 2020 show operates as a black box in a few significant ways. First, the black box, in its association with cinema and theater, is an architecture of virtuality. The smoothness of interface between the human eye and the projection screen achieves a sensation of immersion that goes beyond the spatial necessity of the Globe. For Balenciaga, climate collapse is scalable within a fashion show and evocative as a visual branding strategy. The LED-screen weather simulations are taken from the perspective of drones and satellites, or possibly artificially generated. This type of machine-oriented vision feels like a logical progression from *The Blue Marble* as a visual artifact, as it is simultaneously holistic and reductive. Even though these images are not (human) embodied perspectives, they feel familiar. Perhaps the familiarity stems from the visual memory of IMAX planetariums or GoogleEarth explorations in a dark room. And despite the prophesying of climate catastrophe, no real danger is imminent inside. The Balenciaga black box is immersive theater, after all. Nonetheless, sensations of destabilization and disembodiment are highly palpable. From the destructive visions above to its distorted reflection below, there is no solid ground to re-orient oneself. Machine-vision may be a lucid perspective on climate transformations, but the view from above is vertiginous.

Beyond cinema and theater, it's fascinating to consider the expanded definition of the black box within cybernetics. In modern computing, the black box is defined as an "opaque space", or "a device, system or object which can be viewed in terms of its inputs and outputs [...] without any knowledge of its internal workings."[9] In this sense, the Balenciaga black box functions not only as a visual device, but also as a kind of opaque, condensation machine. The internal workings—networked, human, or climatized—are intentionally obscured. Computers are black boxes, as well as refrigeration units. While the black box theory is applicable to countless technological, infrastructural, and operating systems, the data center is perhaps its most direct architectural manifestation. The data center, a climatized storage space for computing systems, is also an ideal spatial model for "climate interiorization." Its highly regulated facilities maintain stable temperatures and relative humidity through an internal feedback loop. Secured by physical and virtual protocols of CCTV networks, multi-factor authentication, single entry point access, data encryption, and on-site security guards, etc., data centers are nearly impenetrable and entirely opaque. Nonetheless, the black box remains susceptible to other systematic deviations. Namely, the indeterminacy of climate.

In 2013, the media reported an anomaly at the Facebook Data Center in Oregon. During an afternoon heat wave, the HVAC system of the data center attempted to compensate for the dry air and inadvertently executed "relative humidity exceeding 95%."[10] As the cool air inside the vents condensed, water began to drip down onto the servers, causing them to short-circuit. "For a few minutes, you could stand in Facebook's data center and hear the pop and fizzle of Facebook's ultra-lean servers obeying the ultra-uncompromising laws of physics."[11] In other words, Cloud computing manifested its own rain clouds. This "humidity event"[12] collapses the outside inwards, invoking a sense that the boundaries of interior and exterior are not as hermetic as we were led to believe. Despite the apparent mundanity of HVAC systems within black boxes, an inexplicable agency of chance (weather) persists. The enclosed black box remains an open system.

The Balenciaga black box shares certain parallels to the data center "humidity event." On one hand, the show operates as an enclosed system with an interior environment that is as highly regulated as its guest list. The aesthetics of climate collapse are staged primarily through visual devices. On the other hand, the flooded runway is tangibly damp, murky, opaque, and quite possibly reeks of mildew. This form of a leak, unlike the data center "humidity event," was intentionally designed. However, as liquid seeps into improbable physical spaces, other ontological questions begin to emerge. The uncanniness of the scenography appears remote from the usual semiotics of a fashion show. It is unclear whether the Balenciaga black box engulfs the aesthetics of catastrophe more effectively as a social critique or as a provocative campaign. Perhaps that distinction doesn't matter. The unlikely coupling of couture garments and stagnant water is as grotesque as electrical servers and rain. In all its grotesqueness, it is also seductive. Material conflations of such disparate objects and bodies begin to dissolve the boundaries between them, potentially creating substances or situations that are ambiguously defined, open-ended, perhaps even swamp-like. The viscous surface of the runway melds into glossy leather. Projected images of water become indistinguishable from liquid water. Subsequently, the boundaries of interior and exterior collapse and fold into each other.

Opposite left: Balenciaga Fall-Winter 2020 Look 103. **Right:** Look 85 detail. The gloss of latex garments against the wet surface is visually striking. While Balenciaga is often known for its deviance from the usual semiotics of luxury, it also reinforces its status through fashion's commercializing of "subversiveness." The use of "fetish" materials—such as leather and latex—with priestly silhouettes is understood through this lens. The critique of fashion's contribution to climate crisis could also be interpreted as a form of subversive commentary, though its position from within the fashion industry remains ambivalent. (Photos by Alessandro Lucioni, 2020.)

The unfolding events of the climate crisis necessitates new models in reimagining the perverse, polluted ontology of objects and bodies. If cultural images are a distorted reflection of scientific realities, then the Balenciaga black box serves as a beguiling forecast for contingent futures. In this instance, "nature exceeds our grasp but only through our staging of the fantasy of ecological collapse."[13] A fashion show which employs the dark aesthetics of "eco-catastro-porn"[14] does not bring one any closer or further from imminent crisis, rather we may find ourselves even more inextricably entangled within it. As these speculations continue to infiltrate the realms of fashion, data centers, and avant-garde architecture, they also call for heightened sensitivity to other forms of agency, i.e. non-human or artificial. There is, for example, the agency of malfunctioning HVAC systems or mildew propagating within textiles. Further, one could consider hybridity within a multitude of ecologies and timescales: styrofoam in ocean water, probiotics in our gut, CFCs in the ozone, Teflon in bloodstreams, mycelium networks in a forest, and so on. Enclosed systems of any scale, from the body to the planetary, are precarious spaces that are teeming with mutability and intricacy.

Balenciaga Fall-Winter 2020 runway show scenography detail. Photograph by sub.

The pure form of the Globe is an inadequate model of this spatial reality, as it attempts to embody "totality" by suppressing moments of impurity or permeability. In contrast, the black box pretends to be a neutral space; it recedes into the shadows and requires images to perform as environments. In the presence of hyper-real images (satellite, drone, machine-hallucinated, etc.), the black box is nearly imperceptible. Nonetheless, the tendency towards leaks, glitches, and the occasional rain cloud betrays its material presence. It is precisely these malfunctions that makes the black box so compelling as a spatial model in the era of climate crisis. The neoliberal progression towards a platonic black box is overflowing and bursting at its seams. Its structural failures necessitate alternative concepts of "enclosure" that would allow for permeability, fluidity, and indeterminacy.

During the closing of the Balenciaga show, a lonely image of *The Blue Marble* floats in the darkness of the vast interior. In this moment, the black box and the Globe are intermeshed. Meanwhile, as sea levels continue to rise at unprecedented rates, Balenciaga forecasts the endurance of luxury fashion through latex garments. The conflation of clothing and climate into a single space produces another uneasy realization: soon we might not be able to distinguish the boundary between fashion branding and images of climate catastrophe. After all, "it is easier to imagine an end to the world than an end to capitalism."[15] In facing uncertain ecological futures, the entanglement of architecture, climate and technology all collapsing inwards becomes the new, fashionable normal. Yet recognizing the permeable, polluted, perverse material and spatial possibilities that emerge is perhaps a hopeful approach in the aftermath of such a crisis.

1 The writings and ideas of Keller Easterling, Donna Haraway, Ursula K. Le Guin, Timothy Morton, Hito Steyerl, and Anna Tsing were critical to the development of this essay.

Thank you to my editors, Todd Petrie and Zeli Grey, and to Niklas Bildstein Zaar and Andrea Faraguna at sub.

Jennifer Hahn, "Balenciaga floods runway for apocalyptic Paris Fashion Week show," *Dezeen*, March 3, 2020. https://www.dezeen.com/2020/03/03/balenciaga-flood-paris-fashion-week-show-water-set-design/.

2 Etienne-Louis Boullée, *Architecture, Essay on Art*, ed. Helen Rosenau, trans. Sheila de Vallée (Paris, FR: Academy Editions, 1976), pp. 105–107.

3 Anthony Vidler, "Whatever Happened To Ecxology? John McHale and the Bucky Fuller Revival," *Log*, no. 13/14 (Fall 2008): pp. 139–146.

4 Boullée, *Architecture, Essay on Art*.

5 R. Buckminster Fuller, *Operating Manual for Spaceship Earth* (Carbondale, IL: Southern Illinois University Press, 1969).

6 Interiors Agency, "Black Hole Catalog: Tools for Extinction," *032c*, no. 37 (2019): pp. 57–75.

7 Lukas Likacvan, "III. The Globe," in *Introduction to Comparative Planetology* (Moscow: Strelka Press, 2018), pp. 36–59.

8 Ibid.

9 Mario Bunge, "A General Black Box Theory," *Philosophy of Science* 30, no. 4 (1963): pp. 346–358.

10 Several online news sources report the "raincloud" inside the Facebook data center. Facebook's VP of Engineering, Jay Parikh was quoted: "I got a call, 'Jay, there's a cloud in the data center.' 'What do you mean, outside?' 'No, inside.'" Jack Clark, "Facebook's first data center DRENCHED by ACTUAL CLOUD," *The Register*, June 8, 2013, https://www.theregister.com/2013/06/08/facebook_cloud_versus_cloud/.

Planetology (Moscow: Strelka Press, 2018), pp. 36–59.

8 Ibid.

9 Mario Bunge, "A General Black Box Theory," *Philosophy of Science* 30, no. 4 (1963): pp. 346–358.

10 Several online news sources report the "raincloud" inside the Facebook data center. Facebook's VP of Engineering, Jay Parikh was quoted: "I got a call, 'Jay, there's a cloud in the data center.' 'What do you mean, outside?' 'No, inside.'" Jack Clark, "Facebook's first data center DRENCHED by ACTUAL CLOUD," *The Register*, June 8, 2013, https://www.theregister.com/2013/06/08/facebook_cloud_versus_cloud/.

11 Ibid.

12 Ibid.

13 Ben Woodard, "Uncomfortable Aesthetics," in *Speculative Aesthetics* (London: Urbanomic Media Ltd, 2014), pp. 84–85.

14 Ibid.

15 Quote attributed by Mark Fischer to both Fredric Jameson and Slavoj Žižek, and popularized by Internet memes circa late 2010s. Mark Fisher, *Capitalist Realism: Is There No Alternative?* (Winchester, UK: Zero Books, 2010), p. 2.

146

(-125—P)

LIOR
GALILI

CATHARSIS REIFIED: THE OMNIPRESENCE OF PAST THEATER IN MANHATTAN'S TIMES SQUARE

And so we are already living out the *coexistence of a past not only present but omnipresent*, a past that gets in the way of the future...

—Bernard Tschumi, foreword to *A Landscape of Events*, 2000.[1]

Theater as the public program of Manhattan's Times Square ceased to function by the end of the 1920s, but the *phenomenon of theater* has shaped (and still is shaping) the site's identity since its inception. The transformation of Times Square's theater-houses into movie houses during the 1930s marks the beginning of what would later be identified as the site's DNA: a site shaped by a constant shift of its ruling media. Despite this endless shift, a persistent presence of the collective memory of theater is inscribed in and creates new urban forms. During the early 1990s, a massive redevelopment plan called the *42nd Street Development Project* dramatically changed the nature and characteristic of the site's public space. The preserved theaters in Times Square emerged as a key component of that plan. Carrying the social task of retaining the spirit and reputation of the original Times Square, the theater preservation plan is a symptom of the reconstruction of collective identity through an interiority, which is set against a diffused social and spatial background. More than anything, the preserved theater resulted from the recollection of the social practice of empathy—or identification with the hero on stage. Asserting that empathy is both a practice (enhances social exchange) and a matter (manifests in spatial form) allows for a unique discussion of the interplay between the inscribed experience and the inscribed construction of the theater. Empathy at the core of the inscribed experience of theater functions as the precondition that instigates the Aristotelian Catharsis—the relief an audience feels after an emotional purgation of pity and fear.[2] As the producer of these public emotions, catharsis is ultimately linked to the inscription of the theater construction.

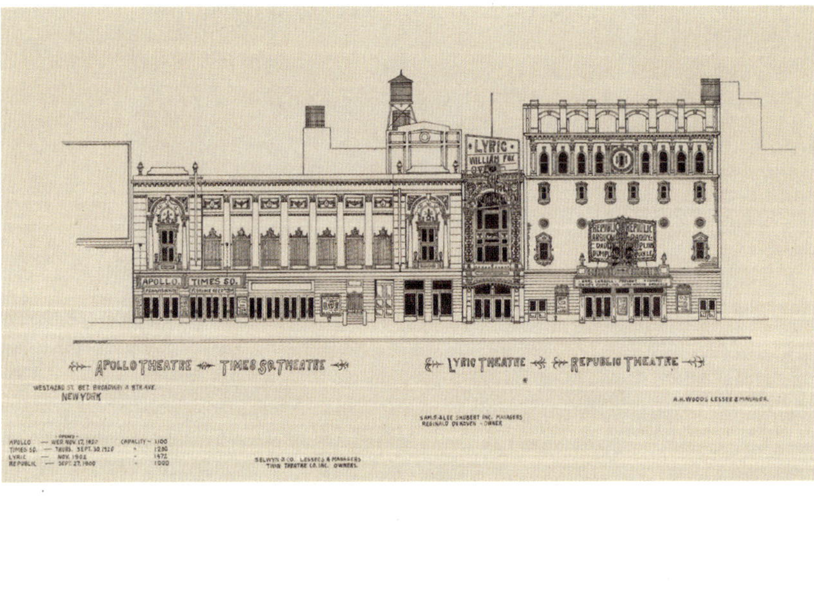

Historical Theaters Along 42nd. (Anthony F. Dumas, *Apollo Theatre, Times Sq. Theatre, Lyric Theatre and Republic Theatre*, 1916–1936, pen and ink drawing.)

A Glimpse into Times Square's Reconstruction: The Cut of Time Square Theater's Original Ceiling Dome. (AYON Studio [preservation architect], *Times Square Theater*, New York, 2019. Photo by Alexander Severin.)

In response to Aristotle's concept of Catharsis, in his 1979 *Theatre of The Oppressed*, Brazilian director and theorist Augusto Boal points out the political use, effect, and power of people's activation through collective purgation.[3] Catharsis as a medical metaphor was first introduced in Aristotle's *Poetics* to portray the dynamic power of the audience's identification with the hero in Greek Theater.[4] While Aristotle declares the artistic independence of poetry and theater from politics, it is precisely through the act of catharsis that Boal claims, "Aristotle constructs the first, extremely powerful poetic-political system for intimidation of the spectator, for elimination of the 'bad' or illegal tendencies of the audience."[5] According to him, the exploitation of the identification with the drama's hero that results in catharsis serves not only to apply but also to inscribe social ideologies and agendas. Furthermore, "This system is, to this day, fully utilised not only in conventional theatre, but in the TV soap operas and in Western films as well."[6] The social agenda that underpins the preservation of the theaters in Times Square is the object of my observation. The preserved theater emerged in response to decades of perceived "bad" and illegal tendencies—from porn to prostitution to all sorts of crime and sleaze. Since the preservation plan attempted to rectify a social and urban affliction through media, it begs critical questions as to the political agency applied through the return of the theater—both as media and as metamorphosed interior public space, and on the functioning of what stays *after* the lived experience has already gone.

In 1895, producer and businessman Oscar Hammerstein I erected a game-changing theater in the middle of what would later become known as Times Square.[7] Hammerstein's Olympia Theater marked not only the physical center, but also the center of gravity and identity of the future theater district. The building spanned an entire block between 44th and 45th Streets on Broadway Avenue, the most central—most contracted—spot within the "X" shape of the streets. First its magnitude, then its location, ensured its kinetic and optic domination of the site. Thus, although it chronologically was the second theater on site (the first was the American Theater built in 1893),[8] it functioned conceptually as the pioneer-attractor and precursor to the formal arrival of Times Square. In 1899, a second Hammerstein construction, Victoria Theater, was erected across from Olympia Theater.[9] The Victoria Theater marked a no-less-significant location, the corner of 42nd Street and 7th Avenue—which would later become the symbolic gate to Times Square. With the center and the essential corner occupied by Hammerstein's theaters, a predominating cultural infrastructure was ready to underpin the future urban construction of the site.

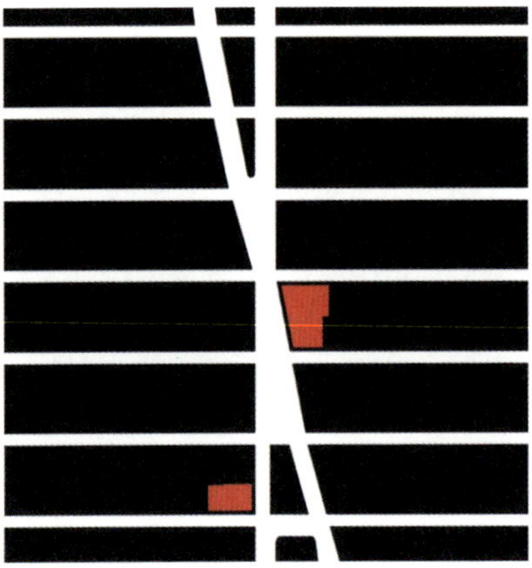

Illustration by Lior Galili. *The Emergence of Theaters' Infrastructure in Times Square*, 2020, mixed media.

Officially announced on April 8, 1904, Times Square emerged as a new urban site following the erection of the Times Tower and the opening of the Interborough Rapid Transit Station.[10] At its inception, it was already well established as the city's Theater District. Contrary to this glorious reputation, the actual fabric of Times Square materialized a social schism: while the theater industry governed its interior spaces, the sex trade dominated its exterior streets.[11] In this unique urban configuration, physical and psychological boundaries collapsed. The interior spaces inspired virtual life while the street provided its actualization, and on a different level, the theater was where one exercised empathy, while the street allowed for the opposite social practice.

Attempts to define the psychological nature of empathy in relation to perception have preoccupied German philosophers since the late eighteenth century, but only in 1873 did Robert Vischer first discuss it in terms of shape.[12] Expanding upon earlier studies of aesthetics, Vischer releases the relations between object, subject, and gaze from an assumed fixed end into an imagined vivid space.[13] More significantly, he introduces the functioning of this space as an autonomous spatial unit comprising a closed, dynamic, and surprisingly symmetrical interaction. This symmetry, according to Vischer, is formed when the perception of an object's exterior limits evokes "the sensation of my own physical boundaries, which I feel on, or rather with, my own skin."[14]

"Vischer's preoccupation with the dermal threshold of the human body," writes cultural theorist Patrick Anderson, "his [...] focus on the active engagement of the skin in seeing—was directly related to [...] *Einfühlung* [the German term for empathy] as a boundary crossing experience by which the subject both entered and was entered by the object."[15] Thus, the skin serves a site of sensation and negotiation between object and subject, and the shape of that interaction is marked by the void existing between their ends. In this way, the shape of the empathic exchange arrives in the form of a collision between the temporal, the dynamic interplay between subject and object, and the spatial, the space between their ends. Since the exterior skin of Times Square's historical theaters marked the end of a legitimate fantasy, it functioned as a site of heightened sensation and negotiation: it marked not only one's own physical boundaries, but also the psychological end of a dream. Correspondingly, the interior vessel of the actual theater hall carried the heightened responsibility of serving as both physical and psychological protective shield. A responsibility reserved for a closed world sustaining an empathic dynamic exchange. This voided vessel would later be inscribed as a social-spatial and temporal unit comprising catharsis (as its media) and the memory of empathy (as its shape).

The memory of the social practice of empathy began to play a symbolic role by the end of the second decade of Times Square, when most theaters had been converted into movie houses.[16] The voided theaters hastened the emergence of a new form of entertainment: the theaters on West 42nd Street specialized in older movies emphasizing action and violence that appealed to a male-dominated rather than a family-friendly audience. Following that, an increasing level of illegitimate activities started filling the streets and on the eve of World War II, West 42nd Street was widely considered unsafe. By the 1970s, the Times Square area was experiencing, in real estate professor Lynne B. Sagalyn's words, the "slide downhill from grinders to burlesque to grit to commercialism to honky-tonk debauchery to sex on the hoof to a market-place for pornography."[17] Since 1937, Manhattan city planners had focused on eradicating crime and sleaze to provide a solution for something that appeared to be out of control. By the beginning of the 1980s, this tension culminated in actual change.[18] The preserved theater in Times Square emerged as part of a comprehensive urban renewal plan called the *42nd Street Development Project* (42DP), which was initiated in the early 1980s, executed in the mid-1990s, and is anticipated to be fully completed by 2021. The plan focused on the two-and-a-half blocks (from 39th to 42nd Streets) that define Times Square's entrance and consisted of the renovation of seven historic theaters.[19] It developed in response to two distinct demands: the social demand to clean up a site afflicted with delinquency and a real estate demand for commercial space. While the theaters' renovations stemmed from a desire to retain the cultural spirit of the original Times Square,[20] their execution reveals a gap between the ideal and the actual theater.

TOWARDS A REVERSED INTERIORITY

In a 2016 Harvard GSD public lecture titled "Interior and Interiority," urban sociologist Richard Sennett discusses the relationship between the physical interior space and the mental state defined as interiority—or subjectivity.[21] Sennett proposes a counter-account to the link made by the nineteenth-century European bourgeoisie between interior spaces and mental interiority. According to him, the modern city gives rise to a new type of subjectivity—one that results from a need to counteract the overwhelming exterior stimuli. The emergence of subjectivity, which is linked to exteriority, forms what he describes as a "divided self": a division between being outside but feeling inside. The radical change to the public space of Times Square that followed the implementation of the 42DP in the mid-1990s created a fertile ground for the arrival of an urban subjectivity that sustains a split between being and feeling. The desire to preserve the site's glory that inspired the theater preservation plan evoked an equal effort to save the site's exterior aesthetics. A struggle to protect Times Square's exterior aesthetics resulted in extensive zoning regulations intended to convey a sense of place through prescribed procedures.[22] Embedded in law, the new imagery of Times Square conveys a distinct visual, spatial, and temporal diffusion—a diffusion that shatters the old center of gravity and identity, namely, the theater as we knew it.

Probing the construction of self-identity, social psychologist Erik Erikson points to the relationship between spatial and identity diffusions. According to him, "diffusion" is inherently a spatial term: "In identity diffusion, ...a split of self-images is suggested, [that is] a loss of center and dispersion."[23] In this context, the preserved theater in Times Square—or, the attempt to rectify its center of origin—is a symptom of reconstructing a collective identity through an interior space situated against a diffused socio-spatial fabric. Hence, it cannot be read merely as the return of a lost interiority, but rather as its re-configured form. If the urban intensification of Times Square created a type of subjectivity that is based on a wall-less mental protection, what kind of physical interiority is shaped in return? In the context of the resurrected theater we must also ask: What role does the memory of the shape of empathy play if the updated cathartic experience is depleted from a symmetrical exchange?

Emerging Media in Times Square's Interior Spaces. (*Aging Magician*, performed at the New Victory Theater, 2017. Photo by Jill Steinberg.)

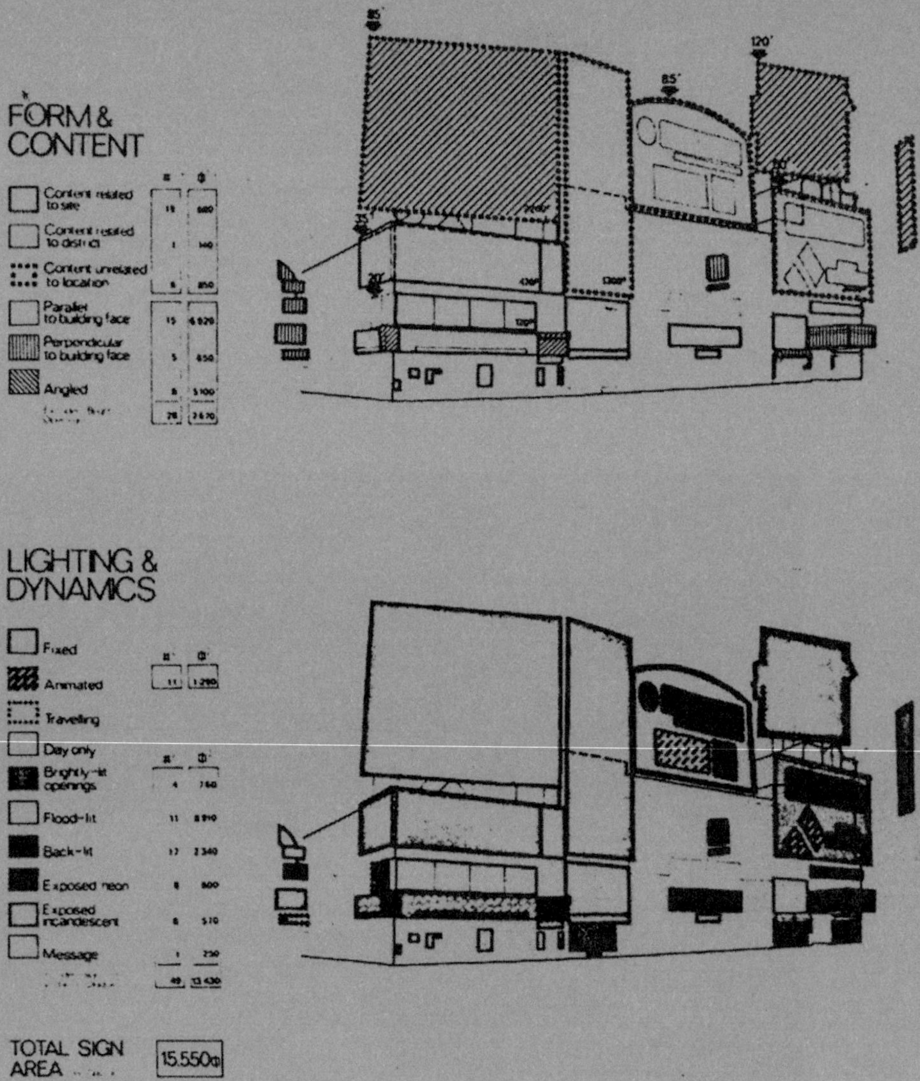

New Regulations for Times Square Exteriority. (NYC Department of City Planning, "Midtown Development Review," July 1987. Reproduced from Lynne B. Sagalyn, *Times Square Roulette: Remaking the City Icon* [Cambridge, MA: MIT Press, 2003], 254.)

Distinct from the surrounding buildings, the three adjacent theaters along 209–215 West 42nd Street create an urban sequence that testifies to the existence of a different era. Their preserved shells, however, do not reveal their function or shelter authenticity.The means, modes, and methods of the resurrected theater exist behind those walls. Coincidentally or not, this syntactic cluster encapsulates a full-circle closure of the mid-1990s theater preservation plan—now spanning over twenty years—as the New Victory Theater, restored in 1995,[24] was the pioneering project of the 42DP, and the renovation of the New Times Square Theater, which is yet to be completed, is its closing chapter. This chronological gap grants us a unique opportunity to explore the social and political agencies of the resurrected theater through a generous temporal extrusion. On the ground of what is now New Victory Theater, in 1900 Hammerstein erected Theatre Republic as an extension of Hammerstein's Victoria. The playhouse opened in September of that year, with *Sag Harbor* by James A. Herne[25]—a play centered

Aging Magician, performed at the New Victory Theater, 2017. (This image was taken at MASS MoCA, 2016.) Photo by Jill Steinberg.

around the ethos of marriage and motherhood through the story of a love triangle among two brothers in love with the same (orphan) girl.[26] A cathartic moment arrives in the form of her declaration of independence from both brothers—an act granted only by the power of her motherhood.[27] While evoking a feminist sentiment for the protagonist's newfound assertiveness, this sort of catharsis makes use of the ordinary boundaries reserved for females of that era, dooming them to redemption through the will to sacrifice their individuality for their kids. Kids as the cleansing cure for moral affliction would arrive later in the history of the theater, in the context of a much greater social wound. Using similar themes, for over a decade, dramas and melodramas on family, women's traditional roles, the adaptation of immigrants to American life, and other manifestations of bourgeois standards continued to play at the theater.[28] In 1914, the theater was subleased to the Universal Film Manufacturing Company,[29] marking the beginning of the end of the centrality of the theatrical play to the venue's identity. An inevitable downhill slide from film, to grinders, to burlesque, to pornographic films inscribed a social shame in the collective memory that only a radically different program could heal. Following the logic of cathartic rectification, this theater, which was symbolically renamed "Victory" after World War II but was most vividly inscribed as a notorious porn house, could only be resurrected in the form of New York City's first theater for kids and families.[30]

Beyer Blinder Belle, proposed design for second-floor interior of the New Times Square Theater, New York, 2018, rendering.

In December 1995, the New Victory Theater reopened with the Canadian circus production *Cirque Éloize*.[31] This show unveiled the new venue's agenda and shift in artistic form: a spectacular choreography of bodies in space; a scattered dissemination of actors on stage; a lavish stimuli of lights, colors, and sound effects; and, most essentially, a replacement of criticality by sensational sensuality. Over the course of the twenty-five years since its inception, the vast majority of the productions in the new theater rendered an ecstatic expression of spatial and temporal diffusion of all kinds. A new relationship, not only between audience and actors, but also between media and construction, emerged.

An Old Construction Displays A New Media. (Hardy Holzman Pfeiffer Associates, *Interior, New Victory Theater*, New York, 1995. Photo by Elliot Kaufman.)

WICHES
SALADS
FOODS

TIMES SQUARE
WELCOME TO THE SHOW
NEW VICTORY
NEW VICTORY
NEW VICTORY
HARRY POTTER
AND THE CURSED CHILD
mazda
Subway

Previous: Beyer Blinder Belle, proposed façade design for the New Times Square Theater, New York, 2018, rendering. This page top: Byron Company, *Hammerstein's Olympia*, 1895, gelatin silver print. Bottom: The Arrival of a Returned Theater. (Beyer Blinder Belle, proposed design for third-floor interior of the New Times Square Theater, New York, 2018, rendering.)

Twenty-three years after the reopening of the New Victory Theater, in 2018, Stillman Development International released a new architectural vision for the adjacent Times Square Theater in the form of a new glass box wrapped around the existing limestone façade.[32] Designed by Beyer Blinder Belle Architects, the renovation converts the original theater, designed in 1920,[33] into a five-story shopping mall.[34] While the project is yet to be completed, its press-release images evidence the transformation of a collective memory of the shape of empathy into a built form. In its new incarnation, this shape defines the spatial boundaries of the experience of shopping. Central to that experience is a rounded circulation area delineating an organic and smooth embarkation on the ship of shops and sales. The historic playhouse, which opened in September 1920, with Edgar Selwyn's *The Mirage*, a melodrama about a country girl who arrives in the big city and ends up being kept by a wealthy married man,[35] now offers a similar cathartic reward to its millennial shoppers: a guarantee of true love in return for submissive devotion to the loop and hook of the circulation of commodities.

Two design decisions reveal the social agenda underpinning the metamorphosed form: the original façade is lifted and transformed into a cantilevered space surrounded by a glass curtain wall, and the original proscenium arch and ceiling dome were selected to be restored and displaced. This dual focus of the restoration, which on the one hand elevates the external wall, and on the other, retains the elements of the interior container that were responsible for the cathartic event, renders clear the relationship between the proposed and historical theaters. The exterior skin of the New Times Square Theater is a densified and intensified site of negotiation, but rather than dividing between reality and fantasy, it heightens their ambivalence. The interior theater hall has returned in the form of select pieces forcing an extrapolation regarding its whole. This whole is based on the inscribed boundaries between audience and actors, on the distance between the dramatic action and its recipients, and on the outline of the void—now a mold—created by a social empathic exchange. It is through this extrapolation that one witnesses the arrival of a reified catharsis as a built shape.

It is not easy to argue for the transformation of a fleeting phenomenon such as catharsis, or to prove the materialization of a de-materialized social fabric such as audience's empathy, but the first and last theaters to be preserved under the 42DP exemplify at least two possible—and perhaps opposite—returns of the old theater. At New Victory Theater we see a shell that remains the same, but its media is changed to eliminate catharsis: mirroring the exterior atmosphere, the new programming replaces the theatrical experience of identification with the hero on stage by the sensation of imagery diffusion in space. Since the interior and exterior events share great proximity, the shell's traditional psychological protective function as the boundary between the two is nullified. Furthermore, precisely because it is acting as a neutralized vessel it enhances and intensifies all sorts of exploded modes of expression on and off the stage. Revealing an opposite application of the collective memory of theater, the New Times Square Theater arrives in the form of a renovated shell, which hosts no media. It is at first glance further distanced from its origin. However, its proposed construction suggests that catharsis has returned not only as a shape, but also as a (transformed) system of intimidation. The return of catharsis as an explicit shape is marked by the newly added spiral stairway. It imitates not only the curvature of the last theater's wall, but also the distance between the center of the proscenium and the center of the stage. Against the diffused social and spatial background of Times Square's exteriority, the memory of the original theater creates an interiority which directs, collects, and concentrates. There, the old catharsis is reified, and a new catharsis emerges—one that leverages sentiment for the old theater for a new social agenda, in which the identification with the hero on stage is replaced by an identification with commodities on shelves. Consequently, a theatrical public emotion is replaced by a neoliberal, anxious—yet centered and still—public motion. Anxious and futile, this motion is what persists after the lived empathic exchange is gone—a vestige of collective purgation of fear, once through the dread and the dream in drama, and now through the imagined power of trade.

1 Bernard Tschumi, foreword to *A Landscape of Events*, by Paul Virilio, trans. Julie Rose (Cambridge, MA: MIT Press, 2000).

2 Aristotle, *Poetics*, trans. S. H. Butcher (The Internet Classics Archive, 1994), http://classics.mit.edu/Aristotle/poetics.mb.txt.

3 Augusto Boal, *Theatre of the Oppressed*, trans. Charles A. McBride and Maria-Odilia Leal McBride (New York: Theatre Communications Group, 1979), xiv.

4 Aristotle, *Poetics*.

5 Boal, *Theatre of the Oppressed*, xiv.

6 Ibid.

7 Mary C. Henderson and Alexis Green, *The Story of 42nd Street: The Theatres, Shows, Characters, and Scandals of the World's Most Notorious Street* (New York: Back Stage Books, 2008), 21.

8 Ibid., 35.

9 Henderson and Green, *The Story of 42nd Street*, 51.

10 Alexander J. Reichl, *Reconstructing Times Square: Politics and Culture in Urban Development* (Lawrence: University Press of Kansas, 1999), 5–20.

11 Lynne B. Sagalyn, *Times Square Roulette: Remaking the City Icon* (Cambridge, MA: MIT Press, 2001), 31-2.

12 Patrick Anderson, "I Feel for You," in *Neoliberalism and Global Theatres: Performance Permutations*, eds. Lara D. Nielsen and Patricia Ybarra (London: Palgrave Macmillan UK, 81–96.

13 Ibid.

14 Robert Vischer, "On the Optical Sense of Form: A Contribution to Aesthetics," in *Empathy, Form, and Space: Problems in German Aesthetics*, 1873-1893, eds. Harry F. Mallgrave and Eleftherios Ikonomou (Santa Monica, CA: The Getty Center for History of Art and the Humanities, 1994), 98–99.

15 Anderson, "I Feel for You," 86.

16 Sagalyn, *Times Square Roulette*, 40–42.

17 Ibid., 42.

18 Ibid., 170–205.

19 William J. Stern, *The Truth About Times Square*, Perspectives on Eminent Domain Abuse, vol. 5 (Arlington, VA: Institute for Justice, 2015), 5–7.

20 Sagalyn, *Times Square Roulette*, 240–44.

21 Richard Sennett, "Interiors and Interiority," YouTube video, 1:00:32, April 26, 2016, https://www.youtube.com/watch?v=hVPjQhfJfKo&t.

22 Sagalyn, *Times Square Roulette*, 252–62.

23 Erik H. Erikson, *Identity: Youth and Crisis*, Austen Riggs Center Monograph 7 (New York: W. W. Norton & Company, 1994), 212.

24 Henderson and Green, *The Story of 42nd Street*, 75.

25 Ibid., 63.

26 Ibid.

27 James A. Herne, *Shore Acres and Other Plays*, rev. ed. (New York: Samuel French, 1928), 125–254.

28 Henderson and Green, *The Story of 42nd Street*, 63–75.

29 Ibid., 70.

30 New 42, "Theater History," The New Victory Theater, https://newvictory.org/about/theater-history/.

31 Lortel Archives, "New Victory Theater," Lortel Archives Internet Off-Broadway Database, http://www.iobdb.com/Theatre/43.

32 Stillman Development International, "Times Square Theater," 215 West 42, https://www.timessquaretheater42.com/.

33 Henderson and Green, *The Story of 42nd Street*, 195.

34 Stillman Development International, "Times Square Theater," 215 West 42, https://www.timessquaretheater42.com/.

35 Henderson and Green, *The Story of 42nd Street*, 195.

IHWA
CHOI

BLIND SPOTS

164

(-150—A)

"Parcel 408" is a nameless lot in Ithaca at the intersection of Plain and Court Streets. It emerged as an intermediate zone after toxic carcinogens, a consequence of the city's early petrochemical industrial days, were discovered in the earth. It is among many intermediate zones that punctuate the landscape of Ithaca and exists as a vague specter with previous life cycles embedded into the seeming void. Defined by indeterminacy, the plot of land reflects Sola Morales's concept of "Terrain Vague," where its physical manifestation provides a case study to explore how residual, unofficial spaces can hold multiple, and often conflicting memories and perceptions from the public.

A deeper investigation into the site reveals stories, previously hidden, that provide clues to the history of the landscape, while also evoking new imaginaries within the ordinary. This thesis investigates the unexpected ways indirect and blurred language exposes public space as an accumulation of memories, rather than an absolute image or remembrance of events or sites. The project fosters thresholds that challenge clear definitions of classification, thereby fracturing hard boundaries, liberating illusions of stasis, and making room for personal interpretations, misreadings, unpredictability, and fantasy.

Rather than a singular intervention, the design focuses on provoking multiple experiences and interpretations through different scales of engagement within everyday spaces. Exploring concepts of the peripheral image and temporal multiplicity, each intervention engages with the past histories of the site, while also acting as portals into uncanny realities. Looking forwards and backwards in simultaneity, the project acts on the peripheries of memory—registering traces, revealing the palimpsest that composes the site, and carving out space for ongoing change and growth. The reincarnation of an underground tunnel, the void of a demolished coal house, and the ever-fluctuating site perimeter become characters that participate in the ongoing fuzzy story of Parcel 408.

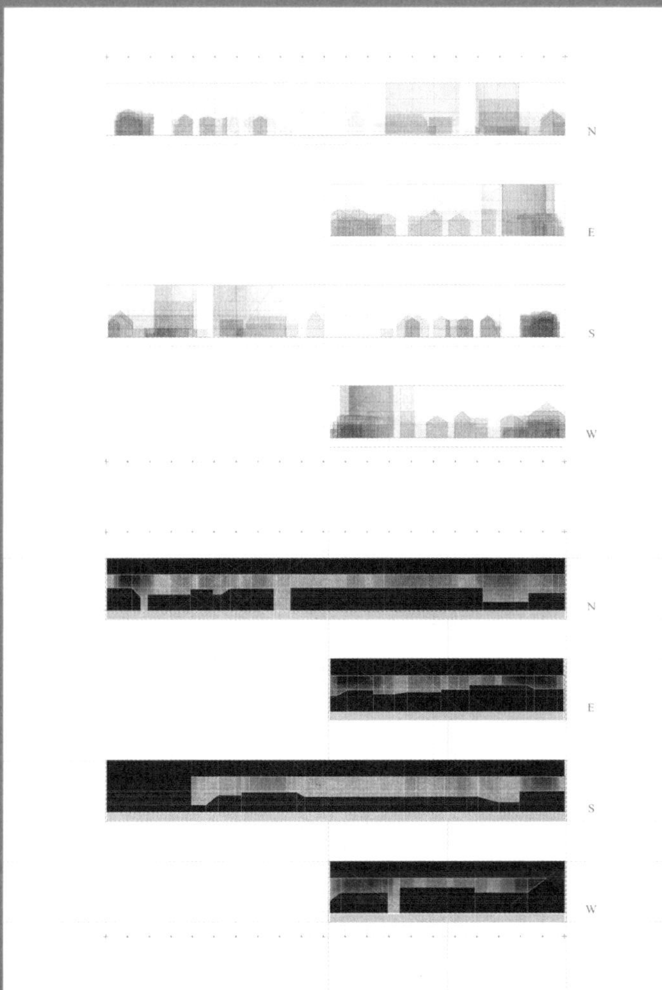

All images by Ihwa Choi, 2020. **P.165:** View into transformed Parcel 408. **This page top:** Acetone collage. **Bottom:** Elevation diagram of the historical built structures and the proposal.

Previous spread: Elevational vignettes. This page top left: Imagined effect onto surrounding Esty Street house, dawn. Bottom left: Imagined effect onto surrounding Esty Street house, day. Right: Imagined effect onto surrounding Esty Street house, night. Next spread: Looking down Esty Street.

(-150—A)

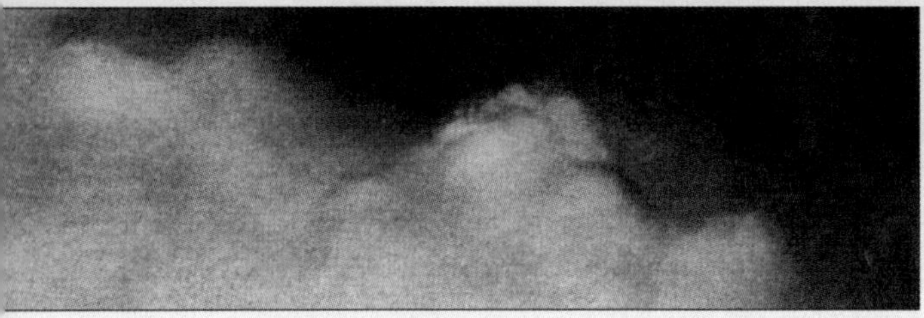

Previous spread: North elevation collage of Markle's Flats. This page: Ithaca Journal collage documenting site history. Opposite: West elevation collage of Markle's Flats.

SEDIMENT SAMPLE LOCATIONS

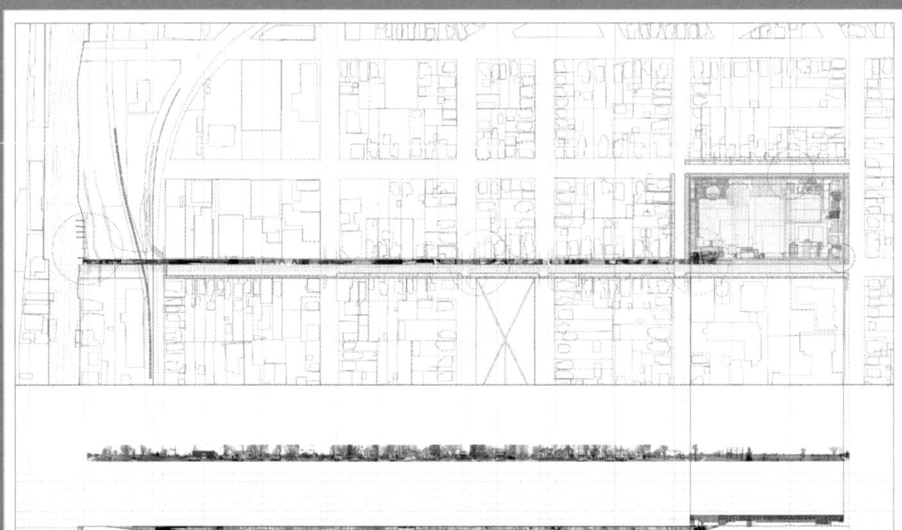

This page top: Existing pavement extended to create a new boundary of the lot. **This page bottom:** Long section from Cayuga Inlet to Parcel 408. **Opposite top:** Vacant lot in between two Court Street houses. **Opposite bottom:** View into proposed utility tunnel and museum hybrid.

180

(-100—P)

JAMES
BIBER

ON CREATION AND LOSS, IDEAS AND ACTUALITY

CORNELL JOURNAL
OF ARCHITECTURE

ISSUE 12
AFTER

Architecture is a curious thing: assembled by builders, orchestrated by architects, commissioned by owners, paid for by banks, celebrated by publications, and occasionally considered the common property of a nation/culture/users. Stakeholders (to use a word I hate) each profess a unique claim to the architecture, many believing they possess a controlling interest. The law attempts to navigate among these with overlapping yet minutely parsed constellations of ownership but can't address the contrapuntal subtext at work among these players.

While architects author these endeavors and may own the documents (effectively, the "building instruction manual" including the drawings, models, specifications, schedules, etc.) they have only limited rights to the final product, while the ideas developed for its creation can be neither copyrighted nor patented. Builders own the physical components until payment (the process, for some, is the most transactional of all transactions) and have seemingly limitless rights to ensure payment. Owners, as the legal name implies, own the finished product, with some caveats. Banks, bonds, and other lending finance nearly every built structure (a claim I can't back up with data but sounds correct) today or at some point in their history, in large part because tax codes provide economic incentives for using OPM (other people's money).

Ownership (in every project more complex than a settler building their own house on the prairie) is distributed among a range of players overshadowing the architect. Architects operate

Previous: *Woolworth tower in clouds, New York City*, May 22, 1928. Photo by Fairchild Aerial Surveys, Inc. This page: *The Cathedral of Commerce*, 1925. Stereograph print on card mount, 9 × 18 cm. Photo by Keystone View Company.

(often unwittingly) in a field of play that is really more power politics than artistic auteurism. Architectural stars ("Starchitects" here, "Archistars" elsewhere) avoid this problem by becoming a power player (but the rest of us, and that is nearly 100% of all architects, are subject to subjugation when power tips away from us).

At an unforgettable 1995 panel moderated by Jonathan Barnett, Philip Johnson, I. M. Pei, and David Rockefeller all took the stage at the Caspary Auditorium of Rockefeller University. The context alone should have been the "tell": Rockefeller University was founded by David's grandfather and the auditorium was designed by Wallace Harrison, who designed Rockefeller Center. Octogenarians Philip Johnson, I. M. Pei, and David Rockefeller regaled the mostly young audience.

The moment of truth came when, after Johnson and Pei had gone on about their own careers (exuding false modesty while solidifying their own position in the architectural firmament), David Rockefeller cleared his throat before saying "When father donated the land for the United Nations…" (a jaw dropping prologue to whatever he said next, which we have all forgotten). The nexus of power shifted visibly on the stage and the quiet voice of David Rockefeller held it all.

Even among eponymous buildings, rarely is the structure built and paid for in cash and "owned" outright. Rockefeller Center required outside financing, but The Woolworth Building, in Lower Manhattan, remains an exception to the convention. The Woolworth Building (where, full disclosure, my own office was once happily situated) is worth considering as an artfully documented hybrid of overlapping interests. Built by F. W. Woolworth in 1913 for $13.5M in cash, it features an ecclesiastical lobby, aptly reflecting the moniker "Cathedral of Commerce." In addition to the lobby's mosaics, carvings, paintings, and elaborate gothic references, it is lined by twelve stone grotesques of the building's multiple "owners" or "apostles." They caricature and celebrate the building's participants including owner Frank Winfield Woolworth, architect Cass Gilbert, structural engineer Gunvald Aus, banker Louis Pierson (whose Irving Bank stands in, appropriately, for the high altar), builder Louis Horowitz, broker Edward Hogan (this was, after all, a commercial leasing venture) and others whose names are lost but whose likenesses remain.

The Woolworth Building is a diagram of "distributed ownership." Those twelve "apostles" and nine hundred other luminaries dined the night of the opening high up in the tower (reported as the "highest dinner ever held in New York" in an almost too cute triple entendre) and closer to God, where Woolworth presented Gilbert with an enormous silver cup and Gilbert toasted Woolworth expressing astonishment that the building was owned free and clear of financing.

It was an interesting exchange: Gilbert, we imagine, in the midst of experiencing the separation anxiety of "losing" "his" building to the public, perhaps grasping for some other encumbrance (to make it a bit less Frank's than his own) while receiving a chalice from the Owner to lighten the loss. (In childrearing it would be called a 'transitional object,' something to grasp while losing their *first* attachment, i.e. mom. In architecture it is sometimes called a cornerstone, swapping ownership with compensatory pride. In religion it might be called transubstantiation.)

References to the divine are not entirely accidental. The cruciform lobby, appropriately entered from the east (NYC-grid east, to be precise, anchoring it in realms cosmic, corporeal, and commercial), features twenty-four elevators posing as chapels; a skylit altar and stairs leading up (rather than down) to the Irving Bank "crypt" (where lucre, rather than relics, are ensconced); and elaborate interior mosaics, sculpture, filigree, and embedded iconography, all announced to the street via an entrance archivolt lined with allegorical figures, a trope borrowed from the architect's favored cathedrals.

The Woolworth Building's inaugural Last Supper, with all Twelve Apostles in attendance (actually held on Passover, 1913, just to bolster the subtext) celebrated both the finality of construction and the christening of the world's tallest building. The simultaneous death and resurrection marked the moment of transfiguration from darkness to light (with an assist by Woodrow Wilson signaling its illumination) and its consecration as the highest, and literally the tallest, of all human endeavors.

L'Ultima Cena is the moment of *transfigurazione*, elevation from what was a mere "building site" to something more venerated, an icon of architecture and an apparition of heavenliness on earth.

Cass Gilbert, half-length portrait, standing, facing front, January 17, 1931. Photo by Bain News Service.

Tiffany & Co., presentation punch bowl commemorating the opening of the F. W. Woolworth Building, 1913. Stirling silver and gold, 9.625 × 17 in.

(Too much? Perhaps.) But that internally conflicted sense of loss is a familiar, if rarely acknowledged, feeling for anyone who has built anything. The slipping away of a project, i.e. the commutation to the legal Owner, is a moment of real separation and quiet interior grief for architects, in spite of the hopes for success of one's progeny. After tasting something as close as possible to the original power architects once had (when "Master Builder" was aptly applied) its sudden revocation can be as disorienting as it is distressing. (Wile E. Coyote knows the feeling well, while hovering yards from the cliff edge and miles above the canyon floor, suspended between time and gravity, not to mention the suspension of disbelief required to defy, or deny, these universal constants.)

As Christo put it; "You have to understand: Art is alive, and if art is alive, it must die."[1] The "completion" of a project stops all forward progress; it's an ice bath for the cooked meal, the end of what seems like an organic, living process that creates a building. It is, in a real sense, the death of a process in the subconscious of the architect. It is quite the opposite in the psyche of the owner; it is the birth. This simultaneous loss and gain, a kind of balance sheet accounting of the project, timestamps a precise and shared moment, perhaps not as fully elaborated as in the Woolworth Building tale, but real nonetheless.

To the architect, everything beyond that point is "after." The building has an "afterlife" but the architect ceases to be its life force. With the atrophy of control, the inability to make any further adjustments and decisions, the process itself dies in the afterlife.

The imperative to continue the design process while realizing a project, to overinvest in the faithful fulfillment of an architect's idea, is obvious to the experienced. We may issue the instruction manual for making a building, but realizing it is a bit more complicated than assembling an IKEA bookshelf. The illusion that the assembly guide is the watertight, self-actualizing DNA of a building implies it can be built without any ongoing assistance from the creator (not *that* Creator…the design creator, though the confusion is not entirely accidental). That illusion of comprehensive completeness is more about the contractual structure assigning responsibility than it is a reflection of what it takes to make great architecture. Great architecture is not a spectator sport.

Pierre Chareau famously moved his office, with collaborators Bijvoet and Dalbet, into the Maison de Verre as soon as the steel was in place. The case could be made that this remarkable construction could not have been made any other way.

A.D.

If architects don't own the design of a building, don't own the building itself, and are sidelined from its operative (performative?) aspects, then what—other than a silver chalice—are we left with? Possibly some part of our fee: that other universal constant, money.

While researching a house designed by Richard Neutra in 1934 for our work on a twenty-first century restoration, I came across a worksheet enumerating the increased budget of $9,332 (yes, the *increased* budget) and noting the original budget with a doodled bit of math on the page. Neutra was calculating his upwardly revised percentage-based fee! This is something (a) every architect does, (b) every architect can recognize, and (c) by now most can do in their head (or more likely on a phone).

These interior machinations affect all of us who manufacture ideas in exchange for something more fungible; we are never quite sure what exactly we are losing in spite of being fairly certain of what we are gaining.

Other than the unlikely excess profit remaining from the fee, we are primarily left with photographs. Neutra, in the Sten-Frenke House above, photographed the project—before the owners had moved in their objects of questionable taste—by moving the same bits of his own furniture (lamp, chair, rug) around the house to appear in every anemic image. His spartan aesthetic undercuts the luxury of the house, something we tried to correct seventy-five years

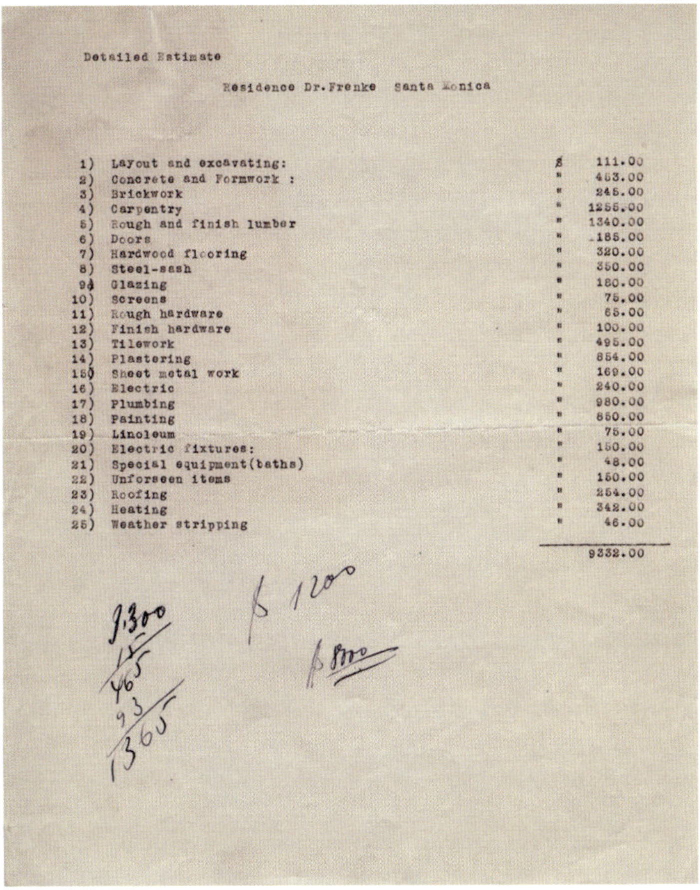

Detailed Estimate

Residence Dr.Frenke Santa Monica

1)	Layout and excavating:	$	111.00
2)	Concrete and Formwork :	"	453.00
3)	Brickwork	"	245.00
4)	Carpentry	"	1255.00
5)	Rough and finish lumber	"	1340.00
6)	Doors	"	185.00
7)	Hardwood flooring	"	320.00
8)	Steel-sash	"	350.00
9)	Glazing	"	180.00
10)	Screens	"	75.00
11)	Rough hardware	"	65.00
12)	Finish hardware	"	100.00
13)	Tilework	"	495.00
14)	Plastering	"	854.00
15)	Sheet metal work	"	169.00
16)	Electric	"	240.00
17)	Plumbing	"	980.00
18)	Painting	"	850.00
19)	Linoleum	"	75.00
20)	Electric fixtures:	"	150.00
21)	Special equipment(baths)	"	48.00
22)	Unforseen items	"	150.00
23)	Roofing	"	254.00
24)	Heating	"	342.00
25)	Weather stripping	"	46.00
			9332.00

9,300
15
465
93
1365

$ 1200

$ 800

Richard Neutra, detailed estimate for the Sten-Frenke House, Santa Monica, California, c. 1934. Reproduced from *Pentagram Papers 38: The Russian Garbo* (New York: Pentagram, n.d., c. 2006).

later when Julius Shulman circled back to one of the only Neutra houses he hadn't photographed. But Neutra's private note makes clear the slightly desperate need for some talisman, however inadequate, to maintain even a tenuous connection to our work.

Photographs are our own transitional objects; most of the architecture we "see," including our own, we experience through photographs.

We accept this downgrade of one dimension (or possibly two, if we include time) from the architectural experience without much resistance. We need portability from the world's least portable art (though I suppose landscape architecture is even less portable), but we have come to think of images as architecture. As transitional objects they keep us preoccupied, sated, in full possession of our work even after our loss of the original. That they become the architecture itself is the ultimate bait and switch.

This was driven home in a *Turncoats Debate* I participated in at The Cooper Union. "Buildings Don't Matter" was based on the proposition that the power of images transcends the impact of built reality; that images are, in fact, architecture. There is something to that (which I argued for, until I argued against it, in the *Turncoats* style) as publications, awards, portfolios, and even education depend on images, not reality. In another world this would be like a restaurant critic reviewing the menu, not the food and place, or awarding the PEN/Faulkner prize based on a book review, not the book itself. A photograph is an interpretation of architecture, by unrelated artists, who use our work to make their own art; and *they* own the images they make!

For unbuilt projects images are all we have, and they have the potential to impact the history of architecture as much, occasionally more, than actual built works. Ownership of renderings, drawings, and models is clear; they remain the sole intellectual property of the author, usually the credited architect. Not building turns out, ironically, to be the only way to fully protect one's ideas! Once an idea enters the complex field of "distributed ownership" it is a lot less clear.

There are even cases of the architect losing the rights to build works similar to their own built portfolio. Donald Trump (and why is *that* name no surprise at all?) sued and prevailed over Philip Birnbaum, an architect of no particular repute (his obituary was emblematically subtitled "Builder Celebrated for his Efficiency"). Birnbaum tried to mirror his Trump design (pun intended) catty-corner (or kitty-corner or cater-corner, variations I still don't get, but apparently refer to four, as in four corners of an intersection) to the original, in a dubious attempt to create a "gateway to Third Avenue."[2] Trump sued him claiming Trump himself had in fact contributed all the salient features of the design, and Birnbaum was stealing these ideas! A case of an architect being enjoined from his own work may be unique (and, of course, who better than Trump to grab credit for *everything* done by others) but illustrates the fragility of what architects consider the only thing they can own, their own design work.

Part of the confusion about design ideas versus built ideas is warranted. US copyright law allows us the ownership of the drawings but not the underlying ideas, yet—in some rather confusing circumstances—also protects aspects of the built result of those ideas. EU copyright recognizes the ownership of ideas embedded in finished projects, in perpetuity, but of course "auteur" is a European, not American, concept.

When plotted against particular moments in the course of the realization of built work, this nebulousness raises some issues that go to the heart of what we, as architects, actually own and what we lose in the process of making architecture.

A project "belongs" (part literally/part figuratively) to the architect as long as it remains an idea, or drawings or even a building site or an unfinished construction. Our ownership diminishes as the builder begins the realization of the architecture, but in an ideal process still relies on the architect to solve and clarify the myriad issues that arise in construction. In fact, the architect is (again, ideally) a kind of celebrity (sometimes infamously) on the building site. In Italy the architect is personally responsible for site safety and is more than a celebrity (always referred to as *Signore Architetto* and occasionally as *Professore Dottore Ingenier Architetto*... it is Italy, after all) and is a figure of legal accountability. We litigious Americans prefer much reduced accountability accompanied by much reduced ownership.

That esteemed status can evaporate as the building is completed. Ownership is technically and legally transferred to the Owner (capitalized, in case there was any doubt, in all contractual documents) in the steps leading up to full possession or occupancy. What remains with the architect? What has the architect lost (or reluctantly relinquished)? More than the technical change would belie. It is a point at which the architect no longer owns significant aspects of their own direction. Just ask Mr. Birnbaum.

As architects we may be commodified IRL, but the motivation for architects to do the impossible—making architecture that fully satisfies the inner and outer requirements of all the overlapping interests—requires both an enduring optimism and a sense of ownership that transcends the reality of corporeal economics. We believe, to some degree, that authorship is ownership, something law school courses (and the courts, in the unfortunate case of *Trump v. Birnbaum*) don't fully acknowledge.

Quoting Michael Graves, copyright protection covers only the "poetic language" of an architectural work, which includes those parts of the design that are "responsive to issues external to the building, and incorporates the three-dimensional expression of the myths and rituals of society."[3] This is more a description of the alternate reality in which architects reside than a useful distinction for establishing ownership.

Smart clients recognize the alternate reality of the architect (not necessarily in its fully obfuscated detail) and its effect on the process of architecture: most architects would do *anything* to get their project built faithfully to their ideals. Anything.

Once a client recognizes this truth it is "game over." Owners can elicit infinite effort for very finite compensation when the stakes are faithfulness. Architects will, unfortunately, sacrifice everything to keep their ideas intact. This emotional vulnerability is elided only to forestall the likely manipulation we will face once a client recognizes it.

Standing heroically against the corrupting powers (Owners, Finances, Codes, Taste) that might alter one's vision; turning the architecture we orchestrate into an extension of the inner soul of the architect; shrouding design in language intended to both aggrandize and obfuscate ideas and motives (a subject for another essay): these are the tools not of a participant in a conscious collaborative endeavor, but the mark of one struggling alone against the internal fears of loss.

I am less interested in Howard Roark than I am in how interested architecture students are in Howard Roark. The cost of architectural impurity, buildings identified as the architect themselves, and a melodramatic fascination with sexual and political power are the embedded tropes in *The Fountainhead*. Most students think it is a tale of righteousness, with Roark a model of what any principled architect would (or could or should) do.

I think of it more as a parable celebrating the physical death of a building privileged over acceptance of anything less than perfect fidelity to the architect's vision. (It's a kind of preemptive Kübler-Ross mash-up; Anger causing death, Denial of *impending loss*, an end run around Acceptance. Bargaining and Depression are just sideshows). Anything to mask the loss integral to our chosen profession.

Loss, after all, isn't a bug in the process of architecture, it's a feature.

John Marin, *Woolworth Building, No. 31*, 1912. Watercolor over graphite, 47 × 39.8 cm.

1 Farah Nayeri, "It's Christo's Final Show. But Is It the Last We'll See of Him?," *New York Times*, July 8, 2020, https://www.nytimes.com/2020/07/08/arts/design/christo-pompidou-arc-de-triomphe.html.

2 David W. Dunlap, "Philip Birnbaum, 89, Builder Celebrated for His Efficiency," *New York Times*, November 28, 1996, https://www.nytimes.com/1996/11/28/arts/philip-birnbaum-89-builder-celebrated-for-his-efficiency.html.

3 Michael Graves, "A Case for Figurative Architecture," in *Michael Graves, Buildings and Projects, 1966–1981*, ed. Karen Vogel Wheeler, Peter Arnell, and Ted Bickford (New York: Rizzoli, 1982), 11.

COMMON
ACCOUNTS

REFRESH, RENEW: FUNERARY CATAFALQUE FOR THE DIGITAL AGE

192

(-100—A)

COMMON ACCOUNTS: **IGOR BRAGADO AND MILES GERTLER**
ATHLEISURE APPAREL: **ARMICHE RODRIGUEZ**
PERFORMANCE: **RENNIE JONES**
TECHNICAL SUPPORT AND FABRICATION**: FONDERIA NOLANA**
REFRESH, RENEW WAS REALIZED AS PART OF A SPANISH ACADEMY IN ROME FELLOWSHIP.

All images by Common Accounts. Previous: *Refresh, Renew Pavilion*, exploded axonometric view. This page: *Refresh, Renew Pavilion*, Piazza San Pietro in Montorio, Rome, Italy, 2019. Opposite: View of Piazza San Pietro in Montorio from the Spanish Academy. Next spread: *Refresh, Renew Pavilion*, Piazza San Pietro in Montorio, Rome, Italy, 2019.

Installed in San Pietro in Montorio square, *Refresh, Renew* is a funerary pavilion that observes the fitness and construction of the self on a continuous spectrum with the death and deconstruction of the body. This pavilion, a public platform for exercise and its digital preservation through casual, self-initiated recording, simultaneously articulates a human self, living and dead.

The pavilion hosts exercise infrastructure and a memorial server that catalogs videos uploaded to its virtual coordinates in recognition that the most active cemeteries today are the accidental spaces where memorial and ceremony takes place subtly, accidentally, on the day-to-day. *Refresh, Renew* proposes alternatives to mainstream funerary protocols to foster ceremony both online and IRL. It manages the digital remains of a life lived online, acknowledging the explosive multiplication of images of the self—mementos that persist after biological expiration.

By re-articulating the role of fitness technologies, *Refresh, Renew* focuses on the capacity of images to construct personal archives as a project of eternalization. Recent cases of online memorialization through the practices associated with fitness point to a long historical lineage of the relationship between body-culture and death that spans millennia: consider the athletic events held during Etruscan funerals, or the development of contemporary mass fitness aesthetics by the North American military apparatus. In this context, Facebook's first significant encounter with death—prompted by a YouTube fitness enthusiast's viral plea for access to the profile of his dead son—shows the displacement of spaces of mourning to areas like the comments section of a social media channel, a home-gym, or muscle fiber itself.

Refresh, Renew re-imagines the architectural tradition of the catafalque for its notion of an absent occupant. Historically, catafalques were often constructed in European urban centers upon the death of a public figure in absentia, as a remote instantiation and marker of one's death. The body was implied, but not necessarily present in a material sense. The virtual archive consolidated by *Refresh, Renew* resonates with this substitute funerary performance focused around the articulation of the self.

REFRESH, RENEW

This page: *Body Processing Facility*, "Il Lutto del Tuo Archivio," model. Opposite: *Body Processing Facility* (detail), "Il Lutto del Tuo Archivio," model.

This page: *Landscapes of Infrastructural Eternities, AKA Phillip the Fourth's Funeral Catafalque.*

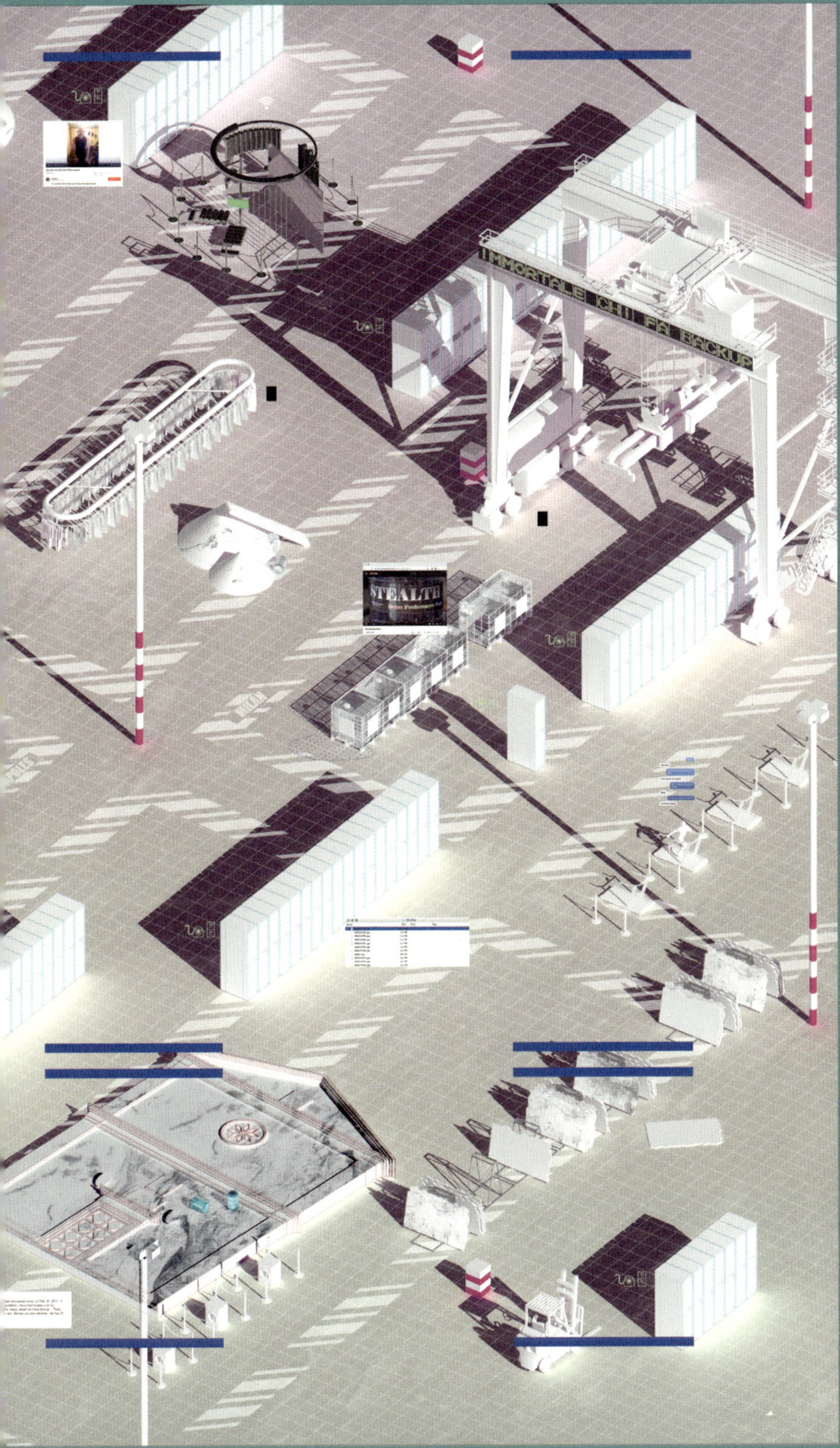
IMMORTALE CHI FA BACKUP
STEALTH

202

(-75—P)

BRUNNO
DOUAT

ON CURUPIRA'S STEPS: LINA BO BARDI IN VILA VELHA

In Brazilian indigenous folklore, one of the most known myths is that of the *Curupira*, his most remarkable characteristic being the fact that his feet are turned backwards. Hence, although Curupira moves forward, his feet—responsible for his movements—keep pointing to the place where he came from. Adapted in such a way to mislead hunters following him, Curupira's dynamics result in a non-linearity in which *before* and *after* overlap and blend each other continuously. Once the Curupira becomes aware of its contradictory condition and uses it as a favorable value, the myth becomes an *anthropophagic*[1] reading of Walter Benjamin's *Angel of History*. The angel figure is described, through the image of Paul Klee's painting *Angelus Novus*, in Benjamin's famous essay "Theses on the Philosophy of History":

> [...] His face is turned toward the past. Where we perceive a chain of events, he sees one single catastrophe which keeps piling wreckage upon wreckage and hurls it in front of his feet. The angel would like to stay, awaken the dead, and make whole what has been smashed. But a storm is blowing in from Paradise; it has got caught in his wings with such a violence that the angel can no longer close them. The storm irresistibly propels him into the future to which his back is turned, while the pile of debris before him grows skyward. This storm is what we call progress.[2]

Benjamin's scene depicts the angel's despair over its complete inability to rebuild the ruins that keep multiplying under his feet. The scene suggests a tense and eternal moment where the angel figure is doomed to a condition marked by the impossibility to constructively connect with past events. As will be seen, although the physical condition of both characters simultaneously faces an idea of *before* and *after*, Curupira's metaphor shows that through the embracing of this condition—apparently adverse—one is capable of not only transiting freely between these two instances of time but also creating new possibilities in the present by using the condition as a favorable value.

A non-linear dynamic—similar to that of the myth—can be found in Lina Bo Bardi's design for the Chame-Chame House, built in Salvador, Brazil, in 1958, and its here proposed relationship to her trip to the geological site of Vila Velha, in the same year. After analyzing its 300-million year-old geological structures, characterized by its naturally sculpted ruin-form shapes, Lina establishes architecture as an expression of the natural environment. She embraces non-linearity as a narrative to design and presents the possibility of moving forward—on Curupira's steps—while questioning the concept of *after* as a unidirectional idea of progress.

Throughout her career, Lina's built and theoretical work was structured by her thoughts on a flexible idea of time, as shown beautifully in its full complexity by Olivia de Oliveira's work *Lina Bo Bardi: Sutis Substâncias da Arquitetura*.[3] As Oliveira states, Lina's architecture acts as a time condenser: for example, through the constant use of spirals such as the ones represented by large stairs that create secondary spaces within themselves, she designs structures not only of passing but also of permanence. These structures then cease to be unidirectional and progressive, and become a hurricane with an abundance of things happening at the same time. Through the use of specific forms, symbolisms, connective elements, and by proposing alternative user paths in space, Lina's architecture can then be seen as permeated by "devices to collapse time."[4] She would later even state that "linear time is a Western invention, time is not linear, it is a wonderful tangle where, at any moment, points can be chosen and solutions invented, without beginning or end."[5] Time can be perceived as a wonderful tangle where one could transit free and consciously as shown by the influence that the ancient geological structures at Vila Velha's site had on the design of the Chame-Chame House.

Previous spread: Vila Velha's geological formations. (Vladimir Kozák, geological formations, Vila Velha, Brazil. Undated Kodachrome slide, 50 × 50 mm.)

Lina's commission for the Chame-Chame House coincided with an invitation to teach at the architecture program at Universidade Federal da Bahia, starting a period of intense research in Bahia that would last from 1958 to 1964.[6] At the beginning of 1958, Lina traveled to Salvador to visit the chosen site for the house, which she immediately praised due to the presence of a large *Jaqueira* (jackfruit).[7] Shortly after, she developed a first study for the house, which refers, conceptually and spatially, to the design of her own Glass House. Chame-Chame's early design is characterized by an orthogonal plan distributed in three different floors resulting in a rigid block located on the top of the site's hill. The façade is defined by a continuous balcony that connects interior and exterior spaces, a variation of the belvedere-house exemplified by the unbound relation between the great salon and the tropical forest at the Glass House.[8]

As pointed out by Zeuler Lima, one of the first perspective drawings she sketched seems to match perfectly—in all its proportions and structural elements such as slabs and columns—with a famous photograph, taken by Peter Scheier, of the Glass House "standing as the Acropolis on the hill soon after it was built."[9] Although the drawings suggest a complex natural environment at the site which interacts with the house at certain moments, the house assumes the position of being *placed* in nature. Lina later defines this inorganic approach to architecture as "relating to nature with a certain reserve, which is its reserve to the irrational."[10] This relation is also illustrated by the presence of a dendroid (tree-shaped) column on the entrance façade that dialogues directly with the *Jaqueira* situated at its side.[11] Within this context, the column seems to represent a statement that, once within the boundaries of the building's footprint, the natural and organic automatically transform according to architectonic terms. The design was approved with enthusiasm by the clients, but shortly after, and without their request, Lina collected the drawings and changed the design completely.[12] Lina's discomfort with the approved design and its subsequent action cannot be underestimated. More than just a formal decision, this decisive moment can represent a complex reflection on her own idea of architecture and its relation to nature and time.

The change is radical. Where once there was a rational grid guiding the position of walls, columns, slabs, and stairs, now one can only see an organic form that dialogues—through curves, voids, and bended shapes—with the site's topography and its natural elements, especially the *Jaqueira*, which continues as one of the only reminiscent references from the previous design. During the first sequences of the new studies, the plan is defined by two inverted C-shape volumes that originate, in their voids, two courtyards with specific symbolisms: an oratory and a fireplace.[13] Protected by the curved walls, both voids represent, more than enclosed spaces, recesses caused by a sort of erosion that made it possible to connect these two cores with its surroundings.[14] This was the first time that such free forms appeared in Lina's work, and it would follow her designs from this point onwards. But what stimulated this point of inflection towards a more organic approach to architecture? On a lecture held at Salvador that same year, Lina mentions this transition:

> [...] Organic architecture, close to nature, seeks to identify with it, surrenders without showing resistance, without wishing to dominate it, accepts it and loves it, takes from it the taste for the prime and rustic materials, and besides all doesn't want to be forgotten and wants to remember every time its laws [that of the nature], into the dynamism of its shapes, on the not completed, on the endless shapes. [...] This acceptance of nature the way it is presented to us, on the spectacle of the continuous mutation, we perceived through the photographs that we made in Vila Velha, near Ponta Grossa, in the state of Paraná.[15]

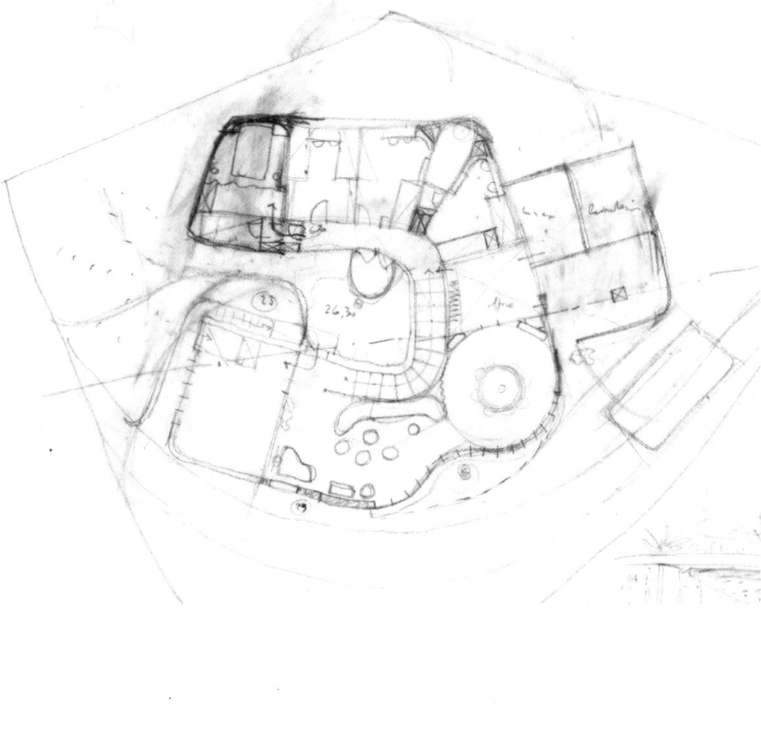

Layout of the ground floor with the early presence of the two "courtyards." (Lina Bo Bardi, ground floor plan sketch, *Chame-Chame House*, 1958. Pencil on tracing paper, 347 × 502 mm.)

Between constant flights from São Paulo to Salvador in 1958, Lina decided to visit the geological site of Vila Velha, located in the south of Brazil, with a group of staff members from MASP.[16] Vila Velha consists of a large group of sandstone formations sculpted by the action of water and wind during several geological eras. The history of these lavish natural sculptures can be divided in two different stages. First, the formation of the sandstone itself and second, its erosion which is responsible for the creation of its forms. Somehow, to understand this geological formation's history and to put it face to face with Lina's design, is to go through this "wonderful tangle" and to pick common points, overlapping even though millions of years apart.

The sandstone that constitutes Vila Velha's geological park is of a specific type called *fluvioglacial sandstone*. This means that its formation is a direct result of millions of years of self-assembling through sedimentation and compaction caused by the action of glaciers movements back when the south of Brazil was attached to Africa and partially covered with ice.[17] The geological history is seen through the recording of specific characteristics on the stones' surface, such as the constant presence of pebbles inclusions and exfoliation forms, making it available to trace its faraway past.[18] These pebble inclusions were created through the flow of defrosted water within the sandstone over millions of years. By visually analyzing the angles created by the inclusions, it's even possible to understand the directions of the continental ice sheet's movement.[19] But these geological memories are not made only from inorganic matter: Vila Velha's area also hosts a significant and large collection of fossil sites. The fossil sites record prehistoric underwater life while rock paintings on the wall's surfaces reveal an archaeological trace of ancient human presence. It is inevitable to relate this geological history, which Lina documented in a variety of scales through photographs, with the design for the Chame-Chame House. The external surface treatment applied to its walls is defined by a textured masonry surface covered with gravel, pebbles, ceramic shards (initially representing marine elements[20]) algae, ivy, tropical plants, and even plastic doll's parts, such as arms, legs, and heads.[21] The result is the creation of a living wall—built upon both inanimate and living memories—which Oliveira calls *muros-relatos* (narrative walls).[22]

After millions of years of sedimentation and compaction, the sandstone surface started to suffer from natural erosion, resulting in the unique forms of this geological archipelago. In ancient times, the whole area of the geological site was a large sandstone

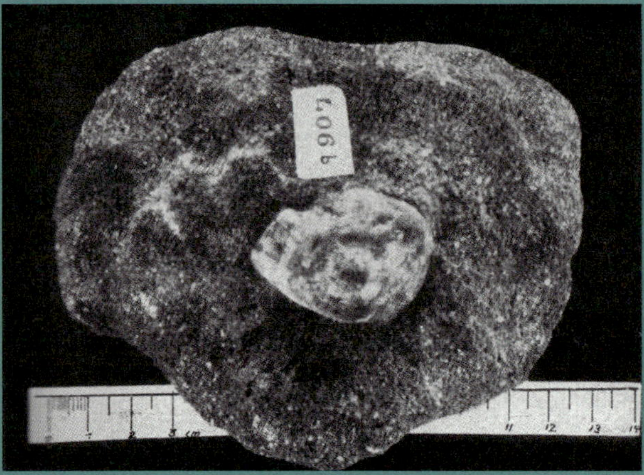

Top: Glacial material propelled in Vila Velha's sandstone surface as proof of its fluvioglacial origin. (Photo by Reinhard Maack, 1944.) **Center:** Detail of the sandstone's surface documented during Lina Bo Bardi's trip to Vila Velha in 1958. (Photo attributed to Luiz Hossaka, 1958.) **Bottom:** Lina Bo Bardi, view from the upper terrace, *Chame-Chame House*, Salvador, Brazil, 1958-1964. (Photo by Hugo Segawa, 1982.)

plateau that protected the lower layers made of a softer mineral. Through the constant exposure to water, initially from the glacial defrost and later from rain, this monolithic plateau was subdivided into large blocks. With this constant flow of water scouring straight lines on the rocks, valleys similar to streets were created between the larger structures which are now sculpted in a variety of shapes. This resulted in Vila Velha giving the impression of being a "fossil city" as defined by pioneer researcher Reinhard Maack in 1946.[23] This slow and natural process is directly related to Lina's design. Viewing from the outside, the house is characterized by a set of overlapping rounded shape volumes that seem to have been outcropped from the site itself. Thus, to walk around the house and to ascend to its upper levels is to walk "on a mountain path"[24] exacerbated by the almost symbiotic relationship between the house and its natural surroundings; the house itself becomes nature.[25]

Left: Lina Bo Bardi, view from the western side, *Chame-Chame House*, Salvador, Brazil, 1958–1964. (Photo by Hugo Segawa, 1982.) Right: Vila Velha's sandstone sculptures documented during Lina Bo Bardi's trip to Vila Velha in 1958. (Photo attributed to Luiz Hossaka, 1958.)

It's almost as if the house was a product of natural interaction, shaped by water and wind just as much as by the hands of a craftsman. Erosion slowly revealed memories originating within the walls, excavated the imagined courtyards, and directed the rainwater through a series of gargoyles distributed all around the house. The design process characterizes a "condensation of time" through an endless shape that synthesizes millions of years of geological transformations and memories represented by the surfaces seen on Vila Velha in one act.

The design's condensation of time can be seen as a back-and-forth action occurring in a single movement, like Curupira's steps. The house is transported to a place faraway in the past and borrows patiently crafted memories to design and build a structure at the present. The structure seemed to always have been there, just waiting to be inhabited. Lina's own personality represented a non-linear backwards rush as she once declared that "I never wanted to be young. What I wanted was to have history. When 25 I desired to write my memories, but didn't have enough material."[26] And why not a desire to design her own archaeological discovery? Just as Vila-Velha's sculptural shapes are defined precisely by its dissapearance, it is almost as if, from this moment, Lina's architecture starts to have its form defined by its erosion more than its sedimentation. The design is a creation act tied to its own condition of finitude, working with what is left.

Left: Lina Bo Bardi, view from the front façade, *Chame-Chame House*, Salvador, Brazil, 1958–1964. Photo by Rubem Rodrigues Nogueira Jr., 1983. Right: Vila Velha's sandstone sculptures documented during Lina Bo Bardi's trip to Vila Velha in 1958. (Photo attributed to Luiz Hossaka, 1958.)

Lina's understanding of the relation between nature and architecture is attached with several time references: to be forgotten, to remember, on the not completed, on the endless shapes, and continuous mutation. Time is precisely the prime element that connects, conciliates, and even equates her architecture with nature. Borrowing de Landa's reflections on the idea of a non-linear history,[27] it is possible to understand the creation of both inorganic and organic memories responsible for the formation of Vila Velha's sculptures and the design of the Chame-Chame House. Their creation was not a result of the idea of a *linear progress*, but of a constant dynamic of self-assembling and phase change which makes it possible to condense millions of years in one overlapping moment. The idea of *before* and *after* can be dissolved to see both natural and human-made manifestations as different ways in which nature's matter-energy, not to say time, expresses itself.[28] In other words, *before* and *after* result in forms of the same value, overlapping points on a "wonderful tangle," to walk freely—and to design—on the spectacle of the continuous mutation. What differs mostly between these two expressions would be precisely the speed of the recycling and changing of this constantly flowing reality:[29] several more millions of years for the conclusion of Vila Velha's erosion and the mutation of its memories (which already happened before) or—unfortunately—less than thirty years for the Chame-Chame House.[30]

The result is a house-manifesto that implies a critique of the current idea of progress, with its destructive wind that constantly leaves ruins to erosion while simultaneously preventing one from touching, addressing, and rebuilding them: a condition well represented by Benjamin's angel. It is a critique to an *after* characterized by the complete disintegration of memories, cultural homogenization, and the creation of a future without a past.[31] The alternative would be to fulfill the present with memories—to "consider the past as historical-present."[32] In other words, to tangle a linear concept of time and to embrace this non-linear dynamic by, just as Lina, walking on Curupira's steps while questioning the idea of progress as an *after*, after all.

1 The term *anthropophagic* here refers to the artistic movement that originated with Oswald de Andrade's *Manifesto Antropófago* (1928). Considered by critics as an authentic Brazilian philosophical thinking, the movement suggests a process of cultural appreciation based on the constant "swallow" of the *other* (mostly personified by Eurocentric references) with its subsequent reinterpretation through an understanding of the local context. The manifesto's motto "The inversion of tabus into totens" exemplifies its idea of a persistent inversion of opposite values into favorable ones.

2 Walter Benjamin, "Theses on the Philosophy of History," in *Iluminations*, ed. Hannah Arendt, trans. Harry Zohn (New York: Schocken Books, 2007), 257.

3 Olívia de Oliveira, *Lina Bo Bardi: Sutis Substâncias da Arquitetura* (São Paulo: Romano Guerra Editora; Barcelona, ESP: Gustavo Gili, 2006).

4 Ibid., 282, 349.

5 Marcelo Carvalho Ferraz (Org), *Lina Bo Bardi* (São Paulo: Empresa das Artes, 1993), 327.

6 See Julieta González, "Quem não tem cão caça com gato," in *Lina Bo Bardi: Habitat*, ed. Adriano Pedrosa, José Esparza Chong Cuy, Julieta González, and Tomás Toledo (São Paulo: MASP, 2019), 136–149.

7 Rubem and Gilka Nogueira to Lina Bo Bardi, in Oliveira, *Lina Bo Bardi*, 83.

8 Oliveira, *Lina Bo Bardi*, 83.

9 Zeuler R. M. de A. Lima, *Lina Bo Bardi* (New Haven: Yale University Press, 2013), 79.

10 Lina Bo Bardi annotations for the conference Arquitetura e natureza ou natureza e arquitetura, in Oliveira, *Lina Bo Bardi*, 96.

11 Oliveira, *Lina Bo Bardi*, 85.

12 Ibid., 86.

13 Ibid., 88.

14 During the following design studies, that would culminate on the built project, both recesses disappeared, being "swallowed" by the house's volume that was characterized by a single built mass.

15 Lina Bo Bardi annotations for the conference Arquitetura e natureza ou natureza e arquitetura, in Oliveira, *Lina Bo Bardi*, 95.

16 Zeuler Lima, *Lina Bo Bardi*, 77.

17 This geological formation occurred after successive alterations from being a flatland covered by a shallow ocean to a mountain range of intense volcanic activities. See Reinhard Maack, "Geologia e Geografia da região de Vila Velha e considerações sobre a glaciação carbonífera do Brasil," in *Arquivos do Museu Paranaense vol. 5*, (Museu Paranaense: Curitiba, 1946).

18 Reinhard Maack, *Geologia e Geografia da região de Vila Velha e considerações sobre a glaciação carbonífera do Brasil*, 97.

19 Ibid., 224.

20 Lina Bo Bardi to Rubem and Gilka Nogueira, in Oliveira, *Lina Bo Bardi*, 85.

21 Oliveira, *Lina Bo Bardi*, 107.

22 Ibid., 142.

23 Reinhard Maack, *Geologia e Geografia da região de Vila Velha e considerações sobre a glaciação carbonífera do Brasil*.

24 Oliveira, *Lina Bo Bardi*, 88.

25 Ibid., 91.

26 Lina Bo Bardi, "Curriculum Literário," in *Lina Bo Bardi*, ed. Marcelo Carvalho Ferraz (São Paulo, SP: Empresa das Artes, 1993), 9.

27 See Manuel de Landa, *A Thousand Years of Nonlinear History* (Cambridge: MIT Press, 1997).

28 Ibid., 21.

29 Ibid., 257.

30 The house was sold and demolished in 1984. A residential building was built in its place.

31 Eduardo Subirats, *A existência sitiada*, trans. Flávio Coddou (São Paulo: Romano Guerra, 2010, 125).

32 Lina Bo Bardi, "Uma aula de arquitetura," in *Lina por escrito: Textos Escolhidos de Lina Bo Bardi*, ed. Silvana Rubino e Marina Grinover (São Paulo: Cosac Naify, 2009), 162–177.

Lina Bo Bardi, Luiz Hossaka, and Carlos Paz on a trip to Vila Velha, Paraná, in 1958. (Photo by Luiz Hossaka, 1958.)

216

JAVIER
PERÉZ PUCHALT

LEARNING FROM BERGHAIN

CORNELL JOURNAL
OF ARCHITECTURE

ISSUE 12
AFTER

I.

The overdetermination in which cities have been planned during the last centuries reached its most extreme point during modernism. Cities planned along the twentieth century, especially after World War II, were often designed as a direct and almost scientific consequence of an enormous quantity of parameters: an economy regarding space, the big amount of citizens to host, or correct sunlit conditions for example. These parameters were read as a list of limitations, generating designs that were most of the time too explicit and very rigid. The opportunity of taking them as a chance for providing freedom through all this complexity was missed.

In general, when staring at any regular masterplan, one can recognize elements like grids, long and monumental axes, or central squares: all of these being elements of the city with enormous compositional potential but, unfortunately, which have been mainly used in stubborn and dogmatic ways in years past. Architects, urbanists, philosophers, and sociologists have been theorizing against this overdetermination, understanding it as a limitation to urban design and trying to avoid a solemn imposition of such a city model in the future. An example of such is Oswald Mathias Unger's concept of *Stadtarchipel*, in which he imagines Berlin as an "Urban Archipelago" of architectural islands floating on an urban sea.[1] Rem Koolhaas, for example, recognizes this concept as "being the absolute model for the European city"[2] probably because this theory gives a scheme, or is able to propose a model in which the complexity of the European city, with its historical strati, all its diverse parts and objects and all its intricate layers, are included harmonically.

Because of its dramatic history in the twentieth century, Berlin has become a truly centerless city: its parts have become very evidently fragmented and de-centralized. As Fritz Neumeyer puts it, Berlin is a "collection of centers, of mass and void, of history and destruction that actually becomes a true metropolitan laboratory."[3] One could state that cities are composed by fragments. Actually these fragments, as Anthony Vidler could define, "are layers of formal and cultural complexity contributing to the accumulated experience of the city."[4]

Beyond the planned city—made of alignments, grids, and axes—particular places exist that seem firstly just hopeless environments, but where buildings and spaces are reconverted in quite a spontaneous way, and are endowed with big potentialities.

Previous: The "ready-made" architectural object establishes powerful relationships between the surrounding urban substance and all the objects composing it. (*Parking lot, Berghain*, Berlin, Germany, 2020. Photo by Marie Benaboud.)

These places are examples of what could be called an "automatic urbanism,"[5] fragments of the city composed in themselves by several different parts in a spontaneous and free way, with what is available onsite, and that even offer an alternate way of envisioning the city, somehow overcoming Unger's *Stadtarchipel's* concept. They aren't anymore islands in an urban archipelago but appear as an Oasis in the middle of a desert. Amongst the desperation of the inherited urban condition from the twentieth century, these places appear as fragments of hope, metaphorically featuring the situation in which, when divagating amongst the dessert, one finds water to drink. Once again, Berlin, as the "extreme city"[6] that it is, and as a city made out of opposites, is the background for reflections on a different and more sensitive way of planning: an urban design that accepts the imperfections and the "disorder,"[7] and that discovers new possibilities of the city. This essay will explore a particular example in Berlin of an urban Oasis generated rather "automatically," proving like this a kind of superiority of the so called "automatic urbanism" over the rigid modernist urban planning. This example will be taken as a clever prophet of the city-to-come and shown as a portal directly connected to the before which is undoubtedly the true portal to the *After*.

II.

Not very far from where the Berlin Wall once stood, hundreds of young people queue religiously each weekend in front of a former power plant. They hope to be welcomed inside one of the most internationally famous techno clubs still in existence: Berghain. Surrounded by a landscape of car parks and low-cost supermarkets, a non-paved path welcomes all candidates wanting to take part of the nostalgic disconnections from reality taking place inside. Constructed during the 1950s in a completely devastated and destroyed context which was Berlin, the cube-like object was placed with great liberty. It was built against street alignment and the grain of the surrounding façades, becoming a freestanding autonomous entity. Berghain is situated between the districts of Kreuz*berg* and Friedrichs*chain*, neighborhoods situated rather in the middle of the city, that are representatives of what once was West and East Germany, and in which nowadays, in particular, a freedom of expression tries to survive. Both areas are characterized by monotonous extensions of pseudo-regular streets and their austere "Mietkasernen"[8] facades. But even though the former power plant

appeared in the middle of two rigidly planned neighborhoods, it seems that Berghain and its surroundings are "off-the-grid."[9] They are a fragment of instability under constant development, especially in a city that from the second half of the twentieth century tried to re-construct its image through the idea of the urban block, big protagonist of the past Prussian city model.

Berghain and its neighboring surroundings conform an own entity, a coexistence of opposites, an active space for endless possibilities, which is not defined as a goal but as a process, where "what exists"—the existing—has a potential to be developed. Berghain's location it is essential for understanding it as the metropolitan laboratory it is in itself, as a one more center of the city, symbol of a counterculture resulting from the complex and historic hostility. It is surrounded by tens of leafy trees, several car parks next to commercial sheds which host supermarkets, an alcohol store, a do-it-yourself store…There is a fire station too, a gymnasium, some headquarters of a couple of foundations and other cultural projects. Here, in East Berlin, and apart from all the existing leafy and spontaneous vegetation, two big supermarket advertising poles are visible from afar: "Metro" and "Hellweg." Both German businesses have drawn upon this North American advertising strategy planting these poles next to their big sheds that host the items they have for sale, becoming almost kind of contemporary capitalistic bell towers next to each other's hut or nave. There are several additional vertical elements like lampposts, traffic lights, or fence poles, that in the surroundings of the techno club have been "intuitively planted without any prior plan or geometrical system."[10] All vertical landmarks, the rough and raw materiality of the ground, some abandoned containers, and the big amount of fences, conform a set-up. Together with the strong former industrial block standing with great autonomy and majestic appearance in the middle of the landscape, this place, extraordinarily, at a certain moment, has become another one. It is a place generated without big premeditation, that does not constitute a closed system and which singularity builds an exception in the city. Berghain's improvised "urbanistic-architectonic organization"[11] represents an accidental but highly sensitive example of acquisition of what "was already there,"[12] of what was spontaneously existing, but also a high awareness of the present, and by it, of the *After* too. It is a "ready-made"[13] urbanistic-architectonic organization. It is a re-composition of several subsequent fragments into a new context. It is a place of condensation where an old industrial facility has been retransformed

Previous: Constructed during the 1950s in a completely devastated and destroyed context which was Berlin, the cube-like object was placed with great liberty. It was built against street alignment and the grain of the surrounding façades, becoming a freestanding autonomous entity. (*Access to the club, Berghain*, Berlin, Germany, 2020. Photo by Marie Benaboud.)

into a non-productive equipment for the city: where leisure has been glorified alongside consumerism, discounts, bad taste, education, culture, and exclusive techno music.

These are some of the reasons why Berghain, together with its surroundings, constitute a "heterotopy."[14] It conforms "another space (Des espaces autres[15]), a different space of illusion that denounces the reality as being even more illusory still". It juxtaposes opposite entities or spaces in one same set-up; it never sleeps, remaining alive during the day in a certain way and at night in another. The spontaneous and unplanned urbanistic-architectonic organization of Berghain and its surroundings incarnate an artificial ensemble that could even be labelled as a "Third Nature."[16] It has become a pause, a disconnection from the city that paradoxically becomes extremely urban; the vertical poles and lampposts freely displayed here are conceptual reminders of the ensemble of slender palm trees of an Oasis, generating in this case an urban forest of technical and utilitarian elements. In the middle of the imagined nothingness, "where there is nothing…everything is possible."[17] In this metropolitan emptiness (which is not empty at all), the city is understood as a conceptual Nevada[18] or an urban dessert, which happens to be the perfect scenario for the apparition of this *Oasis*. Berghain is not an urban island anymore but a fruitful and prosperous urban *Oasis* in the desert that is the city, a rather unstable entity, a consequence of diverse processes which are even opposite, irradiating an enormous sense of vitality to the rest of the city. It is a city fragment acting as a paradoxical manifestation, which enables transformation and discoveries through the potential of the existing. Berghain is a legitimate example of a way of constructing the city, adapting easily to the conditions of unpredictability that characterizes the present civilization and its "liquid life"[19] style.

III.

In the middle of the two neighborhoods of the German city, Kreuzberg and Friedrichschain, and very close to the river, next to some train tracks and to the former Wall that divided not only the city, but the whole Europe in two, this area of Berlin is today a result of past hazardous procedures. It is "automatic urbanism,"[20] where the objects arranged freely and without following any masterplan guiding their exact position, together with the rest of artificial and natural elements and all different kinds of materiality

With its equivalent facades and with its elongated and very high windows, one is able to look at the east of Berlin when inside of Berghain. One is able to feel the "urbanity" of the surroundings and of the industrial object. (*Back side, Berghain*, Berlin, Germany, 2020. Photo by Marie Benaboud.)

meet the city, provoke it, shake it, awaken it, and reveal a powerful way on how "architectural objects do become active members in the urban fabric."[21]

As the big pioneer he was, Karl Friedrich Schinkel[22] already predicted the futility of city planning back at the beginning of his century. Looking closer to his architecture and the urban strength in which he designed and projected his buildings as singular entities could be extremely useful for understanding one more step of complexity in the city and to become aware on how the relationships between objects give an order to urban space. The equivalent four facades of the Bauakademie make the architectural object a radical freestanding cube, almost like a Palladian villa, to tease and awaken the city. Thanks to its huge windows, the Bauakademie's users can view out while working inside, looking to the city, to the canal, to the royal palace, and to the streets. It seems that Schinkel knew important things about the conceptual inner strength of the city. "The dialectical principle, (...) the unification of opposites into a whole is the true intellectual background of Schinkel's work."[23]

With its equivalent facades and with its elongated and very high windows, one is able to look at the east of Berlin when inside of Berghain. One is able to feel the "urbanity"[24] of the surroundings and of the industrial object. The "ready-made" architectural object establishes powerful relationships between the surrounding urban substance and all the objects composing it. This example of "automatic urbanism" sheds light on the potential of non-planned places, on accepting instability, "openness,"[25] the ineffectuality of city planning, and the strength of the architectural singular object. It seems true then to state what Neumeyer said, that "urbanity is inscribed within architecture's own discipline" and that the "suggestivity of the architectural object is key for building the city."[26]

IV.

Cities in general and Berlin in particular are an endless becoming. They are "paradoxical manifestos of transformation and instability."[27] The notion of "disorder"[28] is crucial for understanding the way in which it is believed cities should evolve, a way that doesn't look for a definitive shape but for discovering all the possibilities through an unstable and endless process of constant development. Richard Sennett conveys that "the main goal (in life) would be to achieve the freedom that gives you to accept what exists and live in disorder."[29] The city is a process in constant adaptation, antagonistic of overdetermination. In a similar or parallel direction, Rem Koolhaas stated back in 1994 that the urbanism to come would not be about "order and omnipotence" but that urbanism should be looked at more "as a way of thinking, to accept what exists."[30] That urbanism would be about the underdevelopment, the modified, the more, the landscape of impermanence...

Looking at Berghain's *Oasis* carefully, with a cultural hyper sensitivity and a contemporary architectural cultural awareness, it is possible to perceive it as a true portal to understand, reconsider, and conceptualize the *After* of our cities and the potential of their complexity. Berghain offers a full understanding of the power of the relationships established between several objects and with all the rest of cultural layers, awarding even this hopeless place and its surroundings with a new unexpected status, bringing life to it. This rather unplanned and unexpected "management" of urban forces, whose charm resides in the acceptance of what exists, is a call for a way of acting in the city. It is crucial to highlight the importance of being inventiveness, visionary, conceptually curious and aiming to generate new illusions. Like this, potentially, would be possible to deliver a better future, full of yet undiscovered possibilities, having in mind all the learnings from our masters: the unity of opposites, the constant processes of adaptation and appropriation, or the very strong urban potential of architecture. But of course without forgetting all lessons described here, which are as much crucial, predicating the acceptance of the existing and its potentialities as non-planned fragments of the city able to deliver essential qualities in the complex present conditions, especially when looking for the future.

1 Compilation of statements resulting from intense research on the morphology of the city of Berlin (and not only) that has occupied Oswald Mathias Urgers's career since its very early stages. Always dedicated to experiment and understand urban complexity, this concept means to imagine the city as an ensemble of architectural islands floating in a larger context of spatial continuum. Oswald Mathias Ungers, Rem Koolhaas, Peter Riemann, and Florian Hertweck, *Die Stadt in Der Stadt: Berlin - Ein Grünes Archipel* (Zürich: Lars Müller, 2013).

2 Fritz Neumeyer, "OMA's Berlin: The Polemic Island in the City," *Assemblage* 11 (1990): 36–53.

3 Ibid.

4 Anthony Vidler, "The Third Typology," in *Oppositions Reader* (New York: Princeton Architectural Press, 1998), 13–16.

5 Term used by Philippe Oswalt in his essay about Berlin, "city without shape." Philipp Oswalt, *Berlin_Stadt Ohne Form: Strategien einer anderen Architektur* (Munich: Prestel Verlag, 2000).

6 Ibid.

7 Using Richard Sennett's term. Alejandro Hernández Gálvez, "Diseñar el desorden," *Arquine*, April 23, 2020, https://www.arquine.com/disenar-el-desorden/.

8 A housing typology hurriedly built at the end of the nineteenth century to rapidly house the increasing urban proletariat. Alan Colquhoun, "On Modern and Postmodern Space," in *Architecture Criticism Ideology*, ed. Joan Ockman (New York: Princeton Architectural Press, 1985), 103–117.

9 This term could remind in an analogous way to some reflections by Anne M. Schneider, "Off-(Jefferson's) Grid," in *Countryside, A Report*, ed. Rem Koolhaas (Cologne: Taschen, 2019), 210–219.

10 This was the way in which 1,100 new palm trees got planted in the pacific Oasis of Motu Tané, a French Polynesian island to artificially re-generate the landscape for the enjoyment of the occidental owner after some devastating storm. See Ido Avissar, "1,100 Palm Trees," *San Rocco* 1 (2011): 80–88.

11 Term used and translated from: Fernando Chueca Goitia, *Breve Historia del Urbanismo* (Madrid: Alianza Editorial, 1968).

12 Ido Avissar and Freek Persyn, "OMU OMA," *San Rocco* 7 (2013): 101–110.

13 Refers directly to the concept of Marcel Duchamp. The ready-made refers to the everyday object, already manufactured, that the artist elevates to the category of work of art without hardly modifying it.

14 By definition, Foucault explained that a heterotopy has the role of creating a space of illusion, that denounces as more illusory still the real spaces in which human life takes place. A heterotopy has the actual power to juxtapose on one same place different spaces, multiple locations that are between themselves incompatible. Michel Foucault, "Des spaces autres," lecture given at the "Cercle des études architecturals," March 14, 1967. Published in *Architecture, Mouvement, Continuité* 5 (October 1984): 46–49.

15 Ibid.

16 Cristina Díaz and Efrén García from Amid.Cero9 have used this composed term to explain in a coherent way the research on their main interests: the space of mediation between people, objects, constructed surroundings…This term was coined during the Renaissance by Jacopo Bonfadio, Italian humanist and historian, referring to a new kind of garden that was creating a new and unknown reality—a Third Nature—with a new and radical materiality that had been constructed through cultural connections. Cristina Díaz Moreno and Efrén García Grinda, "Third Natures: ten years of mundane, carnal assemblies," *El Croquis* 185 (2016): 23–39.

17 Rem Koolhaas, Bruce Mau, Jennifer Sigler, Hans Werlemann, and OMA, *S,M,L,XL* (New York: Monacelli, 1995).

18 Ibid.

19 Using the term of Polish sociologist Zygmunt Bauman. See Zygmunt Bauman, *Liquid Life* (Cambridge: Polity, 2005).

20 Oswalt, *Berlin_Stadt Ohne Form*.

21 Fritz Neumeyer gives some hints on some of his texts about the potential of the urban *reality*. Fritz Neumeyer, "Reality as Discipline: Metropolitan Architecture and Urban Identity," *Quaderns d'arquitectura* 183, pp. 136–43.

22 Karl Friedrich Schinkel was the architect of the prince back in the early nineteenth century and he was responsible for the generation and conceptualization of the Prussian city-to-be model. However, and probably against what some could directly think, his way of acting with the city was not mainly based on designing any very radical masterplan with big monumental axis facing some buildings.

23 Oswald Mathias Ungers, "Five Lessons from Schinkel's Work," *The Cornell Journal of Architecture* 1 (1981), 118–119.

24 As Manuel Delgado explains, this term stands as well, according to Henri Lefebvre, as a potentiality, as the ensemble of social and mental possibilities of the society which don't necessarily need to be constituted as something tangible. Manuel Delgado, "Lo urbano, más allá de la ciudad," introduction to the Spanish edition of *The Right to the City* by Henri Lefebvre (Madrid: Capitan Swing, 2018), 15–22.

25 Open notion of the city professed by Richard Sennett already back in the '70s. Gálvez, "Diseñar el desorden."

26 Fritz Neumeyer, "Reality as Discipline," 136–43.

27 Oswalt, *Berlin_Stadt Ohne Form*.

28 Richard Sennett's early publication in the '70s, *The Uses of Disorder: Personal Identity and City Life* was a first milestone in his career. Gálvez, "Diseñar el desorden."

29 Ibid.

30 Rem Koolhaas, "Whatever Happened to Urbanism?," *ANY: Architecture New York* 9 (1994): 10–13.

DAN
TOROP

ALEKSANDR
MERGOLD

8TH MTH

228

(-50—P)

All images by Dan Torop. **P.229:** *Falls*, 2020, inkjet print, 18 × 12 in. **Previous spread:** *HS*, 2019, inkjet print, 18 × 12 in. **Opposite top:** *Aurora*, 2019, inkjet print, 18 × 12 in. **Opposite bottom:** *Veery*, 2020, inkjet print, 18 × 12 in. **Next spread:** *RS*, 2020, inkjet print, 18 × 12 in. **P.236:** *HS2*, 2020, inkjet print, 18 × 12 in.

Looking at Dan's photos I had a feeling that I had seen these images before, in my mind's eye, while conjuring up a place with a sense of something very amiss, off, something quietly dangerous. The result of an unfathomable occurrence long ago, no one can remember what and when and how it occurred—and all is quiet for now.

The best written description of this feeling is an excerpt from the Strugatskys' brothers *Roadside Picnic* written in 1971. *Roadside Picnic* is of course better known as the film that it inspired, Tarkovsky's *Stalker* from 1979. Some see this book as a straight-up science fiction: a tale of a place visited by aliens, subsequently converted into a fenced-in, closely guarded Zone, surrounded by the Institute that studies it without much apparent success. Weird things can be found there, and some risk their lives to enter and bring the swag back, to sell, to use for some new purposes, since no one knows what it is and what it is for.

Some argue that it is a political metaphor of the collapsing Soviet project, where everyone is trying to make sense of its ambitious ruins. In 2020 these photographs appear to be closer to the text—mundane, familiar, but off. Something has happened, we do not know what, and all we have left are the aftermaths.

> **When you look at it, it looks like any other piece of land. The sun shines on it like on any other part of the earth. And it's as though nothing had particularly changed in it. Like everything was the way it was thirty years ago. My father, rest his soul, could look at it and not notice anything out of place at all. Except maybe he'd ask why the plant's smokestack was still. Was there a strike or something? Yellow ore piled up in cone-shaped mounds, blast furnaces gleaming in the sun, rails, rails, and more rails, a locomotive with flatcars on the rails. In other words, an industry town. Only there were no people. Neither living nor dead. You could see the garage, too: a long gray intestine, its doors wide open. The trucks were parked on the paved lot next to it. He was right about the trucks—his brains were functioning. God forbid you should stick your head between two trucks. You have to sidle around them. There's a crack in the asphalt, if it hasn't been overgrown with bramble yet. Forty yards. Where was he counting from? Oh, probably from the last pylon. He's right, it wouldn't be further than that from there. Those egghead scientists were making progress. They've got the road hung all the way to the dump, and cleverly hung at that! There's that ditch where Slimy ended up, just two yards from their road. Knuckles had told Slimy: stay as far away from the ditches as you can, jerk, or there won't be anything to bury. When I looked down into the water, there was nothing. This is the way it is with the Zone: if you come back with swag—it's a miracle; if you come back alive—it's a success; if the patrol bullets miss you—it's a stroke of luck. And as for anything else—that's fate.[1]**

1 Arkady Strugatsky and Boris Strugatsky, *Roadside Picnic*, trans. Antonina W. Bouis (New York: Macmillan, 1977; Crpytomaoist Editions, n.d.), 11–12, https://www.cca.org/cm/picnic.pdf.

238

(-50—P)

GESA
BÜTTNER DIAS

EVOCATIONS OF AN ABSENT EVERYDAY: FIFTY YEARS AFTER *THE FOUR ECOLOGIES*

Fifty years ago, in 1971, Reyner Banham published his seminal account, *Los Angeles: The Architecture of Four Ecologies*, on a then-understudied city.[1] In it he declared Los Angeles as unique, without precedent, and non-exemplary: an ecosystem of itself. Written during the first wave of environmental awareness, Banham demonstrated how to read a city as a constructed landscape, an asynchronous geospatial condition. In his manifesto, Banham synthesized his celebration to Los Angeles by dividing the city into four distinct ecologies: Surfurbia, the Foothills, the Plains of Id, and Autotopia. The tone of the text, balancing the perspectives of first encounter, everyday encounter, and studied encounter, was immediate and provocative, making the book ever more difficult to categorize.

TERN LINEN
WEST
St.John's
323-907-7711
BATTERIES
SALE
AEROBICS
CARDIO 4 LIFE

Over the last fifty years both Los Angeles and Banham's ode have become a standard, gone out of fashion and have had their comebacks, riding out the trends of the times. Banham saw Los Angeles neither as prototype nor the apocalypse of all urban landscapes, and while the city might not have changed that much since then, the world around it has. Today, Los Angeles is most similar to metropolitan regions in the Global South and the Pacific Rim, and not just for the climate. The city is rich in civic and real estate development, and yet has a thriving informal, do-it-yourself sector, only recently discovered by the cultural sphere. Thanks to Hollywood, synonymous with popular culture, the image of Southern California urban life has been prototypical far beyond Banham's imagination, with suburbs outside of Shanghai or Chongqing named after Orange County or Palm Springs. Even more pervasively, the everyday urban scenery of Los Angeles has entered the American, if not global, subconscious. As a neutral presence stripped of its geospatial specificity, Los Angeles has been the background of movies set no matter where in the US, past or future. The city is omnipresent yet invisible, as if the object of a non-authored subliminal advertising scheme. Just what is the advertisement is for? What is the everyday of Los Angeles?

I imagine Banham's first encounter with LA similar to mine: from the window of a plane, on a flight from Europe, with a stopover for refueling on the East Coast. Even though I read *Four Ecologies* long after I moved to LA, it was still as if Banham had sat next to me on that first flight over the sprawling city, pointing out the endless vistas of blooming purple Jacaranda, aquatic blue beans of backyard swimming pools, and gridded streets only distorted where demanded by topography and the curved cul-de-sacs of an occasional new urbanist housing development. I was in love, despite better knowledge, despite having lived all my life in dense, post–World War II reconstructed cities. Welcome to the 1950s ideal architecture, unconstrained by historic city layouts.

Banham, born in England, acknowledged his Eurocentrism unapologetically and was fascinated by the image of the traveler during colonial times. His interest in Los Angeles was in what Anglo-Saxon culture looked like when transposed onto a Spanish colonial past on the North American continent. After fifty years, his *Four Ecologies* division of Los Angeles into beachfront, hillsides, plains, and freeways remains as relevant as ever. And the perception

South Los Angeles, 2013–2016. Selection of photographs from work in progress on the everyday architecture of the Los Angeles plains. **Top**: September 18, 2015, 8:58:00 a.m.–8:58:13 a.m., Slauson Ave. **Center**: September 18, 2015, 8:58:19 a.m.–8:58:22 a.m., Slauson Ave. **Bottom**: September 18, 2015, 9:04:35 a.m.–9:04:39 a.m., Slauson Ave. Photos by Gesa Büttner Dias.

ADAMS BARGAIN
98¢
ADAMS BARGAIN

IMITATION GOLD/SILVER LEAF
WATER BASE PAINT

of the hillside, beach, and car culture has changed little—yet the Plains of Id, the city's flatlands, deserve further investigation. There is a gaping absence in the book on the everyday culture in the Los Angeles plains and its stories not just of Euro-American migration, but of Black diaspora, and Asian and South American immigration. Banham neglected to describe the intricacies and injustices that formed a de facto and de juris segregated cityscape, neatly aligned with his division of the ecologies. A few years later, Bernard Tschumi published an essay further investigating the plains, in which he introduced the concept of sanctuaries, or enclaves of distinct cultures, as essential organizational principles of the LA flatlands.[2] In a careful re-reading of Banham's text, a schizophrenic relationship to this, his third, ecology becomes apparent. On the one hand Banham considered the plains as the least specific location, resembling other urban formations in the Midwest. And at the same time, he credited them as home to the LA vernacular and the inspirational resource for the architectural lineage from Rudolph Schindler to Frank Gehry and beyond.

THE PLAINS

The Los Angeles plains are flat like a movie screen in their topography, height of buildings, and depth of geological and built history. Like an empty screen, they have been submitted to many projections, yet rarely allowed to tell their own story in their own words. Having witnessed only one turn of a century, their history is not accumulated in strata of buildings and erasures. It is a sideways history of mobility, connecting most places of the plains to an ancestral home elsewhere. As Banham told it, Los Angeles was settled mainly through overland migration. Implied in his observation that many parts of LA look more like the Midwest is the recognition that the journey extended the built cultures it traversed to the sea, bringing with it the construction techniques of wood framing, originally developed to colonialize the Midwest, where forests (like in LA) were absent. Instead of expanding local building traditions that would be more comparable to techniques of Luis Barragán—found in Irvin Gill's tilt-up concrete wall experiments and Paolo Soleri's earth form works in Arcosanti—Los Angeles got built with wood framing in Douglas Fir.

Yet we would misunderstand the vernacular of the plains if we just interpreted it as an extension of a building technique developed on the east side of the North American continent, decorated with

Left column: April 18, 2016, 7:42:13 a.m.–7:48:01 a.m., April 19, 2016, 7:14:25 a.m.–7:15:13 a.m., Vermont Ave. Right column: April 16, 2013, 7:34:03 p.m.–7:38:58 p.m., Slauson Ave. Photos by Gesa Büttner Dias.

some roadside signage. Instead, the inherent logic of appropriation that comes with a technique based on standardized, lightweight construction elements that can be aggregated and assembled without much specialized knowledge, might have been one of the reasons why the DIY culture, the practice of the everyday, became part of the Los Angeles identity. The role Black artists played in forming this narrative has been discussed in urban and cultural theory since the 1990s, without wider dissemination. In the context of the Plains, Black and BIPOC life demonstrated a resourceful dialogue between the built environment and cultural production. Kellie Jones in her book on the Black diaspora, *South of Pico*, recounts the trajectory of African American Angeleno artists and describes a transformation of Black culture to become synonymous with popular urban culture, moving as far from association with the agrarian past of enslavement as possible.[3] John Outterbridge is an example of a transcontinental transplant who reacted in his art to the encountered and internalized imagery of his journeys across the continent to Los Angeles. Starting in the late 1960s, together with other Black artists like Betye Saar and Noah Purifoy, he explored the medium of assemblage, working directly with materials found in the urban context yet associated with places elsewhere. The material and visual aesthetic of their artworks preempted an architectural style most associated with Frank Gehry. Whereas artists like Ed Ruscha, Vija Celmins, Judy Fiskin, and later Catherine Opie documented the finite forms of Los Angeles landscape (its multistory freeway intersections, roadside architecture, oil derricks, traffic signs, and vast oceanfront) and with their increased fame influenced the perception of the city as stylistic image, the work of Black artists revealed the aspects of process, of a relationship between an object and its making. Instead of documenting the vernacular, they expanded it, made it a practice.

Independently yet coincidentally to the happenings in Los Angeles, Michel de Certeau, a French cultural theorist, developed his theory of the "Practice of the Everyday," expanding theories by Lefevbre, Foucault, and others. De Certeau's work is credited by Kellie Jones in her explorations of the Black diaspora and claim of home. De Certeau expanded what the geospatial history-formalist readings of urban space—even by such a visionary critic as Banham and in extension Tschumi—were missing. The practice of the everyday and its cultural implications, not just in the obvious popular cultures, but in its intertwining with a wide range of cultural and material productions, is fundamental to critical postmodern thinking.

The buildings that make up the fabric stretching over the Los Angeles plains hide in plain sight. They are the ordinary shopfront warehouses along Jefferson Boulevard, where little in its street facades reveal the life of the inhabitants in the blocks shielded behind them. The street lies on the orthogonal one-mile raster that subdivided most of the mid and southwest of America, the Jeffersonian grid named after the same president. It doesn't get any more presidential than that on this boulevard of one- and two-story buildings, constructed in two-by-four wood stud framing. The street fronts are rectangular walls punctured by a single door and sometimes two windows, behind which might stretch a bow truss long-span hall. The street fronts form a continuous photographic reel much like Ruscha's famous series *Every Building on the Sunset Strip*, but without the glamour of consumerist decorations or spaces of consumption. There are barely any neon signs projecting off the facades and no restaurants to eat some ethnic food; there are just spaces of work, of production. Behind the facades are rows of streets, spaced 260 feet apart, and lined back-to-back with single-story bungalows and two-story apartment buildings. The individual lots of each home are not even the width of a basketball court. This urban texture is interspersed with corner strip malls, gas stations, storefront retail stores, the occasional big box store, and shopping malls.

At the geographic center of the plains lies South LA, containing the major part of a contiguous, undisturbed expanse of that Jeffersonian grid. Most street fronts like Jefferson Boulevard still have the patina of vernacular structures saved by disinvestment. South LA's borders are fluid, their interpretation depends on the context in which the name is used. In its widest sense, it combines several distinct enclaves and independent cities, and is bound by mayor freeways. This landscape of built places is the hub of Black culture in Los Angeles, a backdrop in the complex stories of the Black diaspora and resilience in the face of racist planning and policies.

It is not that the everyday structures that dominate South LA and other less affluent neighborhoods were actually magically invisible, but rather that our own everyday being has developed a series of tricks and ruses to overcome the predicament of perpetual repetition. In our mind, much like in the movies, we can overlay what we see with storylines and cut together a spatial continuum. In the cinematic reading of the city, the ordinary structures are the background—the setting—which gives texture to a foreground shot without coming into focus.[4] They are the everyday, interrupted by the storyline.

Very much like how Banham oriented himself in the expanse of the urban fabric by following the cues of its disruptions—the hillsides, coastlines, and freeways collaged into a synecdochic whole—everyday citizens orient themselves inside this fabric by creating their own disruptions. Michel de Certeau called this the tactics of everyday spatial practices. In *The Practice of Everyday Life*, he dedicated a chapter on "Walking in the City" which dealt with the topic of absence and the everyday.[5] For him the everyday was perpetually absent. The everyday existed only in practice and couldn't be recorded. It left no trace. Absence was a tactic of the everyday to subvert systematization. No walk down a street was ever the same, even if it would occur always at the same time and in the same company. The practice of walking fragmented and reassembled one's surroundings, creating makeshift monuments for spatial reorientation while folding away entire in-between sections into insignificance. A street name could open up a door to the imaginary. The everyday was in constant search of its other, its absence, to make its own predicament bearable.[6]

When the eye accidentally refocuses from the personal imaginary to the actual physical environment, like a camera from a portrait to a landscape, what would each of us see? Because of the afterimage of the metaphysical, we would still only see what we are trained to. In this reading of the built environment as something that is responsive and resilient despite its non-elastic physical properties, what is the role of the architect as a specialist for programmatic quantities and phenomenological qualities?

SYSTEM THINKING

A vernacular practice excludes the architect as specialist and relates users and builders directly with each other.[7] It is non-authored, derived out of local traditions. Spatial sequencing and construction detailing are learned from adjacent precedents, and adaptation to changing needs follows the "learning by doing" principle reflected in simple construction. The vernacular is an evolutionary practice; it builds on given circumstances and innovates by adapting a given situation based on available resources. In the premodern vernacular, buildings were stand-alone spatializations of everyday routines. They were part of the landscape and became signifiers of locally available materials, climates, and human activities. In the postmodern vernacular, buildings became continuous spatializations of the everyday routines subjected to globalized market forces. They subsumed the landscape and became signifiers of extensive material distribution networks, mechanical advances in building technologies, and mediations of human activities. A vernacular practice records absence—absence of systematic authority, absence of abundant funds, absence of formulated progress.

In the Los Angeles of the 1960–80s, a group of architects discovered the vernacular as a departure point for a radical practice of tinkering. Rather than focus on decorated sheds—the donut shop in the form of a donut—their exploration of the commercial vernacular was less about the everyday as signage and more about the everyday as material practice. Reinterpreting themes of minimalist and assemblage art of the period, the architects worked within the DIY culture of the early environmentalist movement from the *Whole Earth Catalogs*, a tradition that continues today with McMaster-Carr catalogs and just-in-time production methodologies.

In a 1978 drawing for their 2-4-6-8 House, Morphosis created an exploded axonometric of all the elements that it takes to build a Type V construction house, identifying and labeling every two-by-four wood stud.[8] In its conception as a do-it-yourself kit of parts,[9] this early project by Morphosis embraced the vernacular nature of its construction system and highlighted the role of the architect as a tinkerer within an established code of construction. Through drawing and building models of vernacular precedents, the architects of the time turned the concept of the vernacular on its head. Their vernacular form considered adjacent or precedent structures as prototypes, as full-scale mock-ups, as one-to-one models to copy and improve.

Frank Gehry demonstrated how, similar to Gordon Matta-Clark, the built environment is material for architecture or art. In his project for Gemini G.E.L., Gehry used the standard wood structure and revealed it through glass; he was heir not just to Rudolph Schindler and the organic architecture of John Lautner, but he combined both intellectual construction and creative angst with the relaxation of the California Dream. His early work developed out of experience working with real estate developers' construction systems, from which he established an approach for domestic and commercial architecture born out of the prevalent techniques yet infused with an artist's reading of the contemporary, of surface and color and shapes. Each project probed the capacity

Over three semesters at Cornell AAP, fifty students researched and developed spatial tactics at the blurred boundary between architecture, art, and landscape. The examples included in this essay investigate the extruded box of the Plains of Id and propose operations to reveal the formative processes inherent to the buildings and their hidden stories. Their projects are monuments to an absent everyday. **This page top and bottom:** Taking inspiration from Henri Lefebvre's quote "…everyday life cannot be contained by bureaucratic regimentation, that it harbors the desire that generates transformation," Victoria Clarke confronted the persistent presence of the redlining map of Los Angeles in her work. She exposed the unsophisticated construction methodologies of the 1980s boom era, in itself harboring the potential of being transformed in a DIY manner. Movements such as Buy Back the Block are critical to her approach. (Victoria Clarke, *Buy Back the Block: Redlining, Desire, and Transformation*, 2019.) **Opposite:** Sam Gomez investigated the vernacular shop front building: Colorland Printing Solutions is a shop near Koreatown on Western Avenue in Los Angeles. Their motto is "you make us colorful—we specialize in all your printing needs, such as business cards, flyers, postcards, wedding invitations, invoices, etc, at the guaranteed lowest price in town." Colorland occupies a space on the ground level of a building which is split between housing and retail. It's one of those buildings that John Chase would say is "difficult to see" because it presents the problem of "never having been encountered for the first time, and certainly never in a reified, honorific or even especially focused way." (Sam Gomez, *Buildings that have never been encountered for the first time*, 2019.)

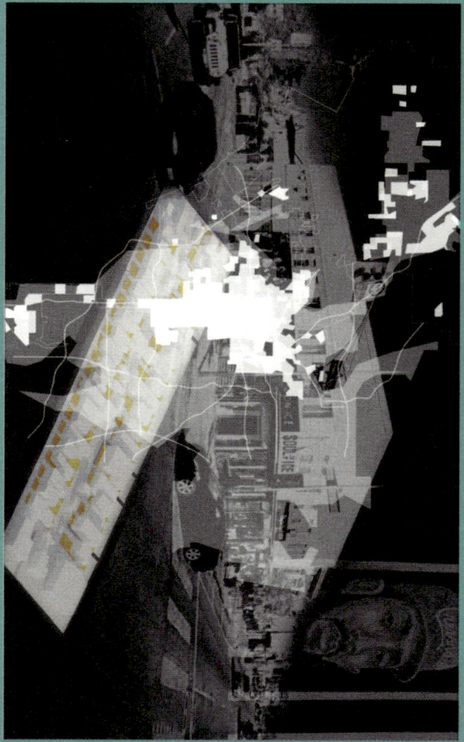

COLORLAND

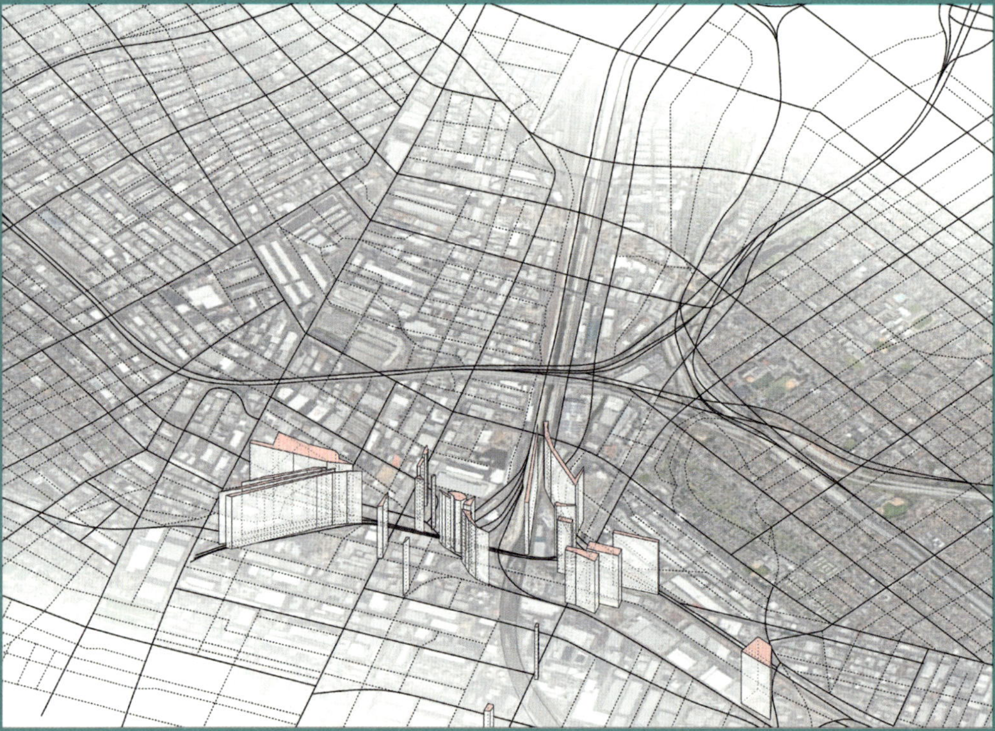

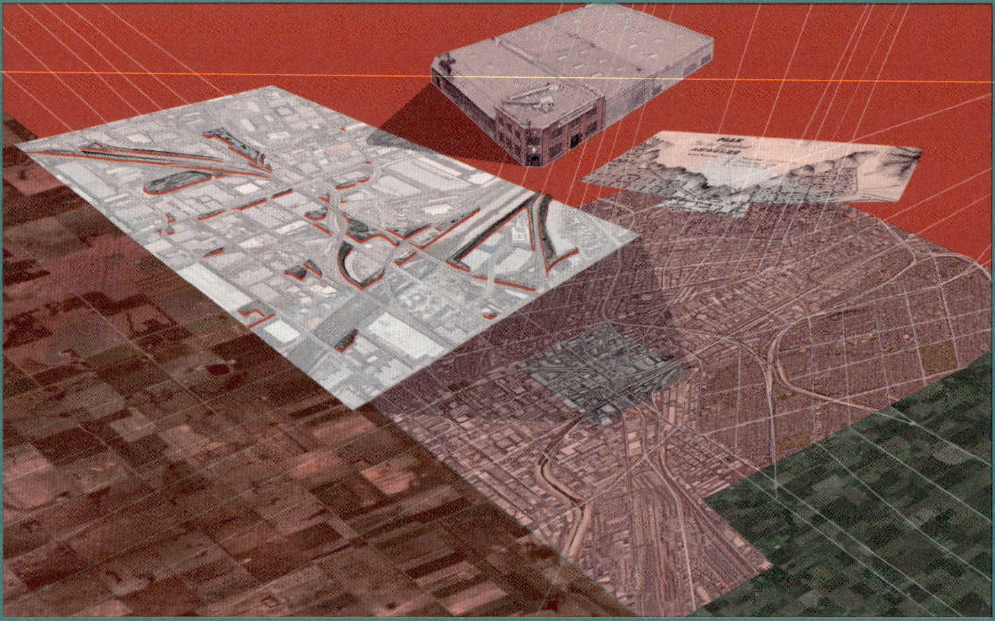

of standard construction materials and assemblies—not to reduce them to minimal detailing, but to tell a story about how he found the materials as if in a catalog and celebrated them. Parallel to the assemblage of the emerging art movement, he combined cheap materials into sculptures. He utilized straight standardized wood members, curved standardized tubular steel sections, and sheet paneling: from the 1990s onward with the support of CAD software developed for aeronautics. Frank Gehry became the most versatile in the art of making something out of nothing, mixing arte povera and minimalism with the fantastic of the movie industry. His vernacular practice was a constant tinkering with systems and processes.

By a beat, Banham missed this shift from form to system as the essence of vernacular architecture. The same as Schindler before, Gehry and Morphosis experimented and expanded the use of available construction systems and along the way developed a new formalistic paradigm. For Banham, the stucco box in its unadorned state was a reflection of the modern architecture of Schindler. Had he written his book ten years later he would have credited the wood system as the vernacular, and not the form. It is here that I find my fundamental critique of this seminal book. Although Banham had been at the forefront to rethink architecture as environment and cities as ecologies, and thus inherently integrated the emerging idea of system thinking into these concepts, his view of Los Angeles and its vernacular structures remained from the outside and formalistic.

EVERYDAY TACTICS

It is ironic that it was the ecology of the plains, which Banham conflated with the ordinary, that provided the materials and systems to have sprung one of the most radical reimaginations of architectural practice of the last fifty years. Today, the plains are ripe to become once more the stage for a radical departure from a spatial commonplace. In the freedom offered by an existence in the margins,[10] their underserved communities have dared to propose a different way of urban development: not top-down, but with bottom-up spatial tactics of resilience. In response to the health and safety crisis from decades of discriminatory and racist planning practices, local community organizations, entrepreneurs, and artists have come together in grassroots initiatives to claim space at all scales for the good of the neighborhood—from the sidewalk to the super block.

Nina Koscica researched the gaps and deviations in the urban grid left by the rail road, and asked how a critical reading of these spaces could make them into anti-monuments or wigs, quoting artist Niamh McCann, "La Perruque; the Wig, alludes to the Certeau idea of slipping tricky tactics into cultural moments and . . . looking at agency from within a moment or from within structures." (Nina Koscica, *Urban Vectors of Los Angeles and the Anti-Monuments They Spawn*, 2019.)

And while the emergencies of 2020, #fridaysforfuture, #shelterinplace, #BLM, all exacerbated the spatial injustice encrusted in the texture of the American landscape, they also brought the issues to the center of attention, out of the margin. The center needs to listen, and learn, and adapt its own ways to accommodate the lessons from the margins, instead of trying to overwrite them.[11]

A sidewalk can be a community kitchen? Check.

A street can be a community museum? Check.

An industrial lot can be used for community farming? Check.

A mall can be owned by the community? Check.

At the start of the COVID-19 pandemic, community fridges suddenly appeared in front of storefronts, not only providing aid to people in need but also inscribing a different identity for the place of provision, an alternate story line. The fridges proved the success of tactical operations: of small scale, non-authored interventions to the benefit of a larger group. As a result of a battle over the route of a light-rail line at grade on the central boulevard of South LA, a local initiative successfully initiated the dedication of part of the boulevard as an outdoor museum for Black culture: Destination Crenshaw. In a cautionary tale, the urban farmers from South-Central Farm, a community farm on a defunct industrial lot, despite thirteen years of lobbying after their initial eviction, just lost a second hearing last year, their land now cleared for redevelopment. But encouragingly, the example of the Crenshaw Mall, where local activists successfully petitioned to transfer the sale of the mall to a group of neighborhood-centered developers,[12] shows that community initiatives can be successful on an urban scale.

In a retake of the systems discussions of the 1970s, the constructed landscapes of the plains can be read as an underdefined system. With their opportunities for adaptation, the Los Angeles plains are fertile ground for innovation, for a much-needed reset, a re-reading of art and everyday practice together to make architecture and a culturally rich everyday neighborhood by and for the local community.

1 Reyner Banham, *Los Angeles: The Architecture of Four Ecologies* (London: Penguin Books, 1971).

2 Bernard Tschumi, "Sanctuaries," *Architectural Design* 43 (September 1973): 575–90.

3 Kellie Jones, *South of Pico: African American Artists in Los Angeles in the 1960s and 1970s* (Durham: Duke University Press, 2017).

4 Jefferson Boulevard intersects with Vermont Avenue and Western Avenue, the two twenty-mile straight running streets that join in the infinity of the long vista from Griffith Observatory in the Hollywood Hills towards San Pedro and the harbor on the Pacific Ocean. It is this view, and its famously captured version by Julius Shulman from the Stahl House, that encompasses all of the plains in their rigid order and yet defiant stance. The view from the Stahl house is a night shot, and we imagine how the sophistically dressed inhabitants of the living room imagine the crime that happens in the city below their feet. For the story behind the photo, see Mary Melton, "A Shot In The Dark: The Unknown Story Behind L.A.'s Most Celebrated Photograph," *Los Angeles Magazine*, December 5, 2016, https://www.lamag.com/longform/a-shot-in-the-dark/.

5 Michel de Certeau, "Walking in the City," in *The Practice of Everyday Life*, trans. Steven F. Rendall (Berkeley: University of California Press, 1984), 91–110.

6 The irony of using a text about walking as reference for thinking about LA is not lost on me. LA has produced its own forms of walking, and the question of access to transportation is a serious one if the city were to seriously try to become equitable to all. See Laurel and Hardy carrying a piano up the steps of a stair in Silverlake. See the idea of driving to walk, the mall being the quintessential replacement of walking in the city.

7 Although my interpretation of the vernacular is purposefully positive, the practices involved with construction of low-cost structures in Los Angeles are often not laudatory. See Douglas McCulloh, *Dream Street* (Riverside, CA: Inlandia Institute, 2009). "In a silent auction, McCulloh won the right to name a street in a new subdivision on the site of a former farm, orchard, and fruit stand in LA county. He documents his street's birth, growth and questionable practice of the construction industry." Quote from Lucy R. Lippard, *Undermining: A Wild Ride Through Land Use, Politics, and Art in the Changing West* (New York: The New Press, 2006), 139. Also see, for example, the commentary to one of the photos on the artist's website: "Justin called it 'slamming windows.' The process moves quickly—wedge the pre-made aluminum window in the framed opening, shove a four-foot level on top, pry and bash with a short crowbar until the bubbles on the level line up, pop the window in place with a nail gun, then move on to the next window. At times, Justin was literally running through the framed houses. He hinted that he got a buck a window. He thought the company owner got five dollars for every window he installed. 'I'm kind of senior man on the crew, so I'm hoping to get a little piece of the action. Talk to the owner, maybe fifty cents or a dollar more per window.' Dave, owner of another subcontractor summarizes: 'A lot of guys piecework their stuff any more, so they don't have to pay all those benefits and stuff. That's why they can save a few bucks. But you don't usually get as good a job from your pieceworker. Because they don't care. Because the more they can get done, the more they get paid, basically. So, there's a strong incentive just to whack through everything.' " Douglas McCulloh, "Dream Street," http://www.douglasmcculloh.com/projects/dream-street.

8 For more on the history of the stud, see Siegfried Giedion, Esther McCoy, Robert Venturi, and Sylvia Lavin, as well as the American Pavilion at the upcoming Venice Biennial 2021.

9 Sylvia Lavin and Kimberli Meyer, eds., *Everything Loose Will Land: 1970s Art and Architecture in Los Angeles* (Los Angeles: MAK Center for Art and Architecture, 2013), exhibition catalog.

10 See bell hooks, *Yearning: Race, Gender, and Cultural Politics* (New York: Routledge, 2015), 147.

11 See Andre M. Perry, *Know Your Price: Valuing Black Lives and Property in America's Black Cities* (Washington, DC: The Brookings Institution, 2020).

12 Roger Vincent, "Developer Drops Plan to Buy Baldwin Hills Crenshaw Plaza and Add Offices, Not Housing," *Los Angeles Times*, June 15, 2020, https://www.latimes.com/business/story/2020-06-15/developer-drops-plan-to-buy-baldwin-hills-crenshaw-plaza-and-add-offices-not-housing.

HALLIE
BLACK

BUILDING UP IN FLAMES

254

(-40—P)

The arson attack on the Genç house fell in the early morning hours of May 29, 1993, in Solingen, North Rhine-Westphalia, Germany. A group of four young men set ablaze the home, killing five and maiming fourteen of its residents. This would be one of several attacks against foreign labor classes, exposing a hotbed of xenophobia across East and West Germany before the turn of the century. The remaining empty lot conceptualizes a blankness within Germany's past and current with only a small plaque next to the neighbor's garbage cans commemorating the victims.

Arson is an act of betrayal, severing the vital connection between architecture and the body. The burning house collapses, bathtubs block exit doors, and bodies defenestrate themselves. Re-drawing, an act of rebuilding or reconstructing, the Genç house in the midst of its destructive calamity concretizes a *Zwischenzeit* space—a space that once was, became momentarily engulfed, and will never be again. The direct translation of *Zwischenzeit* is "between-time." This suspension of time alleviates the binary of the troubling before and the fickle after. Re-drawing the house in the midst of a vital destruction of inhabitant and inhabitation reconciles the memory of human absence within the empty lot in Solingen.

To suspend the duration of the attack on paper, available media documentation became paramount in re-drawing the facades, plans, and interiors of the house. First-person accounts, made-for-TV documentaries, and B-roll video from news outlets are primary sources for examining the interim of formal, bodily, and spatial annihilation. The factual incongruencies in reporting among news outlets led the reconstructions to secondarily rely on other visual media such as typological drawings and real estate listings of identical ready-cut houses. These kit homes scattered throughout Solingen, like living ghosts of the Genç residence, not only illuminate the shadowy remembrance of the attack but also cement memory as both symbolic and material.

By montaging space across time, these four drawings convey a method of seeing through absence—absence stirring within the remaining vestiges of human inhabitation, absence within time itself. It is through these absences, in the *Zwischenzeit*, that the drawings can resolve the emptiness that violence creates and possess an architectural existence suspended in between-time. In a world that is destructive and forgetful of its pasts, the totality of violence prods the possibility for the architecture of memory. Capitalizing on this totality relies on a patient revisiting of that split-second of catastrophe. In this warped, disheartening but expectant, punishing yet hopeful *Zwischenzeit*, "Building Up in Flames" commands its own eternity.

All images by Hallie Black. **This page**: The façades of the house are drawn with precision and later filled in with a series of photographic materials—now without fire damage. The plans are difficult to entirely reconstruct, since program details (kitchen placement, number of bedrooms) were left out of conducted interviews with the residents; however, the circulation route must be adjacent to the front entrance where the fire spread as depicted in the location of the collapsed roof. (*Facades and Plans of the Genç House*, 2019, digital drawing with collage.)

News media were allowed into certain preserved rooms the morning after the arson attack. This room, a children's bedroom adjacent to a family living room, is nearly left intact despite the fire damage, and the personal effects appear to be suspended in time. Architecture as the container of two temporal states, before and after, prods a possibility of conceptualizing loss and memory. (*Bedroom and Living Room*, 2019, digital collage.)

frame g
frame f
frame e
frame d
frame c
frame b
frame a
time by flame

Gürsün İnce defenestrated a chair and ejected herself with her young infant in a desperate and deadly escape from the burning house. The chair, now seen below the attic window, is left among the rubble where they were both found. The future remembrance placard would be placed next to the same trashcans. (*Chair*, 2019, digital collage.)

Within a six-second camera pan of the basement, a bathtub can be seen distressingly perched on the basement stairs. Analysis of the bathtub deduces that a second-floor bathroom was located by the central staircase. When the fire spread through the stair's vertical core, it deteriorated the surrounding structure and collapsed the floor directly underneath the bathroom. The bathtub, a vessel to hold water and cleanse the body, would be instead an object to trap those escaping from the flames. (*Bathtub*, 2019, digital collage.)

262

(-20—P)

SAMIA
HENNI

JARET
VADERA

ON MULTIVALENT IMAGEMAKING

*The following conversation, between Samia Henni (***SH***) and Jaret Vadera (***JV***), took place in the fall of 2020 over email. The discussion centered around Jaret's artistic practice, where his transdisciplinary and transmediated approaches to art consistently challenge our understanding of our environments, both as individuals and as social groups. In their conversation, the two muse over the theme of "after" in relation to Jaret's work and consider their shared interests in speculative fiction, displacement, and decolonial theory.*

SH How do you use color in your work? What is its signified and signifier?

JV I have always been fascinated with color, and how color can be experienced on a visceral, phenomenological, and linguistic level all at the same time. It can set the tone of a work, while poetically telling its own story. Color is also a shapeshifter. That changes in appearance and character depending on which other colors are beside it. Signified meanings also shift as one migrates across borders. In one culture the color white signifies love, and in another it means death.

Vision is political. Our eyes, our memories, our cultures, light, and technology all influence what we see, and what we don't. Images are shaped by all of these biases, and in turn, reinforce them. Every technology renders images and translates color using a different process. Each technology has its own *color space* with its own visual logic that calibrates the internal poetics of color in that medium.

When we look at images, we tend to focus our attention on the most immediate layer of content, while the *color space*, and the imaging process often become invisible. But images and the technologies used to create them are far from neutral, and they all carry their own politics. Images often embed the social and technological biases of their time and place. Amplifying their creators' prejudices about gender, culture, race, and class in overt and subtle ways. For decades, starting in the 1940s, Kodak film technicians used "Shirley Cards" to calibrate color in their film. These internationally distributed calibration cards used a "white" woman as their universal baseline, privileging and embedding a bias towards representing "white" skin tones with a greater accuracy. In millions of photographs, this meant that images of black and brown bodies were visually flattened, reduced into shapes, into symbols, into interchangeable shells, with less detail, nuance, and humanity.

All images by Jaret Vadera. **Previous:** All of the colors on all of the national flags were aggregated and mixed to create a single-color flag. The flag dimensions are the same as the calculated surface area of the outside of the artist's body. (*A Flag for No Country*, 2014, flag, 69.75 × 41.5 in.)

In my work, I often think about how colors can be used to tell multiple stories at the same time, while questioning the quiet, colonial soft power embedded within systems of visual translation.

Left: Multiple photographs of the artist's body were taken from 360 degrees. The photographs were then aggregated, and the colors were averaged horizontally from top to bottom. When translated into the Pantone color space, the skin color of the body was categorically broken down, averaged, and reassembled to form a new imaged skin. The print's dimensions equal the calculated surface area of the outside of the artist's body. (*Self-Portrait in 7 Pantone Colors*, 2011, photo text print applied directly onto the wall, 69.75 × 41.5 in.) **Right**: Multiple photographs of the artist's body were taken from 360 degrees. The photographs were then aggregated, and the colors were averaged horizontally from top to bottom. The new image was then filtered using a blue gradient, derived from multiple images of bodies of water near Toronto, New York, Mumbai, and Manila. The print's dimensions equal the calculated surface area of the outside of the artist's body. (*Self-Portrait in Ocean Blue*, 2016, from the *Pangea* series, photomural fabric print applied directly onto the wall, 69.75 × 41.5 in.)

When I was making *Self-Portrait in 7 Pantone Colors*, I was thinking about my experiences living in post-9/11 America as a brown person. I was thinking about my skin, its color, and how my body was being read as a racialized image in the *color space* of America; and about how racial categorization forces people into boxes, erases complexity, atomizes the self, and colonizes the body.

Self-Portrait in Ocean Blue, was more of a "rude-map" or an imaginary proposition. In this work, I was thinking about how bodies and identities are often territorialized in the same ways that land is; and about ways of imaging the self that could go beyond conventional binaries, to represent identities as fluid, dynamic, and impossible to contain. I created my own quadtone register of blues, culled from images of bodies of water surrounding four of the cities that I consider home.

In the *all that glitters* series I was using color in a different way altogether and was influenced by another constellation of aesthetics. This series was inspired by tricked-out Filipinx jeepneys, and the dollar-store-working-class-immigrant-bling that I grew up

Beyond

ALIEN

around. My lived experiences, and "cultural" color references follow a different logic than the quasi-scientific, ethnocentric, and sterilizing color theory that I learned in art and design school. In *all that glitters* my color palette was serendipitously determined by whatever I could find in "dollar stores" in Toronto, Brooklyn, and Queens.

SH Could you please elaborate on the territorialization of bodies? How are bodies territorialized in the same ways that land is? Can we also think of these acts as systematic deterritorializations?

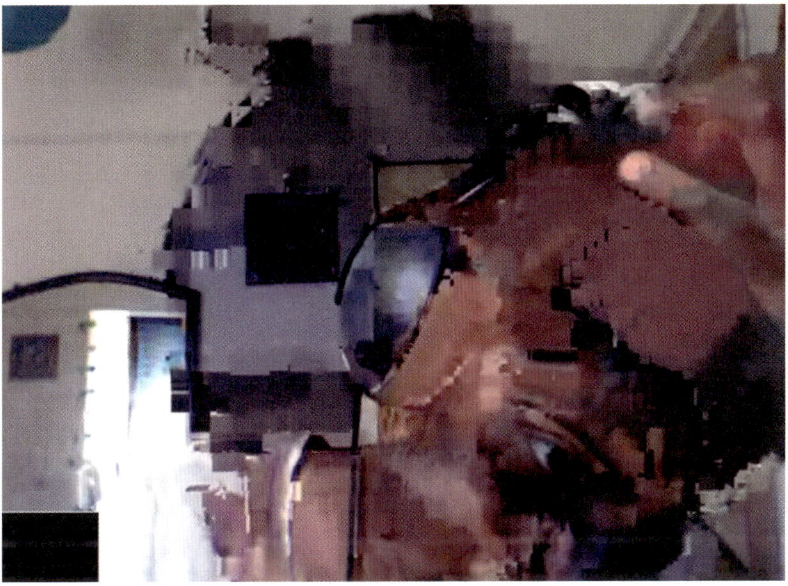

Opposite top: *beyond*, 2018, from the *all that glitters* series, duct tape, mixed tapes, and discarded shoe, size 10.5. **Opposite bottom:** *alien*, 2018, from the *all that glitters* series, duct tape, mixed tapes, and discarded shoe, size 10.5. **This page:** *untitled (I promise, I'll believe)*, 2011, from the *skype* series, inkjet print, 30 × 40 in.

JV Absolutely. I was once told that I make "fugitive images." I like that idea. I think there is something radical about slowing a system down to the point where it starts to fall apart. New potential spaces can open up and new poetics become possible through its entropy. There is also something in the process of unfixing the meanings of images, and reimagining them, that feels emancipatory, and psychologically breaks from malignant narratives and toxic systems of translation.

Throughout history, religious leaders, politicians, and profiteers have been trying to divide people into different constructed categories that they have designed, governed, and policed. As people of color, in America, this systematic process has, for the most part, come from the outside, been out of our control, and weaponized against us. Our bodies are othered, turned into symbols, turned into images, into types—in a system neither created by us or for us.

These constructed images of people of color have been used as propaganda for centuries in this country to manufacture consent in its never-ending wars; to protect its "foreign interests abroad"; to justify slavery and the genocide of indigenous peoples; and to police black, brown, female, and queer people.

The process of identifying, dividing, and ruling was a common strategy used during the colonial era. The underlying algorithms in our current economic systems still rely heavily on resource extraction, exploitation, and population control. So the old colonial machines easily transitioned into our current neo-imperial and neo-liberal ones.

The process of othering and imaging different bodies today shares the same colonial ethos behind the mapping and conquering of lands. Bodies, like lands, are delineated and given fixed borders. They are given clear boundaries of what constitutes a within and a without, a good and a bad, an us and a them. It is this process of territorializing a fluid and nuanced human being into a fragmented and static image—through a paternalistic system of translation—that I am interested in revealing, dismantling, and turning against itself.

This page: *Emperor of No Country*, 2016, from the *Pangea* series, prints of a world map sewn together, 28 × 58 × 6 in. **Next spread:** *No Country*, 2014, from the *Pangea* series, black marker on world map (Mercator projection), 30 × 20 in.

In *Self-Portrait in Ocean Blue*, I unmap, unfix, and deterritorialize my understanding of my "self"—whatever that may be—and decolonize the idea that identities are fixed, bordered, and classifiable. Water as a substance and as a metaphor feels like a natural way to deterritorialize the fixity of signification. Water is malleable. It changes forms, it is fluidly inter-connected, and it is inside all of us. The images I make, and the processes of imaging I use are more like an *impossible object*, or a *pharmakon*, that is a poison, but also potentially a cure.

SH One could say that you make an "impossible object" possible and that's when you turn it into a *pharmakon*. I also often use the term *pharmakon* or *pharmacology*—as a condition—to unpack the practices and histories of institutional oppressions and colonial violence. For instance, in Manifesta 13 in Marseille that opened a few days ago, I titled my exhibition *Housing Pharmacology*. Drawing on Jacques Derrida's essay, "Plato's Pharmacy," which proposed that writing is a *pharmakon*, Bernard Stiegler—who has recently passed away—theorized and broadened *pharmacology* by incorporating a political analysis of and intervention on exploitative imperialist and capitalist systems, which are rooted in colonial pasts and presents. For me, *pharmacology* informs the ethics and politics of care and caring. It is a right to reimagine, reveal, dismantle, and turn constructed narratives against themselves, even though there is a tendency to suppress or marginalize these possibilities. However, I would push it a little bit further and say that "translation" is by definition a "paternalistic system" and that one should not "translate" but rather "unlearn." What do you think about this?

JV The idea that society is a kind of pharmacy, where what is deemed as good and bad is translated through a paternalistic top-down system sounds about right. We see this kind of translation-as-statecraft playing out in the news today when politicians, spin doctors, and journalists try to convince us that peaceful protesters are really crazed and violent mobs. While the world sees uprisings against a failing state, the spin doctors are screaming riot.

It is urgent that we look beneath the surface so we can see who is pulling the strings. It is critical that we unlearn much of what we have been taught, so that we can think for ourselves, write our own histories, imagine our own futures, and define our own poetics of relation. In this spirit, our creative translations can also be seen as liberatory personal and collective acts of reimagining, care, and radical love. For me, breaking images and then putting them back together in new ways feels psychologically freeing, like an act of resistance and invention at the same time.

PLATE XII

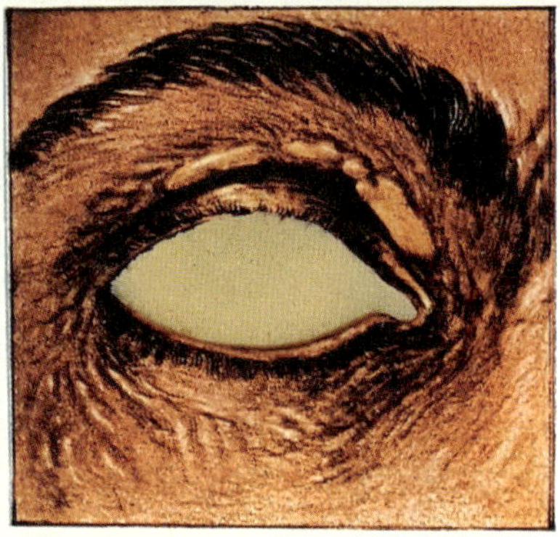

Fig. 130.

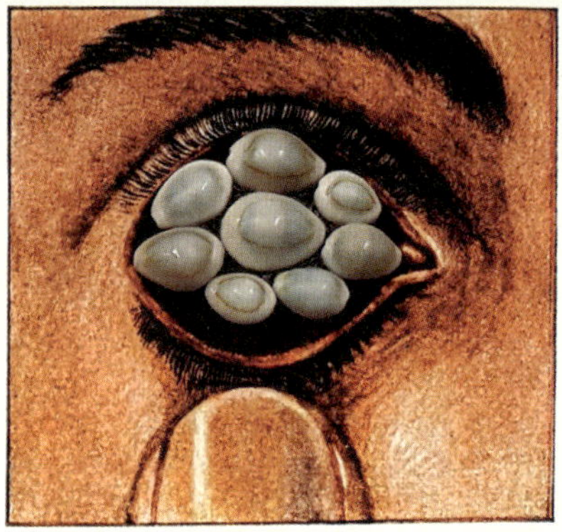

Fig. 131.

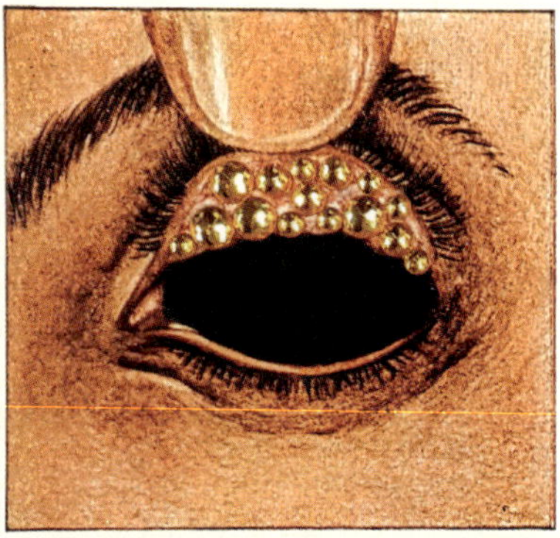

Fig. 132.

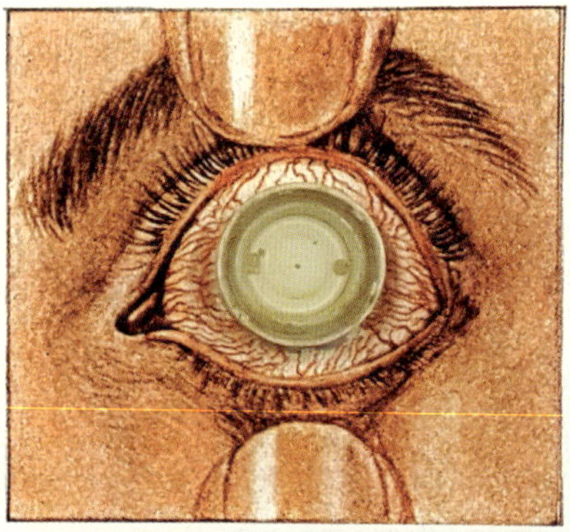

Fig. 133.

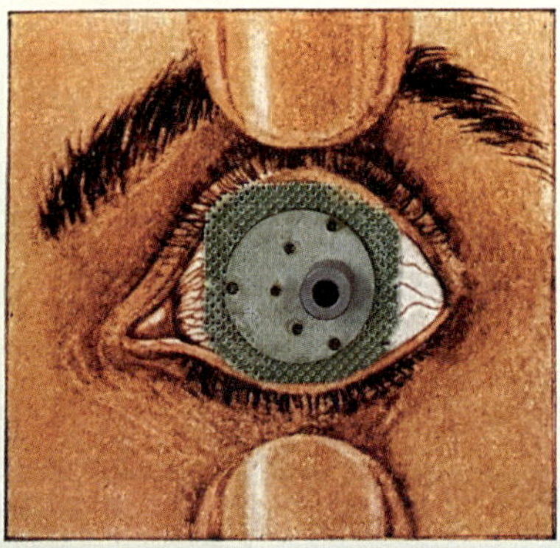

Fig. 134.

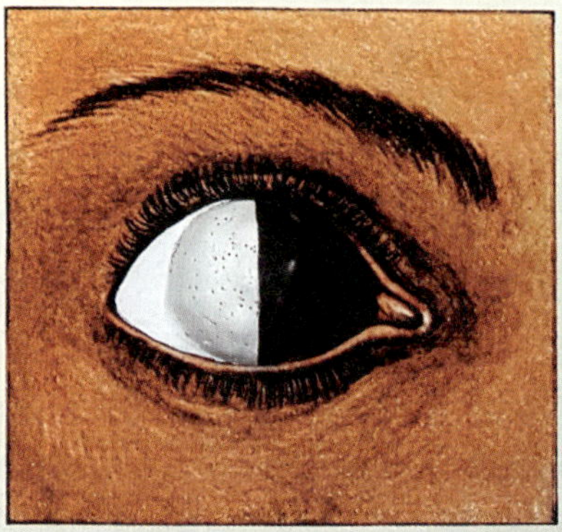

Fig. 135.

I am indebted to Steigler, Derrida, and Plato's theorizing about the *pharmakon*, and am also simultaneously interested in something much less elegant, meta, or Cartesian, something a bit more grimy, messy and confusing. When I think about translation, I think back to the apartment building complex where I first grew up in Toronto, in what some have called a multicultural "immigrant ghetto." I remember walking through those apartment hallways and the savory cooking smells that hung in the air, intermingling and shifting as I walked by, while voices speaking different languages ebbed and flowed from behind closed doors. My parents, both working class, blue collar immigrants had arrived just a few years before I was born. My mother is Catholic from the Philippines, and my father, who came from India, was an idiosyncratic mix of atheist and Hindu. Both spoke three or four different languages each. So translations and mistranslations were always in the air, in a very real, everyday way.

Translation wasn't an abstract concept, or even top-down, for me just yet. All meanings felt like they were in a constant state of negotiation. It was horizontal, perceptual, and cross-cultural. I learned early on that two people could be looking at the exact same thing and be seeing something completely different. It is in these parallaxes that I grew up and why I first became interested in how language, culture, and belief-systems influence how we see, what we see, and what we don't. Or put in another way, in the politics of vision.

Perhaps this is why I am interested in optical illusions, like *impossible objects*, that are seemingly paradoxical, yet still make their own kind of sense. This ability to hold multiple perspectives at once makes new potentials for representation possible that hold complexity and move beyond *either/o*r binaries, towards the *both/and*. These new multivalent images can become a kind of code-switching trigger that glitches and reboots different systems, or keeps oscillating between multiple ways of seeing, like a computer screen that rapidly cycles between windows when something is stuck on your keyboard.

Everything we see or know is mediated through a series of processes and translations. For me, translation is a lens through which one can better understand the layered biological, social, and technological processes through which power is enacted. Translation can also be used as a radical tool that helps us to reclaim our vision, while also serving as a lens through which the world can be seen as a space of magic and new possibilities.

In the *Diseases of the Eye* series, medical illustrations from the early 1890s are redeployed to explore the relationships between desire and disease, enlightenment and violence. (*FIG. 130-135. Diseases of the Eye*, 2017, mixed media, 13 × 19 in.)

SH This is fascinating. Your response makes me think of another layer, that of interpretation, which is very different from translation. I speak seven languages. I grew up with three and I had to learn four additional languages because of my own history of migration. To finance my studies I worked as a language teacher, translator, and interpreter. Today, when I exhibit histories of violence, oppression, and colonialism, I prefer to offer a multiplicity of interpretations rather than translations because the oppressing power refused to learn my own native language. I speak the language of both the oppressor and the oppressed, and therefore, I have the power to interpret that language, but I have no intention to translate it for those who refused to learn it. What is your take on this? Does interpretation affect your work?

JV I remember when I first read Édouard Glissant's writings about opacity and about the violence of translating oneself to become legible to the colonial gaze. After that, I no longer felt the need to answer malignant questions, to respond to the question "where are you from?" or to act as a cultural informant. As soon as I began to assert my right to opacity, to complexity, I felt a great psychological weight lifted and a new confidence. Everything changed after that and there was no going back.

Resisting this kind of translation was echoed in Trinh T. Minh-Ha's idea about the power in being *inappropriate* and *inappropriated*. I embed this attitude using different creative strategies into everything I make, facilitating an interpretative experience for the viewer which is more like a Rorschach test or a koan, that slows down the junk-food processes through which we digest images everyday. But also, if the viewer is open, the work can illuminate the layered processes through which we "make sense." Instead of just being a two-dimensional gesture of refusal, I hope to tell multidimensional, multivalent stories, that offer many ways in, and many ways through an artwork.

I think of my images and installations as "rude-maps," as open and unfixed representations, where all the signifiers are always verbs and never nouns. It is also important for me to keep the holes in my work intact, to present the parallaxes between interpretations, and to reveal the ghostly in-betweens. In my installation work, through the lighting, arrangement, and juxtaposition of different objects, I try to conjure a presence in the absences, to represent the unrepresented, and the unrepresentable.

Minh-Ha also describes "entre chien et loup" as the ambiguous interpretive space of twilight, as the meeting of two lights, when a dog can become a wolf. The two lights of the moon and the sun become a metaphor for the shifting and overlapping of ontologies. This convergence of different ways of seeing overlap for a brief time and open up a new space, like a doorway, or a portal. Where a dog can transform into a wolf, or a wolf into a dog, and thus reveals itself as a mythological third thing, a shapeshifter from a world *beyond*.

SH I appreciate very much your reference to Gilssant's opacity, or "le droit à l'opacité" (the right to opacity). In a plurirelational world, as Glissant argued, recognizing difference (and not diversity) does not entail acknowledging otherness by undressing it, but by accepting the multiplicity and/or impenetrability of its cross-cultural communication. Thank you so much for creating your very necessary "fugitive images," "impossible objects," and "rude-maps."

276

VALERIA RACHEL
HERRERA

THE CONTESTED LANDSCAPES OF MNEMOSYNE: CONSTRUCTING MAPS OF MEMORY

> Perhaps it might be said rightly that there are three times: a time present of things past; a time present of things present; and a time present of things future. For these three do coexist somehow in the soul, for otherwise I could not see them. The time present of things past is memory; the time present of things present is direct experience; the time present of things future is expectation.
>
> –St. Augustine, *Confessions*, c. 400, Book 11, Chapter 20, Heading 26.

We live literally and figuratively in three time spaces—present, past, and future. We exist in the present, are defined by the perpetual conflation of memories that comprise our past, while continuously engaged in a consciousness of what's next—the immediate as well as the infinite future of immeasurable time and of memories yet to be experienced.

My work is informed by both the equivocal spatial realms of Piranesi's *Carceri* series and Constant's optimistic notion of the ideal city as articulated in *New Babylon*. The *Carceri* prints explore imaginary worlds constructed of fluid spaces that defy normative expectations of scale, viewpoint, and atmosphere. The phenomenological dynamism that results from the layers of interpenetrating spaces and overlapping surfaces composed as a receding three-dimensional matrix provides the genesis for my thinking about complex space. The *New Babylon* project explores the notion of the city as a place of absolute self-satisfaction, in which humanity is liberated from the requisite obligations and conventions of "utilitarian life." By incorporating play, creativity, and the saturation of oneself in leisure, time is played out in urban scenarios where one is emancipated from the certainty of life's drudgery to find escape in the deepest recesses of one's alternate consciousness. These ideas provide a parallel mechanism for the conceptualizing and crafting of the *Mnemosyne* series, which is fundamentally about the dichotomy between reality and fantasy, memory and projection.

I am interested in the continuous acts of revision encountered during the process of making and the condition of palimpsest endemic to the practice of etching. This work is a buildup of archeological layers and simultaneous actions of addition and subtraction engaged during the construction and development of the matrix—*i.e the metal plate that is operated on and used to*

All images by Valeria Rachel Herrera. **Previous:** *The Contested Landscapes of Mnemosyne, Episode I*. Intaglio print on paper, drypoint, aquatint, etching, plate mark: 60.96 × 91.44 cm.

transfer the image to print. Moments of superimposition, whiteout, and erasure reveal a differently liberating way to think about plates and prints, narratives and images, space and time. The literal act of palimpsest, both conceptually and technically, motivates my obsessive interest in the medium and my objective to construct multi-layered images and entangled stories. The etchings presented here employ acts of literal and conceptual erasure and destruction in a selective curating of both desired and discarded memories. By retracing a preserved memory of that which was removed, lost, or excluded, one can remember, record, and rearticulate histories as a tapestry of interwoven experiences.

In these prints the notion of the city is reconsidered as an imagined autobiographical construct—one less interested in an idealized utopia than in an urban landscape of dystopian character. A place stark, heavy, chaotic and complex, sufficient to host the playful narratives of an elusive alter ego. It is a place for me and me alone—an inner space within outer space. There is no clear entrance for the viewer into these vast textured spaces of void and that is intentional and significant—the viewer strains to see and understand more. The distance between the viewer and the deep void exists as a barrier, restricting the viewer from access to my inner personal space—there is a story in these landscapes that remains further out of reach.

These deconstructed landscapes are recollections of moments, ideas, places, and feelings that comprise an alternative reality—an "other-world" that operates as a parallel reality to the mundane drama of an unstable childhood. Mnemonic devices populate the spaces, places, and environments of the cinematic imagery providing clues through the *method of loci*. In essence, memories are translated into a contested, congested landscape of episodes and experiences that reconstruct a non-linear memory of the conflation of reality and fantasy that provided the place of survival for my childhood. There are moments, elements, portals, and thresholds depicted that mark tangible memory within an endless timeline, a long take video frame transcendent from a specific curated lineage of incidents. The space is dark, black, and boundless with unexpected collisions between episodic events and spaces—both fast and slow—deep and shallow—then and now. Things are in constant motion: shadows shifting, ghosts oscillating between the here and there, elusive, never captured in a world that does not attempt to illustrate a clear, decipherable space but instead a place that is in flux, unstable, lacks order, and is the

ultimate convergence of the distinct and divergent paths that have contributed to the *medina* that is my personal history—that of a nomadic existence paradoxically confined to a labyrinthine world.

Because of the fallibility of memory, fantasy comes into play. The notion of *after* is an evolving and changing part of one's own collective consciousness. Memory does not end after the experience itself but lingers as part of the person and their development, and when the memory dissolves or disappears it is replaced with fantasy. There is room for time to move away from its linear past, present, and future and to transform into a dream state of fluidity, creativity, invention, and escape—to a place, after time, a place where the film continues to play on... If you look closely you may find these places, hidden in plain sight... or in the far-off space of the imagination.

> Now let us turn to the treasure-house of inventions, the custodian of all the parts of rhetoric, memory. There are two kinds of memory, he continues, one natural, the other artificial. The natural memory is that which is engrafted in our minds, born simultaneously with thought. The artificial memory is a memory strengthened or confirmed by training. A good natural memory can be improved by this discipline and persons less well endowed can have their weak memories improved by the art.
>
> —Frances A. Yates, *The Art of Memory*, 1966.

Previous spread: *The Contested Landscapes of Mnemosyne, Episode II*. Intaglio print on paper, drypoint, aquatint, etching, plate mark: 60.96 × 91.44 cm. **Opposite top:** *The Contested Landscapes of Mnemosyne, Episode III*. Intaglio print on paper, drypoint, aquatint, etching, plate mark: 60.96 × 91.44 cm. **Bottom:** The *Contested Landscapes of Mnemosyne, Episode IV.* Intaglio print on paper, drypoint, aquatint, etching, plate mark: 60.96 × 91.44 cm.

(YOU ARE HERE)

286

(P)

JACQUES
FERRIER

HOW CITIES BETRAYED THEIR INHABITANTS

The COVID-19 pandemic questions the resilience of the metropolitan model. Appearing as the main source of contamination, dense cities have proved incapable of protecting their inhabitants. The piece invites us to rethink the model from the urban planning perspective that is concerned with the body and the scales of action of city dwellers.

The astonishing situation we currently face leads us to question our relation to the urban planet, as the intense and global flows of both goods and people that link metropolises together clearly hastened the spread of the epidemic. It is a subject in itself, just like the media coverage of the pandemic. Indeed, "live" impact on people's reactions similarly directly impacts our urban world.[1] Finally, to complete this overall picture, it is necessary to mention the lack of solidarity between cities. Whereas New York, Shanghai, Paris, London, and the like emblematized a single, united, and transnational club of interchangeable and connected urban elites just a few week ago, cities are now insolated and facing the crisis on their own.

But the responsibility of urban meta-organization in the diffusion and reception of the pandemic is not the topic of this essay. Cities' inability to take care of their inhabitants shall be questioned and our global model rethought. This essay advocates a reinvented urban environment in resonance with the planet, through local-oriented mindset, micro-urbanism, and new dimensions for shared spaces.

CITIES' INABILITY TO CARE FOR THEIR INHABITANTS

The built environment, whose technical sophistication and performance seemed invulnerable, begins to show signs of weakness in the wake of the lockdown. Urban infrastructure—an unprecedented accumulation of buildings, sprawling networks, commercial overabundance, and hyper-concentration of workspaces—appears as the organizing framework for millions of people's daily life. By substituting for most of inhabitants' skills, urban infrastructure has come to create a haunting yet gentle, and eventually accepted, kind of oppression. On the other hand, urban life was at least expected to be protective. It is now clear that this is not the case. We used to raise the dense city as a model of a sustainable city, particularly for the optimization of transports and the magnification of social life, but this pattern is now at the heart of the health crisis. Indeed, extreme density precisely turns out to be the cause of our collective and economic lives' paralysis: alleged powerful metropolises stopped dead. Multiple withdrawals to the countryside actually demonstrate an instinctive mistrust vis-à-vis an urban environment that apparently fails to protect. On the first day of confinement, 17% of Parisians left the capital to return to their ancestral lands, or simply to their holiday home.[2]

The current crisis caught us unaware. However, it is not and will not be an isolated event. Although the health cataclysm outpaced the foreseen and inevitable environmental catastrophe, they are two sides of the same coin: a single problem our globalized society must confront. In the near future, a global stress related to energy, climate, or the availability of drinking water may induce broadly similar—and even more acute—consequences for large cities than those caused by the current pandemic. Our city model needs to be revamped. As the French philosopher François Jullien wrote, "we must tackle the crisis as a danger, but also as a positive opportunity. Perceiving this constructive aspect, which at first may go unnoticed, is key to make it prosper."[3]

Health crises' impact on city planning is neither unheard nor recent. In nineteenth-century Europe, they led to the virtually complete reconstruction of large cities. Both the fight against endemic tuberculosis and the fear of recurrent cholera outbreaks affected entire societies without distinction, and in all countries. Architects, scientists, and politicians gathered in the same spirit to invent and promote massive renovations of deadly city centers. "A city shape changes faster, alas, than the heart of a mortal," Baudelaire grieved in a Paris undertaking complete transformations.[4] Scientific research, notably microbial modelling and the hygienist movement, lucidly contrived to design contemporary town planning. This includes demolition of the inner-city walls to open up the city, introduction of public transport, creation of urban parks, promotion of ventilation and natural light, connection to the sewer system, drinking water distribution and waste collection, but also simply development of bathrooms in apartments. To supersede cluttered, irrational, and dangerously insalubrious old cities, masters of modern urban planning used the tremendous technical arsenal that engineers put at their disposal to make the past a clean slate. They created a new urban model, combining the art of science with geometric planning and economic rationality. For more than a century, the performance of this strategy, constantly enhanced by technical innovations, has accompanied world population growth. Annihilating the sensitive and contextual urban planning of ancient cities, functional urban planning has imposed, as never before in the history of mankind, the same way of conceiving inhabited environments. As a result, an efficient urban world rose everywhere, yet without quality.

All images by Ferrier Marchetti Studio. **Top:** *Impasse d'Amsterdam, Grand Central Saint-Lazare*, Paris, France, 2019. Photo by Myr Muratet. **Bottom:** *Rooftop Garden, Grand Central Saint-Lazare*, Paris, France, 2019. Photo by Luc Boegly.

This way of designing the city has been disproportionately multiplied on the scale of a world of more than seven billion inhabitants caught up in a constant acceleration. Under the fire of environmental criticism for many years now, its dependence on an ultra-sophisticated technique makes it fragile. We just witnessed it. And the fact that all cities are dependent on the same technical sphere makes them all weak at the same time when technic comes to lack.

THINKING LOCALLY

Questions raised are global, so are necessary means available. However, solutions shall be thought out locally. Now oriented towards communication, data management, and complex networks, our techniques totally differ from Haussmann or Le Corbusier's. They can, of course, offer tools for social control—e.g. tracking—to help resolve crises, as Seoul, Hong Kong, and Singapore just demonstrated. But they could and should be requisitioned for a much higher ambition: to move from the generic, fragile, and consumerist international city to a city that offers its inhabitants a richer, freer experience from a sustainable development perspective.

Waking up after the COVID-19 crisis will be difficult. We can augur massive disillusionment with metropolises that have betrayed their inhabitants' expectations. However, we shall not reject our urban civilization. The philosopher Michel Serres wrote twenty years ago that, "On planet Earth, there is now less intervention by man as an individual and as a subject [...] and more massive, immense and dense human patches."[5] Cities created problems; now cities must provide solutions. What will they be? It is too early to tell. But let's get ready now: dealing with the post-pandemic will require different ways to work and think. More than just heaven-sent innovations, we need above all to reassess neglected notions that proved essential thanks to the crisis. The concept of urban density shall be subtlety nuanced by taking into account multiple parameters including natural spaces, biodiversity, agriculture, and climate. As for built areas, we need redeploy, pool, and redefine them to ensure their adaptability to each particular situation. Let's move towards a living density: hybrid, flexible, and shared. In other words, quantitative density—Paris, 20,000 inhabitants per square kilometer—must give way to qualitative density.

This general diagnosis is only sketchy and requires many developments and in-depth studies. But I would like to conclude by addressing the question, which is always risky—and often perilous—of concrete proposals for action for the immediate future. In this respect, the period of confinement points us in a number of directions. These are not spectacular revolutions that an architect who has become providential could take on board, but rather simple things that have already been mishandled in the twentieth century and whose value must be restored. In the light of this crisis, we are better able to identify strategies that, although essential, had ended up being considered negligible. In the continuity of the work that has long been undertaken following a sensitive approach to the city,[6] I propose to return to the evidence that proves vital in the impeded city, and to do so on three interlocking scales: first, the scale of public life in terms of a neighborhood limited to a nearby walking radius, secondly the scale of collective life as contained in the building, and finally the intimate scale of each person's experience.

FOR MICRO-URBANISM

Green space availability and exercise facility accessibility within a close radius are two striking topical examples of criteria that argue in favor of moving away from large-scale planning towards micro-urban planning. Envisioning the neighborhood as an area you can walk through and feel around you demonstrates well the importance we place in our comings and goings, journeys, walks, or strolls. They are the true scale of our perception of urban design products, rather than the city as seen from above.[7] It is precisely this short scale that lockdown imposes in a Europe that limits the average maximum distance for necessary travel to one kilometer.

Cities are nowadays torn between designing architecture as an autonomous object and designing the territory on a too-large scale. Design on the scale of micro-urbanism remains to be invented, but it clearly starts from the scale of architecture, more precisely from the gathering of various architectures connected to a larger urban environment. In a nutshell, the scale should be a modest radius of action, i.e. more or less a ten-minute walk. Thus, measurement no longer relies on the view from sky, but on body's engagement in the city. One must imagine the conception of the city as the weaving of patterns that partially overlap and intertwine to form the overall urban fabric. These human-sized urban patterns, by involving a wide range of resources, provide the resilient neighborhood that is sorely lacking today. Essential resources to human wellbeing, including health, of course, but also landscape, agriculture, education, sports and leisure, etc. must become basic parameters of planning a neighborhood. This approach puts feelings and senses at the heart of any conception.

TOWARDS A NEW DIMENSION OF PROXIMITY AND NEW COMMON SPACES

Collective buildings' lack of convivial space also emphasizes their inability to meet human expectations. It turns impossible for someone at home to escape a cramped flat within the building itself. Thus, is "collective" just a way of saying "accumulative?" An "in-between," i.e. between private life and community life would offer a true common dimension. One could imagine at least two major issues to positively deal with.

First, various kinds of thresholds, from the entrance hall to the second floor shall be designed as places to sit and meet for a moment. Social distancing, a new dimension of proximity between city dwellers, would then no longer be a constraint but, rather, the measure to define common spaces our parsimonious apartment buildings clearly lacked.

Lumière Tower, Tours, France, 2017. Photo by Myr Muratet.

Secondly, we need to institute in every collective building truly collective areas: halls and gardens where several people can stand, shade under trees and meadows that protect from the heat island effect. Shared fountains, game and meeting rooms, and rooftop terraces would therefore become the norm. It is necessary to introduce flexibility in the assembly of the apartments rather than define assignment, whose use and allocation may change over time. The list could easily be extended by what each person may wish to add to his new or old building in order to no longer live, crisis or not, in a confined apartment.

Children's lives seem appear particularly revealing in this question of the lack of common ground in the building. The crisis makes us realize that children themselves have been confined for a long time. For them, the city means going from one confinement to another: school, playground, apartment. The health crisis reveals in its true light city of children's mourning. When there is no longer a square or a school around, a child's space is limited to his or her room, about the size of a space capsule. Consequences are, at best, the exasperation of the whole family in apartments on the verge of implosion at the end of the day. At worst, this situation may degenerate to provoke a 20% increase in calls for violence against children after three weeks of lockdown in both France[8] and the UK.[9]

We are very far from the kids playing in the streets of Paris feeling at home, as shown by the images of Ronis, Doisneau, and Boubat. Children have been excluded from large cities and now today they are suffering the worst of this crisis. By conquering a truly collective dimension, buildings can begin to repair and eliminate harm to the city of children.

Lumière Tower, Tours, France, 2017. Photo by Myr Muratet.

T20 Building, Shanghai, China, 2019.

WELCOMING NATURE

Finally, it is necessary to note the very different experiences that result from having access or not to an external extension. Enjoying a garden, a terrace, or even a small balcony clearly helped to handle confinement. Allegedly trivial and ordinary, this domestic relationship with nature is not sufficiently taken into consideration as key for a possible design renewal. It is nevertheless constitutive of an in-depth reflection on how to de-compact the apartment building to make it porous, crossing, and open. By allowing to welcome nature "on all floors," permeable architecture would hence create a homely place for the living world, in accordance with climate and seasons. Each building would henceforth become the support of its own landscape and offer various possibilities of appropriation: private, shared, collective. Promoting continuity between inside and outside facilitates a controlled constancy of sequences and passages for biodiversity, from the public to the intimate, from the city to the very interior of homes or offices.

These three instances—micro-urbanism, shared building, landscape architecture—are deliberately extremely tangible,

Jardins de la Lironde, Montpellier, France, 2013. Photo by Myr Muratet.

LAKERS
23

anchored in the field of possibilities without utopia. None of them are new, albeit disdained. The crisis just helps shed light on. Good old exterior spaces shall be rediscovered, brought together and intensified. They are a sample of basic solutions that are within our reach to turn the current upheaval into a lever for transformation. Then, although our future action shall be based on local and site-specific actions, it is time for architecture to be part of a global economy capable of addressing the millions of urban dwellers who today all share same anxieties.

Resources, climate, health and the extinction of species are the different facets of the same challenge for metropolises. Let's turn the post-COVID era into an opportunity to create an urban environment that resonates with the planet and the people who inhabit it.

130 Dwellings, Romainville, France, 2011.

1 Michel Lussault, *Chronique Géovirale*, March 21, 2020, www.youtube.com/watch?v=BsaKg8bbgVQ.

2 Martin Hirsch, press conference, March 20, 2020.

3 François Jullien interviewed by Nicolas Truong, *Le Monde*, April 7, 2020.

4 Charles Baudelaire, "Le Cygnet," in *Les Fleurs du Mal*, 1857.

5 Michel Serres, *Le contrat naturel* (Paris: François Bourin, 1990).

6 See Sensual City's publications on www.sensual-city.com.

7 Michel de Certeau, *L'Invention du quotidien* (Paris: Gallimard, 1980).

8 Adrien Tacquet, French Secretary of Children's Protection, April 9, 2020.

9 Data from NSPCC, April 30, 2020.

ELEANOR
KRAUSE

MELTDOWN: GLACIAL ARTIFACTS FOR PROJECTIVE FUTURES

300

(P–30)

All images by Eleanor Krause, 2019. Previous: *Site 4: Valley Plan.* This page: A slice of Gannett Glacier is displaced and partially buried into the ground as an extension of the river. Sited in an expansive meadowed valley and at the first view of Gannett Glacier, the monolith visually projects into a corresponding void in the glacier and a winding river of meltwater stretches between them. This surreal composition amplifies the viewer's experience of glacier melt as a disruptive and monumental displacement of mass, rather than a natural flow. (*Site 4: Valley.*)

Climate change not only radically disrupts systems of energy and capital but also rescales our notions of time and space. While we struggle to grapple with human responses to global ecological crises, architecture carries an opportunity to bring environmental change to visibility, occupying scale as an "in-between."

Operating at two scales, the hiker and the satellite, the thesis proposes a remote trek through the twenty-five-mile valley carved by Gannett Glacier of the Wind River Range in Wyoming. Gannett Glacier and its sister glaciers are melting at an unprecedented rate. Glaciologists believe the remaining glaciers in Wyoming will disappear by the middle of the twenty-first century. Accentuating the devastation of a seemingly "untouched" landscape, a series of five interventions along the river of meltwater registers, catalyzes, and amplifies shifting natural systems. Each intervention creates a moment of pause for the solitary hiker and a sequential measure for the distant public, most of whom may only experience the series through photographs or satellite imagery. Each move is explicitly geometric to clearly mark a moment of human intervention. As a collection, the five sites ask how architecture can register meltwater levels and express the multitude of ecological and experiential changes resulting from glacier loss.

Sites one through three register and amplify soil deposition, rock erosion, and lowering water levels: each sculpted first by glacial movement and then more subtly by meltwater. Sites four and five crescendo the displacement, void, and melting of glacial mass. Each meditation sources construction materials from upstream and serves to build an experiential sequence of passive synthesis—culminating in an empathetic sensitivity to interconnected degradation.

The proposal aims to engage the multiple scales of interconnectivity that climate change challenges us to grasp: planetary shifts, geologic time, and lived experience. Somewhere between metaphorical, observational, and phenomenological, the interventions mediate the scale of individual and landscape in a manner that is not didactic nor performative, but experiential and relational. This ambition for architecture intentionally collaborates along renegotiated timescales to express the intimate and profound changes of local environments.

Opposite: Compressed earth dug from the valley is cast against the void in the ice, creating a U-shaped hall. The ice's ancient strata inscribe the rammed earth walls with prehuman histories, preserving a melting past. (*Site 5: Glacier.*) **Next spread:** Gannett Glacier Valley, Wind River Range, Wyoming.

ELEANOR
KRAUSE

MELTDOWN

site 4: VALLEY

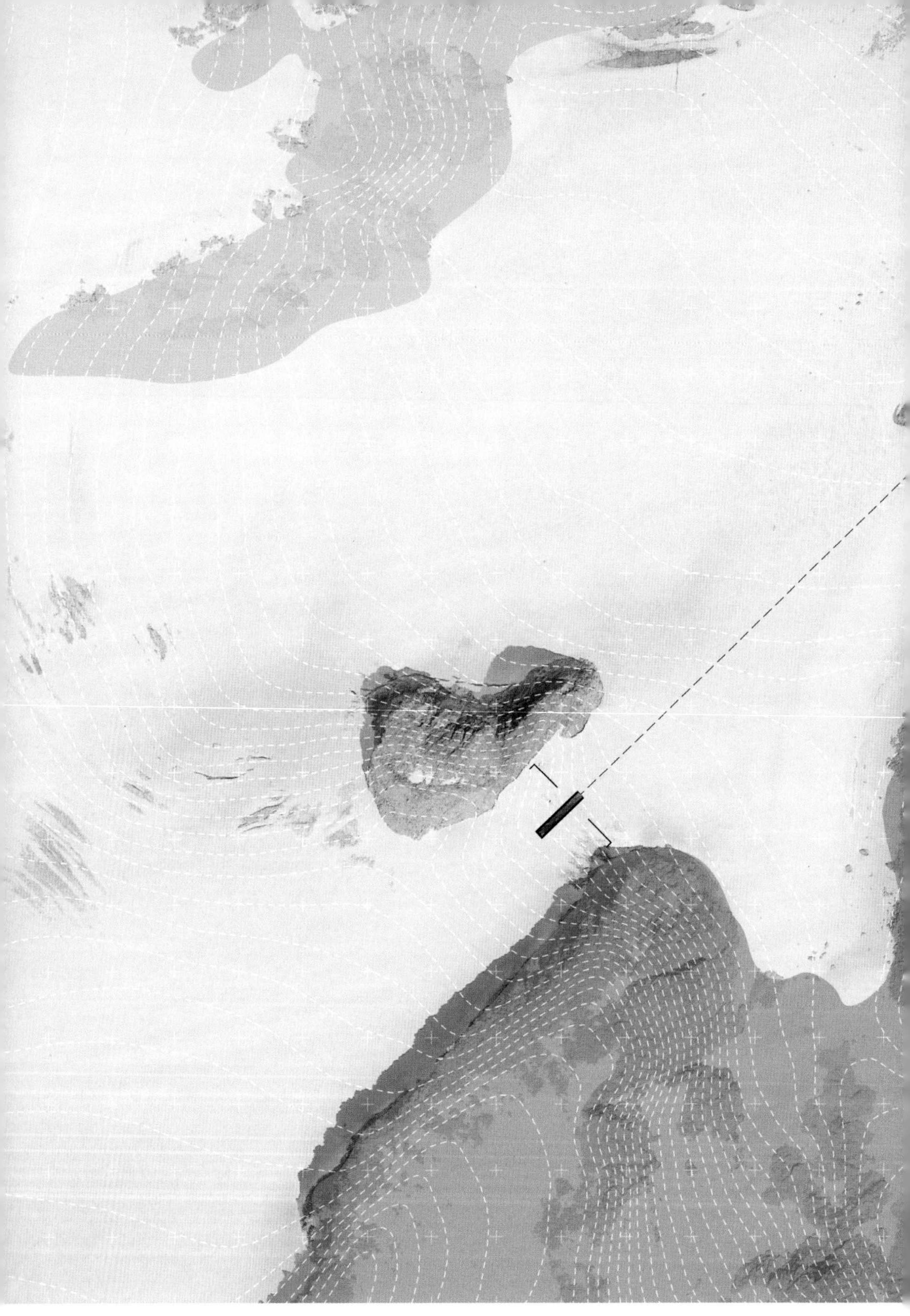

Previous spread: *Site 4: Valley Section.* Opposite: *Site 5: Glacier Plan.* This page top: As the glacier dissolves, the void is experientially inverted and emerges as a mass. What remains is an austere monolith embedded with traces of the glacier: an artifact suspending the ruin of a lost entity. *(Site 5: Glacier in Thirty Years.)* Bottom: When the glacier melts completely, a distinct pool will remain in its footprint. *(Site 4: Valley in Thirty Years.)* Next spread: *Site 5: Glacier Section.*

site 5: GLACIER

314

(P–A)

SAM
CHERMAYEFF

HOW DO WE GET TO AFTER THE SELF?

I have noticed that real community is more economic than I am comfortable with. And, like all problems, this one is self-created.

I have a family. I love my family. I have an office. I love my office. These things are my community. There is nothing controversial about this.

My units, family and office, are relatively new in my life. When I started adulthood and related architectural pursuits as a more or less free entity, I imagined that possible communities were malleable, that I could shape them as an architect. I imagined, and still do, that I can design buildings for people to live, work, and so on very much together. I happen to have found some very likeminded clients and this work goes on. But, my clients, my colleagues, and I have gotten older and our understanding of community is changing.

When people, myself included, are beginning to settle down and have kids, or as parents pass away, I notice that we often feel a need to own things. Fine. I might accept this in my own life without asking too many questions under the premise that this is some version of tradition. This is what my parents did, I thought. But I've been mistaken. Our political society has made something new while perhaps disingenuously implying tradition.

In talking about "family" I do not mean the family the way my parents did. I certainly don't speak about a support network. I wish that I were referring to a group of people with whom I share something and I wish I meant community. What I've been tricked into meaning by any of this is my own economic self and its extension. This idea of family, often defended from many ideological perspectives, is the narrowest view of our (my) interests in history.

Shared value and shared space are still things we should pursue. This mission appeared obvious until this inflection point that I am currently experiencing, new fatherhood and passed parents. I have not wavered in my support for a more collective existence but am clearly abutting the forces against my colorful coexistent vision. I am too young to fully grasp a time before this advanced capitalist version of the self was created but at this personal inflection point I can begin to draw a line backward from my sudden desire for security—private security.

It seems that capitalism requires that I create security for my family, which is my community. I have been drafted as a co-conspirator. I don't feel entirely empowered, much less able, to go much beyond my baby and wife. Again, this is despite my desire for a much larger community-cum-family or family-cum-community.

I imagine at first that this idea of my family versus yours relates Reagan and Thatcher, who apparently had to do away with shared value. They ushered in a world where everything including ourselves (me) would be considered a commodity. This happened when I was just a baby myself. It's unclear whether the people around me at the time noticed their world getting smaller. However, I am sure that the public realm has suffered in the intervening years. It is this paucity of collectivity and intensity of the self that has spurred me to action up until now.

"Value" in this version of free market capitalism has been vague to me, but I worry that its significance to architecture goes much further back than I originally noticed. Maybe modernism is the problem. I believe rather deeply in modernism. I come from a long line of people who believe that abstraction in service of the universal can change the world. It turns out that the universal may be the partner of individualism. In a sense Thatcher and Reagan picked up on an idea that was already there. Postwar suburbia, an undeniable offshoot of modernism was for "everyone" in the smallest terms. And postwar social housing, which might have made complete sense got sold off or put aside from larger community fabrics in the first place. Perhaps people older than me already understand this. Certainly, home ownership as a path to wealth came before 1980s neoliberalism.

We now understand value to be defined by and as discrete things. It is clear that this version of capitalism led us to devastating inequality, but the cultural implications on everyone, rich and poor, are more subtle. I have been privileged. I may remain privileged but not with certainty. This perhaps imagined uncertainty is suddenly part of living with my family, which is many lovely things. These include, perhaps less lovingly, an economic entity that I am meant to, and do endeavor to serve. Now I think of any money saved as an opportunity to buy something that my daughter can then sell.

As I constantly evaluate and redefine objects in the market's terms, I turn myself into an object which subjects itself to the same pressures driving economic growth. I am displaying the possibility for consumption of products and experiences that are commodified. The commercial and personal realms—once more distinct—have collapsed into one. Commodity is reliant on our presented relationship to life and to the lives of others. There seems to be no possibility for shared value, it is rather zero-sum accumulation. In this context I am not lonely per se. But discounting my little family and office, I am very much alone. This structure of the world has me, and possibly you, very close to lonely and in the larger sense we are fighting to be more so.

After realizing the predicament that I am in, one that I believe many of us share, I wish to expand the idea of family as I always have. I am not alone in noticing the implications of our system. I am not alone in a wide embrace of solidarity, a concern for the expansion of society rather than the self and an active interest in identity that transcends the "traditional" notion of family. Despite the fact that a larger view of the self threatens capitalism, I want it.

This is a moment for architecture. Architecture can endeavor to dismantle the self in favor of something larger. Until the aforementioned forces brought me into the fold, I imagined that I didn't care about the structures of our system. My privilege allowed me to believe that I was above this and that the people around me were too. I have discovered, in a hard truth, that I need to work within this reality. And then, not to sound like a used car salesman, suddenly upbeat, I realize that the larger notions of community can work within this system. By this I mean that people can share space and equity. Maybe this is giving up. An earlier version of myself would have said "equity?" and scoffed. I did not believe we needed that.

We confuse what is a self-replicating structure with something producing novelty. But what we need is to make an experiment in the possibility of changing what's expected, in a way that is undeniably charming and thus approachable and convincing. We can propose a way this structure might break down, then examine how that change might be amplified into a greater sense of the shared.

With an amended structure we would allow the possibility for a happy duality between an expansive world and a very specific place. The individual of the twenty-first century calls many places home, desiring connection across the globe without a decision between urban anonymity and culture-rejecting rural. We want to live together without retreating. We wish to live in a world which exists in the glow of the local and vice versa. This may be obvious and uncontentious. What we don't know off hand—because it takes a bigger leap, and here we are trying to understand that leap—is that we can live together with flexible definitions of what is yours and what is mine within capitalism (despite my wish to reject it). We can have a house for many of us living together against an isolated economic self, and to our mutual benefit in all senses.

Place, then, in this shared world must be more than surface, more than a blank slate. It can operate on a universal level while imbuing identity in its interactions. Contemporary space for those with a larger view of the self needs connectivity working on several levels, because we are for better and for worse in a near constant state of public forum. This is not to say a venture-capitalist-tech-start-up community, but a community with much longer spans of equity. We need to invest in our social equity, which means architecture that supports long term interaction and embedded social value.

I want to live in a way that can is calm but can also have friction. It has become necessary to build engagement rather than escape. When we share things, we can have more, not less. Two households have more resources than one. As an architect I have never had trouble convincing people of this. But after agreeing, people start to waver because of their potential lack of control. We've been trained to think of architecture (and much more) as tools for security. This is true in the "asset" sense but also in the day-to-day comfort sense.

Let's agree, for now, that your money can make money. In short that is what real estate and by extension architecture has become. Let's agree that this is easy enough to organize. We can sell our share of the shared. If we agree on that we can just talk about our own control over our own situation. We don't need this. We in fact want some interruption and interaction.

Let's consider a larger view of the self, because it's clear that family's promise of shared value was not futile.

Next spread: Images of author and family. Berlin, August 2020. Photos by Eray Aydin.

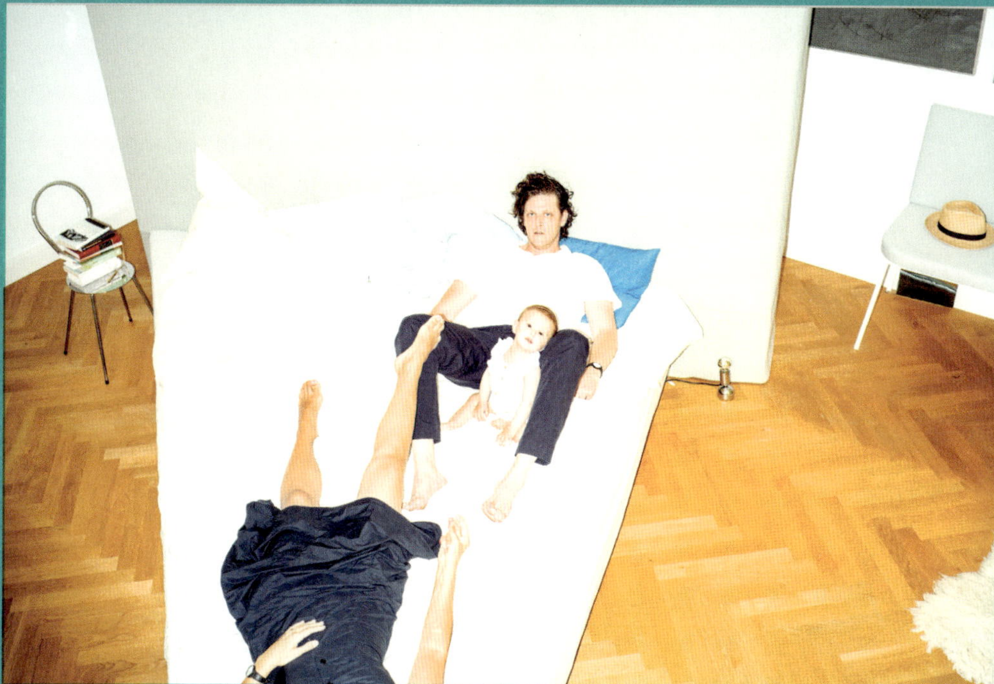

322

(P—A)

LUKE DOUGLAS
ERICKSON

EXODE ARCH: GATEWAY FOR AN AMERICAN EXODUS

[you can't go home again]

> **Our people are good people; our people are kind people. Pray God some day kind people won't all be poor.**
>
> **—John Steinbeck, *The Grapes of Wrath*, 1939.[1]**

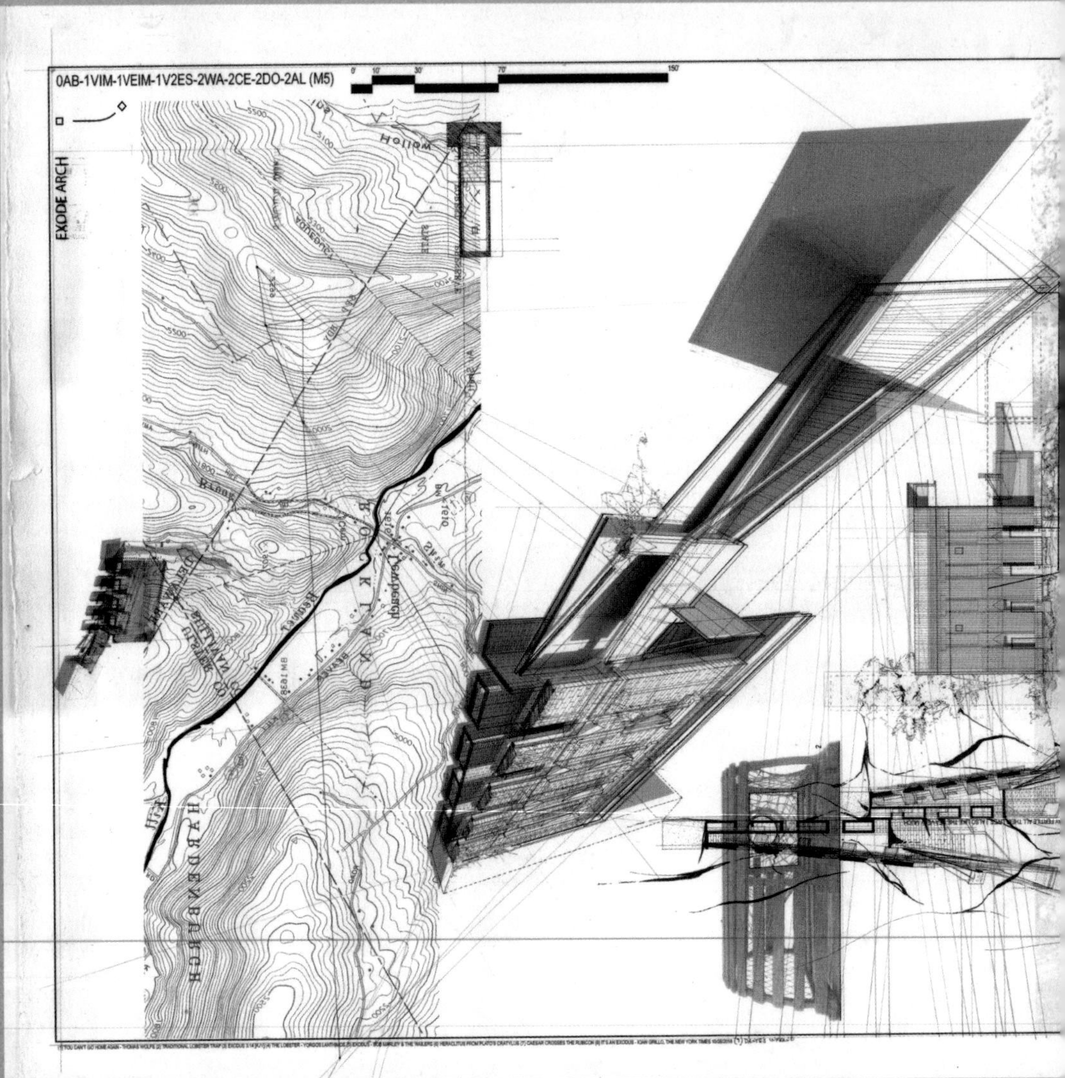
0AB-1VIM-1VEIM-1V2ES-2WA-2CE-2DO-2AL (M5)
EXODE ARCH

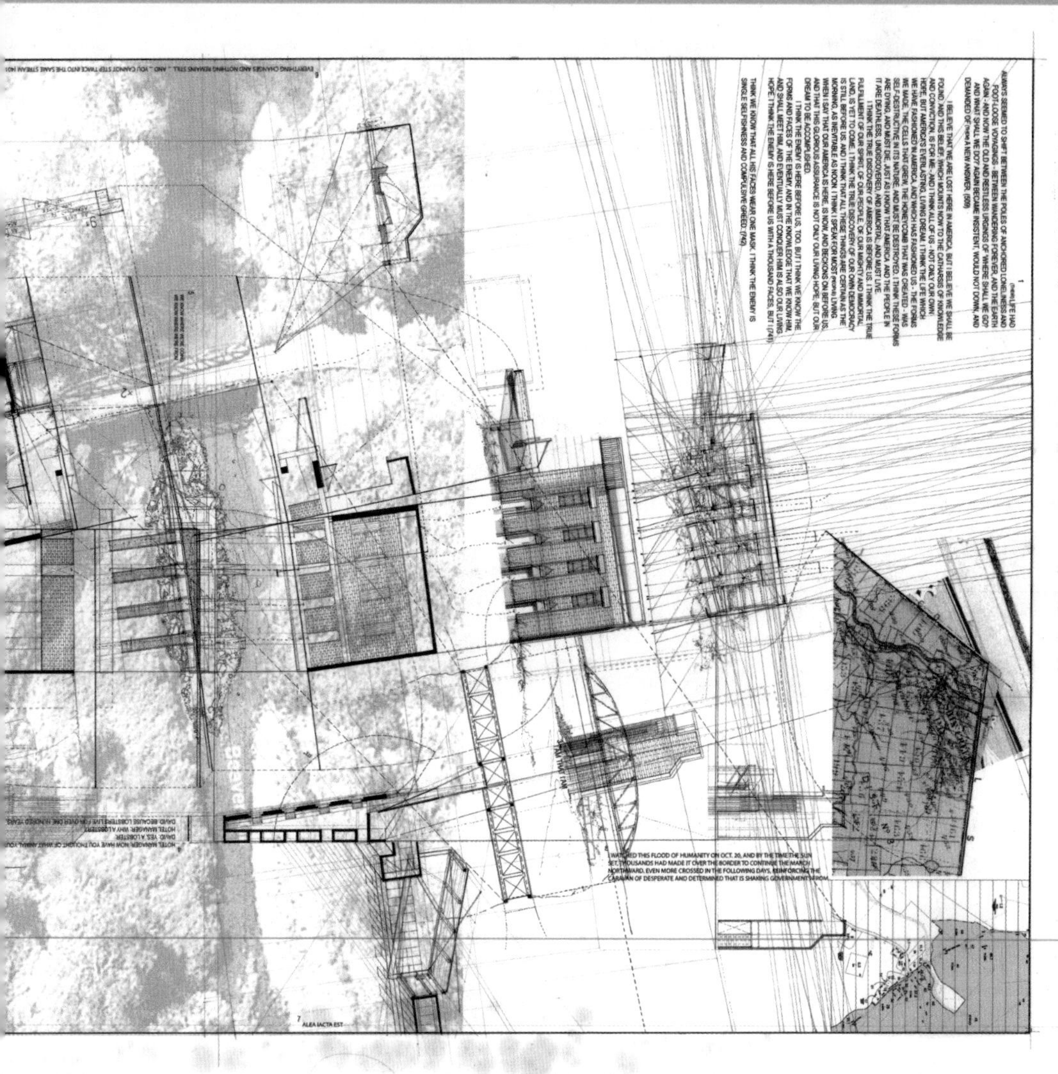

Located at the small crossroads where Beaverkill Road transitions from country road 151 to 152 and Shin Creek Road transforms into Mary Smith Hill Road, Lew Beach, the northernmost village of the fictitious Subsullivan County would be the penultimate stop for any Subsullivans headed north in a time of crisis. Just down the hill from that intersection, planted firmly amid the loose pebbles of the Beaverkill River, rests a monument awaiting future catastrophe. Constructed with a grant from the Subsullivan Post-Historic Landmarks Commission, the Exode Arch was gifted to the sub-county with reference to the past, present and future. The arch stands as a reminder that most current residents are the descendants of émigrés or are themselves recent settlers of the sub-county. The reasoning behind the arch's design is grounded in the global unrest and national fear of the unenviable nomads in search of safety and a better life.

> **As the architectural concretization of a language of memory forces a site to organize repeated gatherings around a repetition of the violence, the spectating public itself is also enrolled to trace this economy of symbolic refraction. The language of monumentality hopes to coordinate for the crowd a pluralized ideal; it is just as much a vocabulary for targeting attacks on built forms that carry significant currency, as it is a way to give form to the memory and mourning of an attack.**[2]
>
> **Give me your tired, your poor, / Your huddled masses yearning to breathe free, / The wretched refuse of your teeming shore. / Send these, the homeless, tempest-tossed to me, / I lift my lamp beside the golden door!**[3]

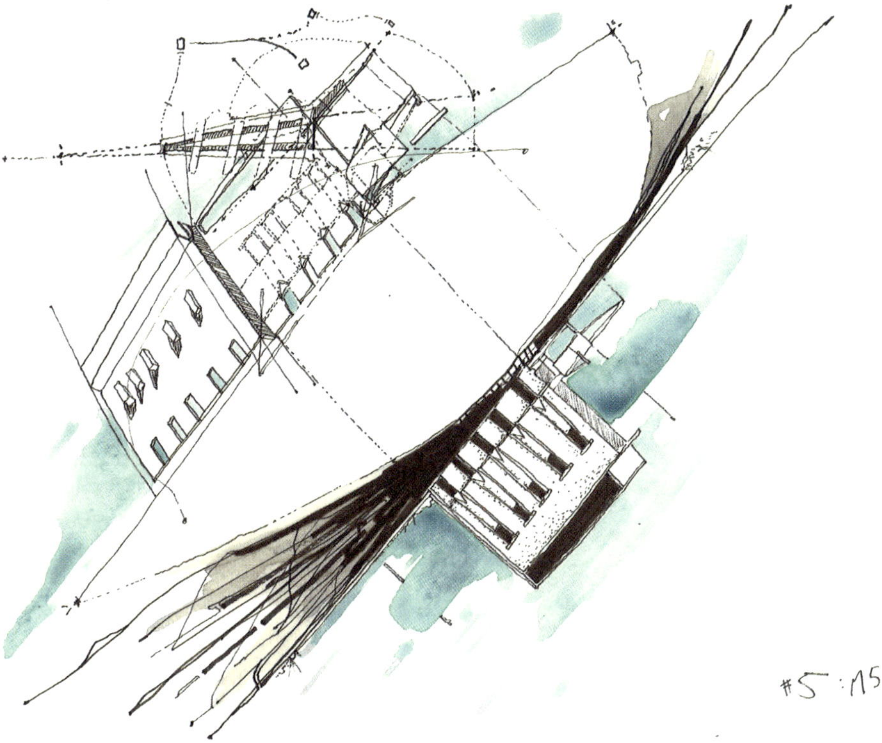

All images by Luke Douglas Erickson. Previous spread: *Exode Arch (Conscientious Objectors #5)*, 2019–2020, acetone transfer, graphite, ink, and watercolor on paper and transparency film, 24 × 51 in. This page: *Exode Arch Sketch*, 2019, ink, graphite, and watercolor on paper. Next page: *Exode Arch Model, 1/32 in = 1 ft*, 2019, basswood, paint.

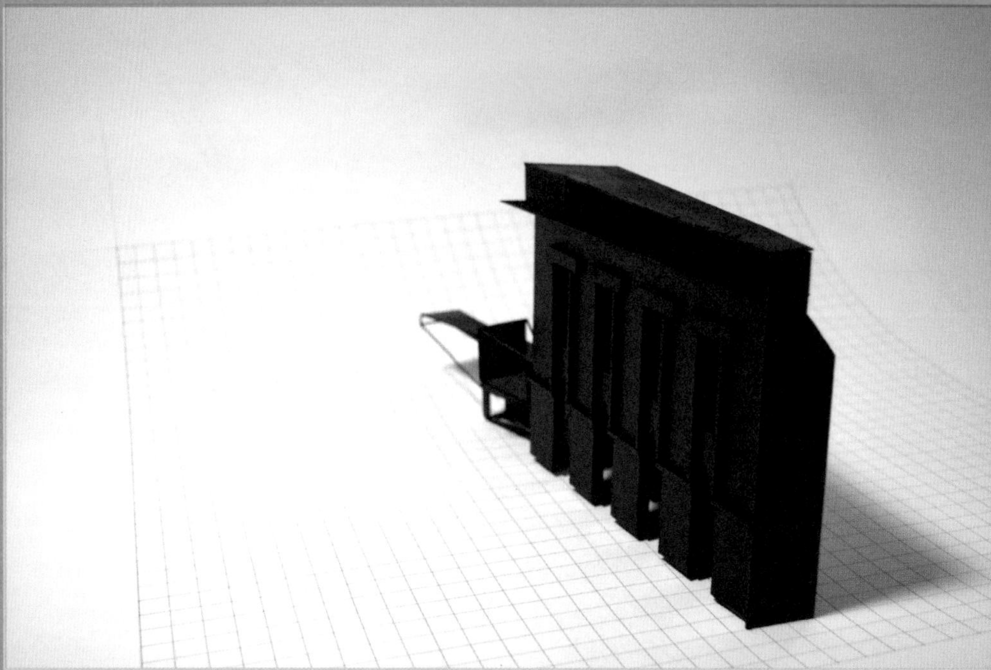

Fear of the unknown has shaped modern politics and been a tool critical to the form-making of the upstate sub-county. By issuing this landmark into the collective unconscious, the Post-Historic Landmark Commission intended to remind residents of their shared humanity and inherent ability to empathize with those in need. The arch represents those unforeseen acts, natural (as in global warming) or man-made (as in war or the dreaded self-implosion that is a vote for disenfranchisement), can drive any individual from their home in pursuit of happiness. Furthermore, those acts could very well affect Subsullivan County, and if they should the Exode Arch will stand ready as a final farewell, a small eddy in the momentum of humankind northwards.

> **We have difficulty changing, even if it's only the position of our furniture. Moving house is quite a business. We stay in the same neighborhood, we miss it if we change... Something extremely serious needs to happen for us to agree to move: wars, famine, epidemics... We find it hard to get acclimatized. Those who arrived a few days before you did look down on you. You stay in your own small corner, with the people from your corner. You remember with nostalgia your little village, your little river, the big field of mustard you could see when leaving the main road.**[4]

1 John Steinbeck, "Chapter 19," in *The Grapes of Wrath* (London: Penguin Books, 2011), 239.

2 Benjamin H. Bratton, "For a Staging of Jean Genet's The Balcony in 2007," in *Dispute Plan to Prevent Future Luxury Constitution* (Berlin: Sternberg Press, 2016), 87–88.

3 Emma Lazarus, "The New Colossus," 1883, poem.

4 Georges Perec, "The Countryside," in *Species of Spaces and Other Pieces* (London: Penguin Books, 1997), 71–72.

GEORGINE
BOTHA

TRACING MEMORIES

330

(P–A)

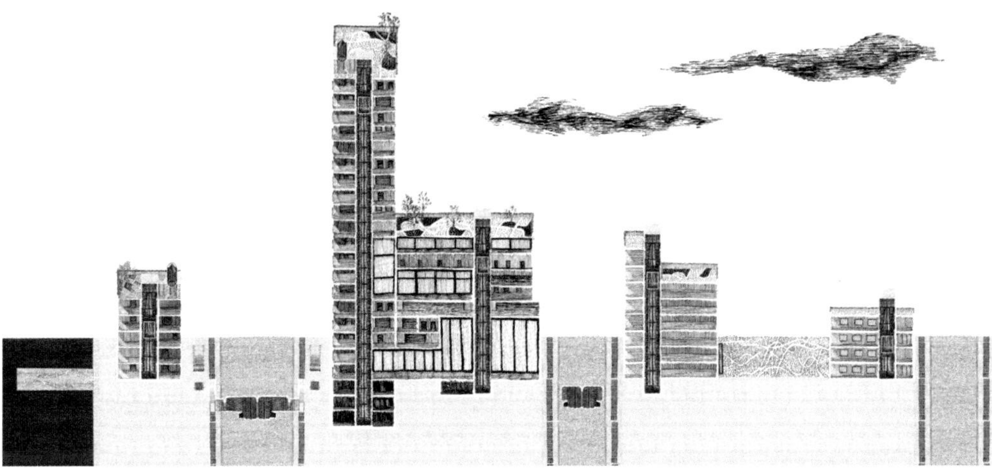

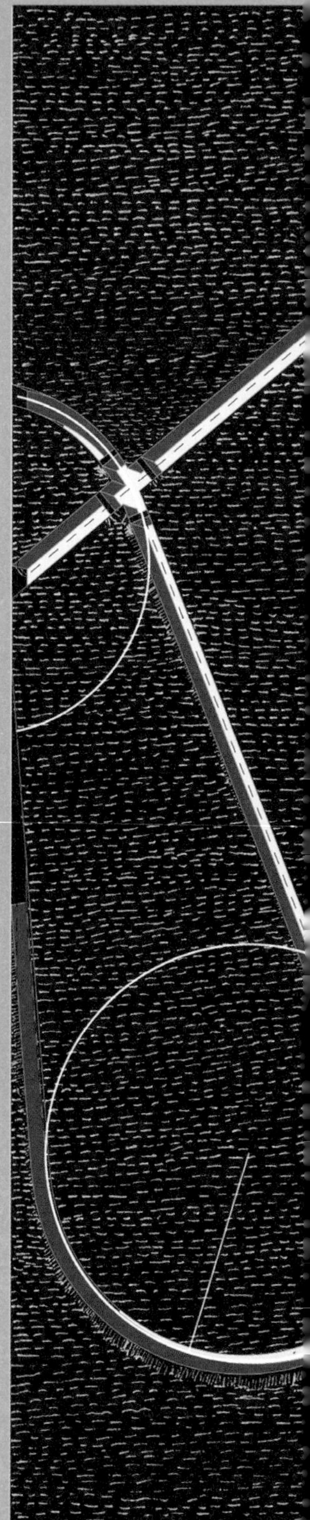

All images by Georgine Botha, 2020. **Previous:** Within the urban landscape, traces that commemorate the individual assemble into a network that traverses from the sky to the water's edge. **This spread:** The ritualistic act of carving the city's surfaces ingrains the individual memories into the city's armature. With time these traces become a network: a network of stories, a network of families, a network of relationships. These traces reveal the physicality of individuals, their relationships to both the living and the dead, and importantly the passing of time.

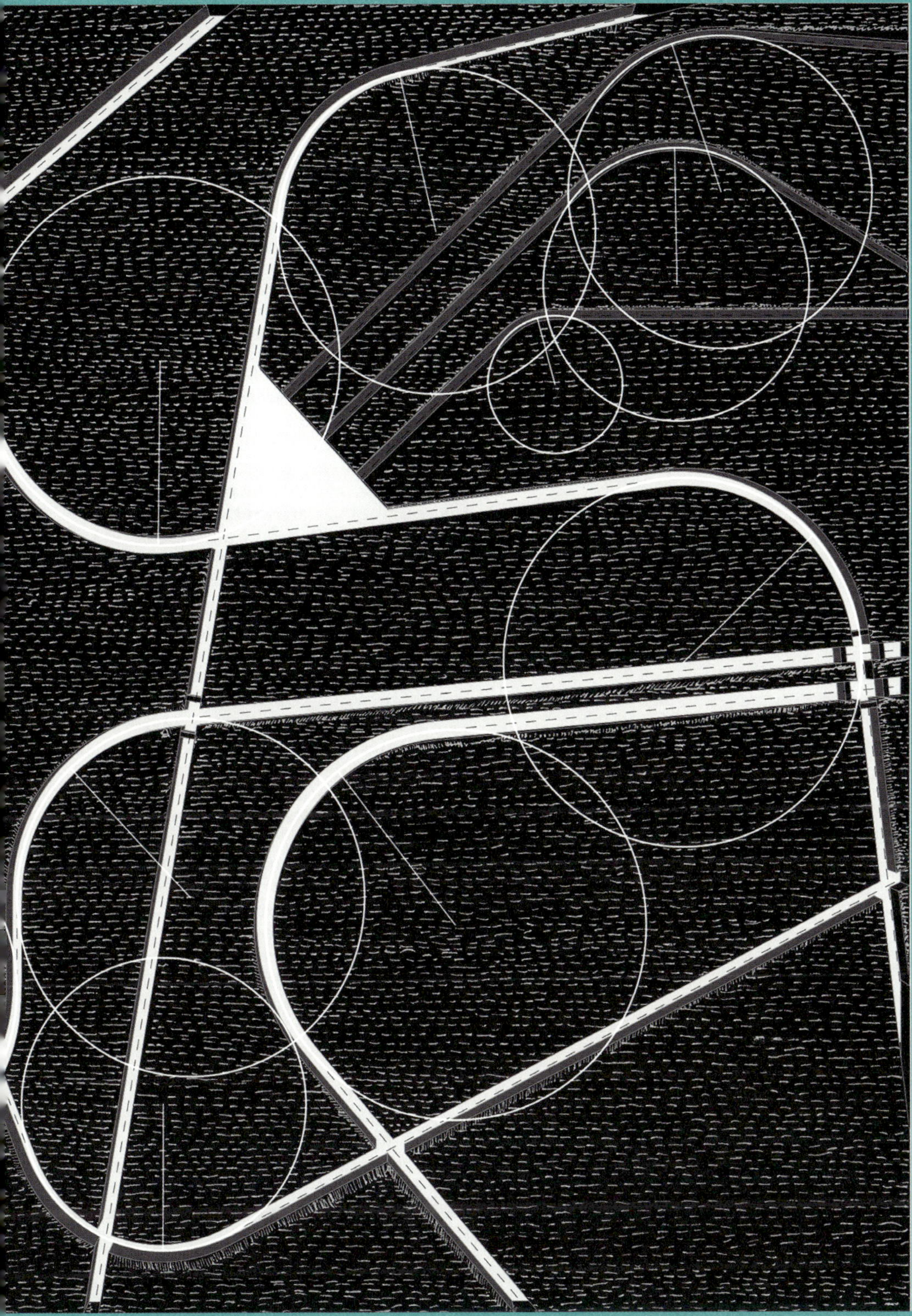

From the street, one cannot distinguish the infrastructure of the water towers from the newly transformed chapels, yet we begin to understand them as both; their function is only revealed as the light escapes through the carvings at night. The walls are systematically etched by the living and punctured in the transition to death. Like life, the conditions within the tower are in flux, shadows move with the cycle of the day, while the continuous flow of water dictates water levels.

The only inevitability in life is death. After we are gone, what do we leave behind that documents our existence? When memories live, the departed continue to live on. When memories die, our departure is final. Long after our last belongings are lost, cemeteries tie individuals to their faded identities. They allow for the documentation of the departed within the urban landscape, preventing the total erasure of memories. Cemeteries act as historical repositories that on greater inspection can reveal settlement patterns, genealogy, and reflect historical events from epidemics to wars. Their physicality fulfills a greater communal need to honor our past and life's transient nature; however, cemeteries require immense amounts of space, and in New York, that space is limited.

"Tracing Memories" explores the commemoration and preservation of memories, without the grounding of traditional cemeteries in light of their spatial, monetary, and environmental consequences. In this thesis, the formation of traces upon the city's surfaces through carving, etching, and erosion allows both the living and the dead to actively generate landscapes of memory. Beyond dealing with the body, traditional death practices allow for deeply personal rituals in which individuals can commemorate their loved ones and preserve their memory. This project reflects upon this condition by simultaneously forming a ritual (the act of constructing traces), and a means to preserve memories (the traces themselves).

PAUL A HARRISON
JOSEPH M LOUGHRAN Jr
EDWARD C MILLER
JOHNNY MILLER
JAMES McDONALD
JAMES P NICHOLSON
DONALD D RANDALL
MARK J ROMAN
ROBERTA ROMO
GREGORY I STARTS
CLYDE J VALSLAD
HOWARD M THOMPSON
LEON C HAMILTON Jr
MICHAEL L HANSON
BENJAMIN A HONEYCUTT
ROLAND R LAFOND
JOHN M MALNAR
THOMAS I LONG
HERBERT L MEADS
EDWARD C MILLER
EDWARD L MUNSON
JAMES P NICHOLSON
HOWARD M THOMPSON

ROLAND RIVALSTAD
CHARLES

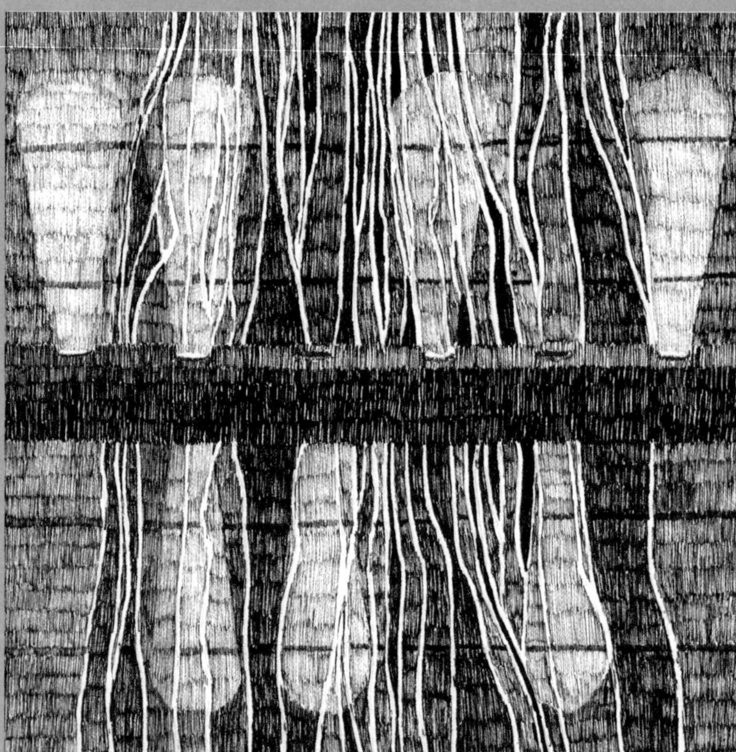

Constructing a trace is a new form of agency. Family and friends participate in the final documentation of an individual by ritualistically ingraining the individual's memory into the city's armature. In a city confronted with a density crisis, these landscapes of memory site themselves within forgotten urban spaces essential to the powering of the city. By reexamining the role of these structures, they begin to take on a new meaning. Within the urban landscape, the traces that commemorate individuals assemble into a network that traverses from the sky to the water's edge. The traces, united by the flow of water, become a reminder of those who came before.

Each trace symbolizes a life. With time these markings become a network: a network of stories, a network of relationships, a network of families. Our cities are full of signs and symbols; we do not just see things in their physical sense, but rather, we understand them as being charged with meaning. In this same manner, the traces intentionally add a new layer of understanding to the city. Their width, depth, arc, and length become entangled in meaning. Understanding these notations is the key to unlocking the stories and networks of the city's past and present inhabitants. The traces reveal an individual's physicality, their relationships to both the living and the dead, and importantly the passing of time. The ritualistic act allows for the preservation of memories within the city's landscape.

Top: Small rooftop Edens become pockets of respite from the hectic streets, their ground covered in a network of waterways. The surface does more than tell stories; each carving is a commemoration of life, each allowing for the more abundant flow of water. With time, the lives continue to positively impact the city—more growth becomes visible and New York's skyline continues to change well after the construction of the last building. Bottom: The elevator is an armature for the flow of water, the flow of people, and the flow of life. Under the glimmer of light, the carvings of time are almost unnoticeable: the rhythmic drip of water slowly eroding the wall. The structure is a receptacle for light; each glow symbolizes a life, creating a constellation up above.

Far below our feet are tunnel networks that traverse the city; we can only imagine what goes on there. Barely visible, we are only reminded of their existence by the gratings that interface the street or the occasional rumbling of the earth as the subway zooms past. But now, when it rains, we are reminded of their presence as we listen to the gushing water down the walls before it returns to an inaudible stream.

In its final act, traces extend out to the water's edge, slicing and fragmenting the pier. The edges move with the cyclical rising and falling of the tides. Like life, these cyclical patterns define the pier. Resembling the horizon line, the edge is indefinable. Time determines what is visible, what can be read, what is murky, and what is lost. But like the clarity of memories, this ebbs and flows, and soon enough, everything is revealed once more.

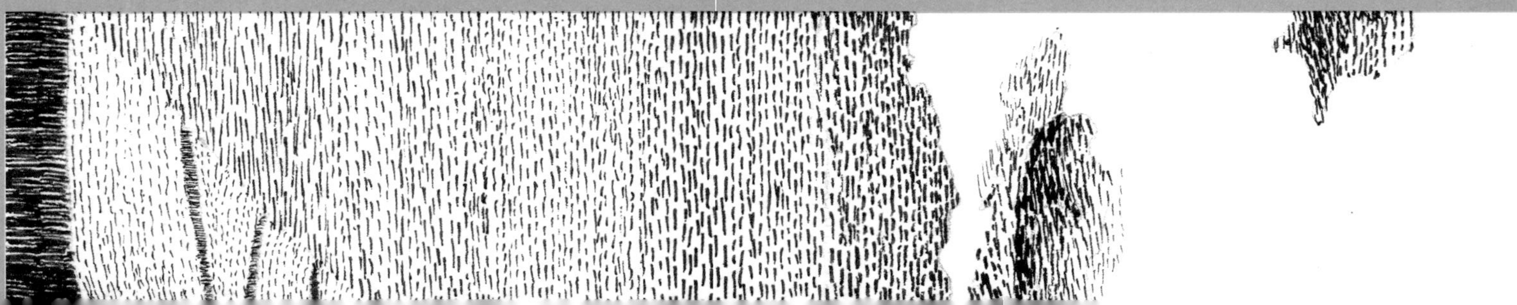

342

(P–A)

MUNJER
HASHIM

CROWDED ROOMS WITH SECRETS

CORNELL JOURNAL
OF ARCHITECTURE

ISSUE 12
AFTER

SPATIAL IMBALANCE

The use of a space is contingent on its occupants' needs: be it for living, work, or play. External economic, social, or global influences have the capability to put architecture's inherent functions into a state of flux. Such a "glitch in the matrix" can trigger a series of events which completely alters the characteristics of the city and shifts tendencies in human consumerism. As spaces are abandoned through changes in programmatic demands, economic situations, and usage requirements, an atmosphere of neglect and silence begins to take over the city. The dramatic shift in world perspectives and needs completely devastates spatial occupancy. People line up outside—six feet apart, trying their best to maintain human intimacy as they socially distance—while above in the skies, office towers lie vacant with their computers whirring in the background. Digital screens with masterless seats in front of them orchestrate commands on their own. Offices which have gone completely remote now have become equipment holders and data centers: they stand like empty vessels. As tenants relocate from buildings, cities, and continents in the hopes of a better future, deserted spaces await their unpredictable fate. With such a dilemma, the urban composition changes shape, teasing the mind to consider alternate spatial uses in this unfolding scenario.

All images by Munjer Hashim, 2020, digital.

NEW OCCUPANTS

The emptiness starts to devour the economic dreams of a once bustling city, but alternate uses for the vacant locations become the survival tactic. As citizens pivot their future goals and aspirations by relocating, so too does space adjust. Fresh uses for these abandoned spaces—as wards for patients, housing for the homeless, hydroponic gardens, and street side restaurants—renews the lifecycle of buildings and the city. Through the game of supply and demand, a few individuals are baited into remaining: they take advantage of lowering costs and more room. This simple pivot begins to shuffle the demographics of the city—all in the hopes that activity returns.

New occupants and uses begin to spur changes in the formerly vacant towers. Office and hotel floors are transformed to equitable private homes for families and individuals. Their interiors are organized into open flexible spaces, lofts, studios, and duplexes. This sequential change multiplies and arrays across each floor plate. Neighbors in other buildings begin to cherry-pick air rights to connect adjacent facades and grab views, therefore reinvigorating the city's vertical fabric. Floors in the clouds initially meant for the wealthy are no longer privatized, allowing the residents to create and live within privileged elevations. The towers' previously empty spaces slowly revive with commotion and community. As the skyline shifts from abandonment to activity, the secrets of the past get plastered over, hiding the skeletons in the closets through the layering of time.

EMBEDDED CHANGES

With significant changes, both spatial and geographic, occurring post-pandemic, the identity of the city as a communal space jolts back into life. Change is widespread, needs are different, the population is diverse, and the future remains uncertain. As more offices adopt four-day work weeks and remote working from home is the norm, demand for private open spaces skyrockets. The typologies of the suburban house take over the city as apartments are retrofitted with vegetated outdoor spaces, their "backyards" facing the skyline. Spaces which lack views have become server warehouses and storage. The utilitarian skyscrapers are slowly transformed into infrastructural obelisks and service nodes. Offices now cease to exist as the servers are placed underground and work happens everywhere. The facades of buildings begin to abandon their traditional continuous symmetry and embrace a patchwork of diverse identities. Concrete cast-in-place walls next to brick constructions next to cut open facades create a unique puzzle of vertical texture. Once an imposing monolith of steel and glass ruling the sky, the tower has become an indicator for diversity and an icon for shifting use throughout its own history.

REVOLVING IDENTITIES

Due to the influx of ad hoc changes and the widespread repurposing of existing infrastructure, loss of spatial cultural heritage and identity becomes a source of concern. Cataloging all existing buildings before, during, and after their modifications becomes the name of the game. Each space's lifeline to prolonged usage is the creation of a family tree that tabulates its flux, structural applications, and load histories. This initiative begins to allow new occupants an opportunity to address idiosyncrasies within their spaces and make informed structural modifications. As beams and walls are modified, remnants of the past are uncovered: drywall cavities unearth items from stuffed animals and clothing to hidden piping and love letters from the '70s. Structural bracings which were used to hold up a duplex now can be utilized to make loft-like spaces. A practical three-dimensional repository of building historical information and metadata propels a space's functionality and continuous modification.

This digital database archives each square foot of a building, as well as its facade transformations, floor and wall compositions, ceiling openings, programmatic history, and tenant habits. The remnants of past usage are leveraged for new functions, possibly giving rise to entirely novel typologies. The built environment is continuous and fluid in its functionality and use. Such is the characteristic of architecture now: discrete, effervescent, and highly adaptable. No longer do particular programmatic identities bind the usage of space. Modifications and constant change promote a nonstop reproduction and reinvention of the city. The new city is not stagnant and does not hold on to the ramifications of the past. The history of its spaces exist in both symbol and physical form while their future fate is endlessly orchestrated and enabled.

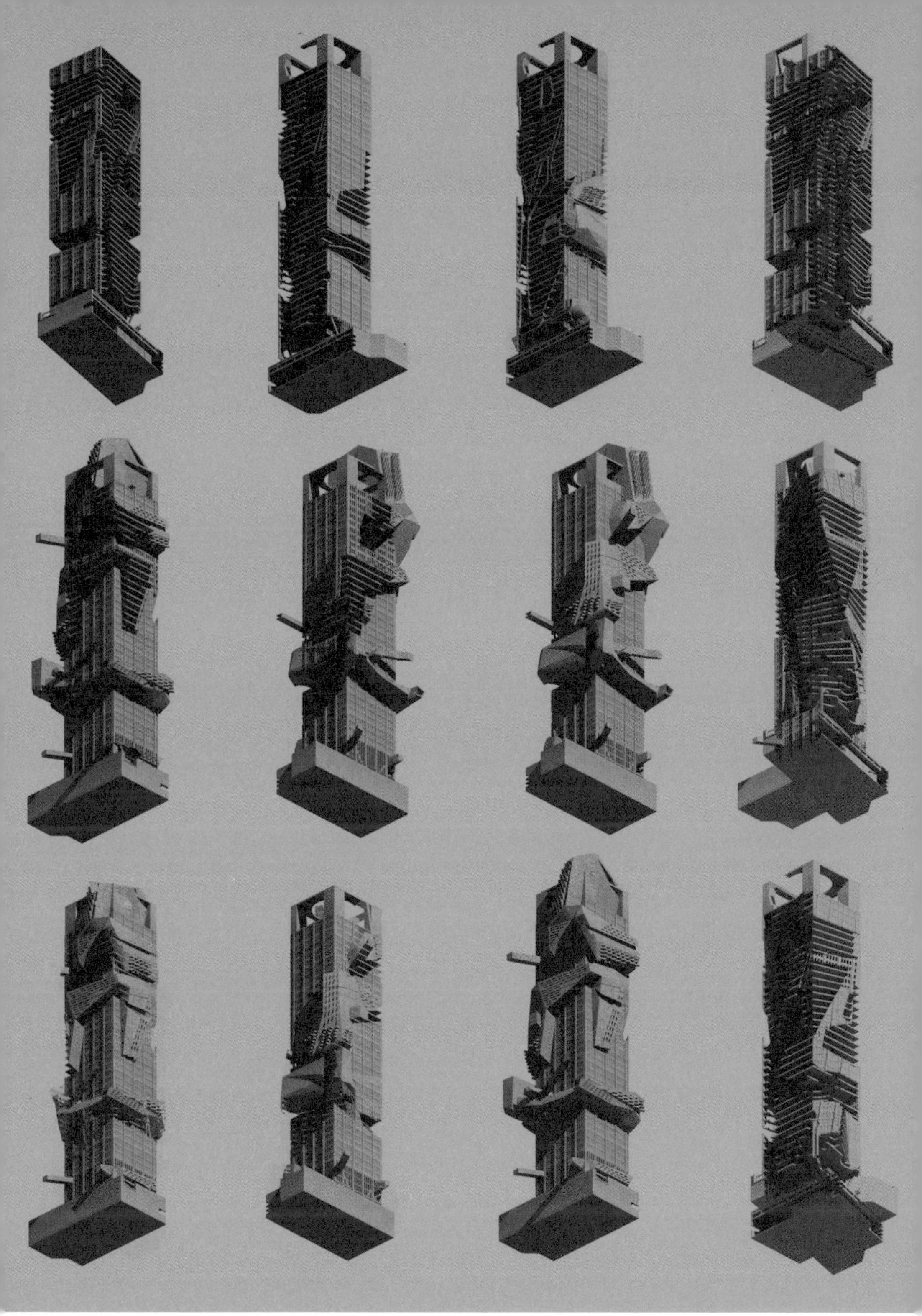

352

(P—A)

OLALEKAN
JEYIFOUS

THE BROOKLYN AFRO / ECO / AGRI FUTURE

All images by Olalekan Jeyifous, 2020. Previous: Open and closed "petals" on a series of rooftop Solar Trees. (*Rooftop Solar Petals.*) Opposite: View of a terra-formed rooftop garden and rainwater delivery drones. (*Rooftop Garden and Rainwater Drone Delivery.*)

Instability and precarity prescribe our current socio-economic, environmental, and political realities, while the physical and systemic infrastructures that sustain us with illusions of security have been revealed as wholly untenable. A global pandemic, the impact of climate change, and rampant protests against (racial) inequities revealed cracks in the principles and practices our capitalist society was built upon, contributing to a growing disillusion with the stability of our existing institutions. These ruptures and fissures in the prevailing order indicate the unquestionable possibility for radical transformation, and it is within this space and moment that the efficacy and the catalytic potential for speculative, sci-fi-inspired imagining, truly emerges.

The Crown Heights and Bedford-Stuyvesant, Brooklyn neighborhoods, which were once predominately Caribbean and African-African enclaves are, as of this moment, among the most gentrified areas in the nation. As such, they provide an appropriate setting for re-imagining technological, environmental, and architectural interventions in a post-pandemic, post-capitalist, yet non-gentrified future. In this future long-standing marginalized communities have not been displaced and the Black folks who inhabited them are placed squarely within the visual narrative. As a result, the notion of whiteness (the western world) is de-centered as the most forward thinking and evolved as concerns technological advancement and environmental practices.

A Brooklyn Afro/Eco/Agri-futurist aesthetic which deploys the vanishing/vanquished urban ephemera of the bodega and storefront properties merges with seductive and suggestive yet indeterminate technologies for rainwater harvesting, biofuel technology, aeroponic and aquaponic systems, self-automated and cooperative farms, along with fresh-water marshes and idyllic gardens. This integration with the existing architecture occurs on, within, and throughout the interstitial spaces of rooftops, alleyways, and the air gaps between brownstones. As a result, sustainability and cooperative economics returns to the fore as they were originally intended and practiced by marginalized communities, before neo-liberal capitalism co-opted the language and began financializing "sustainable practices and technologies" for profit.

This page: Existing photograph of a Crown Heights, Brooklyn rooftop framed by a multi-family high-rise in the background. (*Crown Heights Rooftop BEFORE.*) Opposite: Rooftop and façade rainwater-harvest system. (*Rooftop Rainwater Harvest AFTER.*)

This page: Existing photograph of an alleyway between two buildings in BedStuy, Brooklyn. (*BedStuy Alleyway BEFORE.*) Opposite: A trio of brothers perched on the steps in front of an urban bubble farm (for rare species of plants) peer into the neighboring yard. (*BedStuy Urban Bubble Farm AFTER.*)

EAT
RICH

Opposite: Worm's eye view of a trio of brothers perched on the steps in front of an urban bubble farm. (*BedStuy Urban Bubble Farm AFTER Close-up.*) **Next page:** View of a garden pathway beneath the canopy of a rooftop rainwater-harvest system. (*Rainwater Harvest Delivery.*) **P.363:** Two local residents inspect the lush vegetation beneath the canopy of a rooftop rainwater-harvest system. (*Rainwater Harvest Garden.*)

MEREDITH
MILLER

T+E+A+M

AFTER MODELS

364

(P—A)

T+E+A+M: **THOM MORAN, ELLIE ABRONS, ADAM FURE, AND MEREDITH MILLER**
DESIGN AND PRODUCTION TEAM: **OLIVER POPADICH, DELANEY MCCRANEY, THERESA KAPLAN, REED MILLER, JOHN VIEWEG**

All images by T+E+A+M. **P.365:** *Models on View*, Kent State College of Architecture and Environmental Design, 2019. **Previous spread:** Last year, the chance to display the models for *Detroit Reassembly Plant*, *Ghostbox*, and *Additional Address* all together in one gallery became the impetus for uncrating and inspecting them. However, a plan of the gallery revealed that its single entrance was narrower than the models' smallest dimension. None would fit through the door. *T+E+A+M: Models on View* presents the images of three recent models via digital screens and 2.5D dioramas. Made of paper and printed vinyl, these models of photographs of models, were made to be easy to install, demount, and toss in a recycling bin. Instead, these paper artifacts are also hanging out in our studio, awaiting another exhibition or decomposition, whichever comes first. **Opposite:** Installation view from inside gallery. (*Models on View*, 2019.)

Currently in our studio, a small collection of large models, with their bulky crates and various parts displaced about worktables and shelves, take up over three hundred square feet of space. *Detroit Reassembly Plant* (2016) represents an urban clearing among three buildings made from older buildings, *Ghostbox* (2017) resembles a long chunk of extracted ground with a partially disassembled big box store atop, and *Additional Address* (2018) depicts an additional dwelling unit, surfaced to blend in with a wooded residential landscape not included in the model. These models, built for past exhibitions, now languish in various states of decay. Crumbling, delaminating, sagging, or simply collecting dust, the afterlives of these models offer a parallel view into afterlives of buildings we imagined but never built.

Buildings exist in a state of continuous change. By refraining from placing value on that change (ruination or improvement), our practice tries to apprehend the built thing for what it is and not just what it was meant to be. That is, by understanding a building as a temporary assembly of materials in an environment, we try to circumvent the expectations of permanence or universality that often come with reducing architecture to abstractions.

Some typologies are more vulnerable to changes in cultural or economic circumstances than others. *Detroit Reassembly Plant* and *Ghostbox* engage the entropic life cycles of a vacant automobile factory and an obsolete big box, respectively. The immobility of the former's over-reinforced, early twentieth century concrete structure stands in contrast to the efficient container typical of big box construction. However, the same strategy of reassembling materials and elements recovered from the existing building affords new programs and unexpected visual effects to occur within the existing site. Each project creates an unstable relationship between design authorship and agents beyond the designer's control. The parts are legible, but the whole does not easily resolve, making other histories sensible and allowing other futures to unfold.

Model view. *Detroit Reassembly Plant*, 2016.

Building large models has been a way for us to represent our ideas about materiality in an immersive and experiential manner. The size and the detail of the models is important in making them read as realistic as possible—they are small constructions that demonstrate the strategies and tectonics of reassembly from the scale of an aggregate to that of the site. Our original intent was for the models to be scenographic, inviting exhibition-goers to frame their own views of the project by walking around these large objects and peering in. What we had not expected at the outset was the degree to which the models would become generators of new images. Photographs that simulate eye-level views depict scenes that are uncannily architectural with their level of material richness and detail. While the models now fall apart and gather dust, these images have become the more consequential output, continuing to circulate the projects in a virtual state of arrested materiality, every crumb and peel in place.

Previous spread: Diorama model produced for *Models on View*, 2019. This page: Model view, *Ghostbox*, 2017. Photo by Bruce Damonte. Opposite: Viewing the exhibition occurred only from outside the gallery, along a long glass wall dividing the gallery from an interior common space. Images on screens, printed images, and diorama models comprised scenes behind a full-scale graphic adhered to the glass.

LAWRENCE R. & SANDR
FRAGILE
"MODELS ON VIEW"
2/4 – 3/8
T+E+A+M

MICHAEL MURPHY

JHA D WILLIAMS

THE INFINITE AND THE INTIMATE

376

(P—A)

WITH LOVE TO PAMELA AND ANNETTE, WHO INSPIRED US TO HELP REMEMBER.

A cap, a hair clipper, a stone, a t-shirt, a cigar, a chain, a cap, a shoe. Countless objects, piled among others, left, at the sites of atrocity, trauma, and rest. Left over time, over generations, over cultures, over us.

A human impulse, if not a human need, is to leave objects in tribute to those gone before us.

In the after, we place the rock on the tomb, the stone on the grave, the graduation picture, the memento, the flowers now wilted. We remain by giving something of ourselves and yet this act allows us to let grief go. To reminisce is human.

These inanimate objects, now imbued with deep meaning, become animated and alive.

They transform in front of us, becoming talismanic, charged, embodied with a person's actual legacy, her spiritual life. These objects tether us to them, and them to us.

At massacre sites, we see spaces filled with the remnants of the thousands. Objects are left, contributed, donated, constructed. New homes are found for each of them: the necklace in need of a neck, the shirt in need of shoulders, the stone in need of a strong hand. Each object is the punctum to a life we now begin to see. These objects invite us to consider why, from the universe of objects, each specific one was chosen to represent each specific person. This is the realm of the intimate.

Architects are asked to memorialize often. Memorialization requires space. Cemeteries, mausolea, and graves hold space. But some loss is too traumatic, too violent, too inexplicable and holding space is not enough. We must become part of the story. To address wounds left from generational and cultural injury we must do more than witness.

Objects, names, and compositions compiled together spatialize loss volumetrically. They go beyond what is comprehensible or recordable to the human mind. This is the realm of the infinite.

The infinite is counting the uncountable. It is to know our personal loss as part of some greater shared loss. We need spaces to broadcast these shared linkages across time, across culture. We need spaces that reconfigure publics, launch shared journeys, enact rituals, and demand participation. As such, these spaces can become tools towards a construction of peace.

Successful memorials must oscillate between the infinite and the intimate. In that flicker a pathway reveals itself into the individual life, the story, their spirit. We surrender to the magnitude of shared loss; we feel each loss is also our loss. If, in this process, we are given the tools to engage, the rituals to enact, the stories to hear, and the spaces to hear them, we may find memorials are living actors in constructing cultural transformation. And in this way, architecture can be healing spatialized.

All images by MASS Design Group, 2019. Previous spread: The Gun Violence Memorial Project at the 2019 Chicago Architecture Biennial. The memorial consists of four houses constructed out of seven hundred glass bricks, each house representing the average number of lives taken due to gun violence each week in America. Opposite top: Shirt belonging to a victim of gun violence, collected at a Remembrance Object Collection event. Opposite bottom: Detail of the commemorative objects installed in the bricks of the Gun Violence Memorial Project.

jeans co

DEDRICK DESHON EARL
DEVANTE CARTMAN
LARRY DARNELL
HARPER, JR.
1979-2003
CHARLESQUILL
BALLARD
1985-2018
PHILLIP "PIP" OPSTAD
1975-2001

382

(P—A)

FELIPE ORENSANZ

BOB SCHALKWIJK

MEXICO CITY AFTER MEXICO CITY

I am Death [...]
I have walked at your side for a long time now [...]
Are you prepared?

—Ingmar Bergman, *The Seventh Seal*, 1957.

Although at one point or another most major cities have found themselves on the brink of an irreversible urban collapse, few have walked side-by-side with death for as long—or as close—as Mexico City. It is a city that has lived on the edge for most of its modern history: a crumbling, overcrowded, impoverished, unruly megalopolis of 22 million, built on a rapidly sinking lakebed, in the center of a highly floodable endorheic basin, 7350 feet above sea level, along a deadly seismic corridor, and surrounded by a pollution-trapping range of mountains and active volcanos. As writer Carlos Monsiváis has suggested, Mexico City just might become "the first megalopolis to fall victim of its own excesses."[1]

All images by Bob Schalkwijk. **This page:** Demolition of the Juárez Housing Unit in Mexico City after being damaged by the deadly earthquake that struck the city on September 19, 1985. (October 1985.)

At times, living in Mexico City can seem in itself a near-death experience, and death has become so deeply embedded in its everyday culture that it is barely a tragedy. It is, to a certain extent, a way of life—and at times even a spectacle of sorts. Two narratives—one sacred and one secular—define the backdrop against which this spectacle has been staged. On the one hand, the many syncretic expressions of death emerging from the combined bloodiness of the Mexica and Catholic liturgic traditions have become centerpieces of Mexico's religious landscape—the most important of which are the traditional and colorful *Día de Muertos* (Day of the Dead) and the more recent and obscure cult of *Nuestra Señora de la Santa Muerte* (Our Lady of the Holy Death). Marked by an explicit and crude display of death—from the skeletal figure of *Mictlantecuhtli*, the Mexica's lord of the underworld, to the lacerated body of the crucified Christ—these overlapping traditions have left an indelible mark on Mexico City's visual culture.

One of the towers of Mexico City's Pino Suárez building complex in the aftermath of the 1985 earthquake. (September 1985.)

But parallel to these sacred representations lies a profoundly secular fascination with death or, to be more precise, with the concrete particularities of why and how we die. And nowhere is this spectacle more present than in Mexico City's ubiquitous *nota roja* (red press) tabloids, where the stylized religious images are replaced by a macabre display of mangled corpses and body parts, and its rituals and liturgies by sardonic headlines and disturbingly detailed accounts. They do not depict death as a natural process but as a social act, as the result of human agency. In this sense, it is the images of accidents, murders, and suicides that are most highly prized. In addition, the gruesome images are often interspersed with erotic spreads and centerfolds in a double exposure of the flesh (pleasure and pain overlapping through the violent accumulation of living and dead bodies, pornography meets necrography in a morbid rewriting of the Freudian duality between Eros and Thanatos).

Equally present on the other end of Mexico's cultural spectrum, death has played a crucial role in some of the country's best-known artistic works—including José Guadalupe Posada's engravings, Juan Rulfo's 1955 novel *Pedro Paramo*, and Roberto Gavaldon's 1960 film *Macario*. But unlike the subtle depictions of death in these earlier works, newer generations of artists have started to shift their interests towards the blood-and-guts aesthetics of Mexico's infamous crime tabloids and represent death not as an abstraction, but through the details of the often-violent ways in which people die in Mexico. The work of photographers like Enrique Metinides, writers like Sergio González Rodríguez, filmmakers like Amat Escalante, visual artists like Teresa Margolles, or philosophers like Sayak Valencia—to name a few—all bear the influence of a visual culture defined by the shock-provoking narratives of Mexico's crime tabloids.

Bakery window in Iztapalapa, Mexico City during the traditional *Día de Muertos* (Day of the Dead) festivities. (October 1963.)

Unsurprisingly, these different necrocentric cultural expressions have fueled a highly lucrative industry. Like any other commodity, death has been branded, marketed, distributed, and consumed at an increasingly massive scale, from the Hollywoodization of traditions like *Día de Muertos* (and its subsequent colonization through the pizza-effect[2] of north-of-the-border appropriations, including Charles and Ray Eames' 1957 *Day of the Dead* short film, and blockbuster productions like Sam Mendes' 2015 James Bond film *Spectre* or Pixar's 2017 animated feature *Coco*) to the billion-dollar profiteering of death and its byproducts, often described as "gore capitalism"[3] and best illustrated by the country's rampant narcoviolence.[4]

In Mexico City, this spectacle of death has gradually been scripted around the idea of its own demise, and for many, the only remaining or relevant question consists of predicting the precise time and cause of the city's inescapable downfall. In the past, plagues, earthquakes, floods, droughts, and wars have all delivered deadly blows that have repeatedly left Mexico City hanging by a thread. On top of that, the slow violence[5] of crime, pollution, traffic, and poverty has taken its own toll on the hard-hit metropolis. In this sense, Mexico City is, in more ways than one, a city that should never have been built—let alone been allowed to reach its current behemothic scale. Its continuously ominous state almost gives the impression that history has been trying insistently to correct its past mistakes by wiping the city off the face of the earth.

Ironically, Mexico City's residents have not only become inured to the tragedy of their feeble urban condition but have embraced their tragedy through a form of collective self-satisfaction—what Carlos Monsiváis calls "catastrophe chauvinism."[6] While most cities take pride in their moments of power and glory, Mexico City does so in its ability to survive and/or endure its calamitous fate. This chauvinism has, of course, its own myths and fictions, built around a series of overstated and often misleading facts and figures. For example, contrary to what most residents like to believe—and boast about—Mexico City is neither the most populated, nor the most violent, nor the most polluted city in the world—though it is certainly populous, violent, and polluted.

Mexico City's doomsday narratives follow two dominant storylines. The first is defined by what Monsiváis has called a "post-apocalyptic" rationale—that is, by the idea that the worst of times are in the past, that the city has already hit rock bottom, been to hell and back, somehow managed to trick death, and survived against all odds. As Juan Villoro has suggested, "the best way to deal with tragedy is to suppose that it has already happened."[7] After all, isn't the city's mere existence sufficient evidence of its resilient superpowers? What could be worse than a killer epidemic, a five-year flood, or an 8.0 magnitude earthquake? Haven't the learning experiences of the past left Mexico City more prepared than ever in the event of future catastrophes?

Eastward view of Mexico City with the Iztaccíhuatl and Popocatépetl volcanos in the background. (January 1964.)

The second scenario—which could be called "pre-apocalyptic"—is centered around the idea that Mexico City's death lies somewhere in the near future. And everybody takes turns choosing from Mexico City's "inventory of calamities",[8] trying to figure out which one will eventually give the agonizing city its *coupe de grace*. In *The Lawless Roads*—an ill-tempered and unapologetic account of his 1938 travels through Mexico—Graham Greene wrote of the country's capital city: "how right Lawrence was when he wrote, 'this city doesn't feel right—feels like a criminal plotting his next rather mean crime.' "[9] Despite Greene and Lawrence's preconceived fear and loathing of all-things-south-of-the-border, they were all but alone in their wariness. To this day Mexico City feels somewhat wrong, as if death were still walking closely by its side.

This prevalent fear that Mexico City will sooner than later come to an irreversible end has left a lasting imprint on its morphological structure. Aside from its older inner boroughs, it is a city that seems inherently unfinished and undeveloped, as if, aware of its imminent systemic collapse, it was afraid to fully embrace—or even plan—its future.[10] Like the beauty-parlor-turned-hospice-for-the-dying in Mario Bellatín's 1994 novella *Salón de belleza* (Beauty Salon), Mexico City is something of a transient space. Rather than aiming at permanent or even long-term fixes, planning and design seem to be implemented to offer provisional palliatives for a city that, much like the sickened and dying patients at Bellatín's hospice, is in the end "nothing but a vanishing body."[11]

From the memory of its previous tragedies to the fear of potentially new ones, Mexico City has been forever shaped by the tensions between its *pre-* and *post-apocalyptic* urban visions. Caught between these two overlapping narratives, Mexico City has been time and time again haunted by the idea of its own afterness. Regardless of whether we place the city on the verge or in the aftermath of its overly predicted collapse, afterness has played an increasingly pivotal role in how we plan, design, and inhabit Mexico City. And as the debates over the city's vulnerabilities have multiplied and escalated in the wake of recent events—most notably the 2017 earthquake and the 2020 COVID pandemic—it has become one of the central leitmotifs of the city's urban identity. Today, the ways in which we define and imagine our urban condition have become inseparable from the ways in which we define and imagine Mexico City after Mexico City.

1 Carlos Monsiváis, *Los rituales del caos* (Mexico City: Editorial Era, 2016), 19.

2 The process through which certain cultural expressions are exported, transformed abroad, and then reintroduced into their original context.

3 Sayak Valencia, *Gore Capitalism* (Cambridge: Semiotext(e), 2018).

4 The sheer volume of this business is staggering. To set an example, 2019 was the country's most violent year on record, with a total of 35,588 officially recorded homicides. During the same year, Mexico City's authorities reported an average of 40 daily offenses against life and limb, including assault and battery, attempted murder, manslaughter, and suicide. And in most cases, each one of these events produced some kind of direct or indirect profit.

5 Defined by Rob Nixon as "a violence that occurs gradually and out of sight, a violence of delayed destruction that is dispersed across time and space, an additional violence that is typically not viewed as violence at all." Rob Nixon, *Slow Violence and the Environmentalism of the Poor* (Cambridge: Harvard University Press, 2001).

6 Monsiváis, *Los rituales del caos*, 19.

7 Juan Villoro, *El vértigo horizontal* (Oaxaca: Almadía, 2018), 322.

8 Villoro, 322.

9 Graham Greene, *The Lawless Roads* (London: Penguin Books, 2006), 87.

10 One example can be found in Mexico City's surprisingly low density. While it ranks fifth among the world's most populated cities, it occupies the 27th place in terms of population density. Based on data from www.citymayors.com.

11 Mario Bellatín, *Salón de belleza* (Mexico City: Tusquets, 2013), 23.

B. ARCH. THESIS
ADVISORS: **SAMIA HENNI & ANGELA PANG**

COCO
TIN

NO CURE? CARING FOR BURNOUT IN ~~A NEOLIBERAL AGE~~ HONG KONG 2.0

Before a disease can be treated, it must be diagnosed. And you do not need to know the prescription before you diagnose a disease. Thus it is telling that bad news can be a gift and a step towards hope, as long as that news can be let go when the time comes or the world changes.

—Rebecca Solnit, *Hope in the Dark*, 2016.

All images by CoCo Tin. This spread: Fragmented triptych into nine parts of a whole depicting the Apothecary Grave-Garden in its totality. Panels are labeled A–I, beginning from top left, down, ending at bottom right. (2019, acrylic, ink, dirt, analog and digital collage, 220 × 200 cm.)

Zoom of Panel H. By simply providing light, the Apothecary Grave-Garden breaks the conventional 9:00 a.m.–5:00 p.m. hours of operation of a cemetery and transforms it into a hospitable site for the living—even in the darkness of night. (2019, acrylic, ink, dirt, analog and digital collage, 50 × 70 cm.)

Burnout, as a chronic illness, is a mental and physical state of limbo. "Burn" refers to a position of productivity. Infected by neoliberal attitudes favoring 24/7 efficiency and endless growth, "burn" is a prolonged period of exertion without rest. In contrast, "out" signifies a temporary termination. Unless a final and inevitable death is reached, "out" serves as a warning for mandatory pause. To be cured or released from this limbo is to cement onto a singular state: "burn" or "out". Therefore, the illness is oxymoronic, a physical-mental predicament of being where one fluctuates between two extremes, which when merged can only be *cared* for. By acknowledging this indefinite period without resolution, burnout-limbo emerges as an opportunity to rethink current ways of being, living, and thinking.

Recognized as one of the most work-orientated cities in the world, Hong Kong is not only collectively battling work-induced burnout but also a political one. In addition to wrestling with the global COVID-19 pandemic, the city and its inhabitants (human and non-human) have endured a year of political unrest as response to Mainland China's attempt at integration. Moreover, the recently passed National Security Law foreshadows the end of an autonomous era. The most obvious repercussion of this law manifests in silence. Citywide pro-democracy

Previous spread: Zoom of Panel E. The Commons is the largest of the seven interventions on site. Three unconventional entrances blur the boundaries of this civic space: a pile of rubble to the left, a dirt trail in the center, and impossible stairs to the right. (2019, acrylic, ink, dirt, analog and digital collage, 100 × 70 cm.) This page: Zoom of Panel C. Reusing all found materials on site (soil, broken tombstone, fragments of concrete, plants, etc.) as the base "building" palette, the thesis is conscious of those who clean and maintain the cemetery, in parallel recognizing Mother Earth as the original caretaker nourishing humanity. (2019, acrylic, ink, dirt, analog and digital collage, 50 × 70 cm.)

demonstrations once dominating public spaces of shopping malls, streets, highways, parks, mountains, etc. have been banned. To the untrained eye, one could argue that not much has changed in the day-to-day functions of the city. However, behind the scenes, plans of nationalistic educational reforms and the building of China's great firewall loom at large. In this state of transition and background of fear, Hong Kong is collectively experiencing burnout-limbo; the community is unable to return to prior ways of life, but also not yet entirely integrated with mainland China. Against this magnified context of crisis, the thesis of an Apothecary Grave-Garden can immediately be a place of retreat for victims of protest-induced burnout. Seven architectural alternatives as preventative and aftercare responses to burnout operate alongside a still-functioning urban cemetery. Recalling historic notions of cemeteries as crucial public spaces of reflection, the city of the dead should also be a home for the living, a peculiar sanctuary to recharge. In the most hopeful sense, perhaps the project (a limbo in itself situated somewhere between landscape and architecture, an abode dedicated to the living and non-living) can memorialize a piece of turmoil history—a physical space to commemorate the heroic fight for freedom.

1 Rebecca Solnit, *Hope in the Dark: Untold Histories, Wild Possibilities*, 3rd ed. (Chicago, Haymarket Books, 2016), 24.

2 In the context of religion, limbo is the region on the border between heaven and hell, a midway state or place.

3 Varying side effects of the protest include tear gas, noise pollution, increase in waste production, etc. As such, it is important to note that non-human entities of animal and plant life have also been affected.

4 The National Security Law is a top down, all-encompassing decree passed by the People's Republic of China to protect and prevent anti-nationalistic actions. Passed on June 30, 2020, the law is in conflict with The Basic Law protection freedom of speech and action, signed during Hong Kong's handover in 1997.

5 Lily Kuo, "China's Great Firewall Descends on Hong Kong Internet Users," *The Guardian*, July 8, 2020, https://www.theguardian.com/world/2020/jul/08/china-great-firewall-descends-hong-kong-internet-users.

6 The Apothecary Grave-Garden is a term designed to describe the overall program of this thesis. Simultaneously a space of care for the living, the dead, human, and non-human, seven multi-scalar interventions with non-standardized architectural elements require participation from its users to be fully activated.

CHARISSE
FOO

THE CONSTRUCTED RUIN

400

(P—1000)

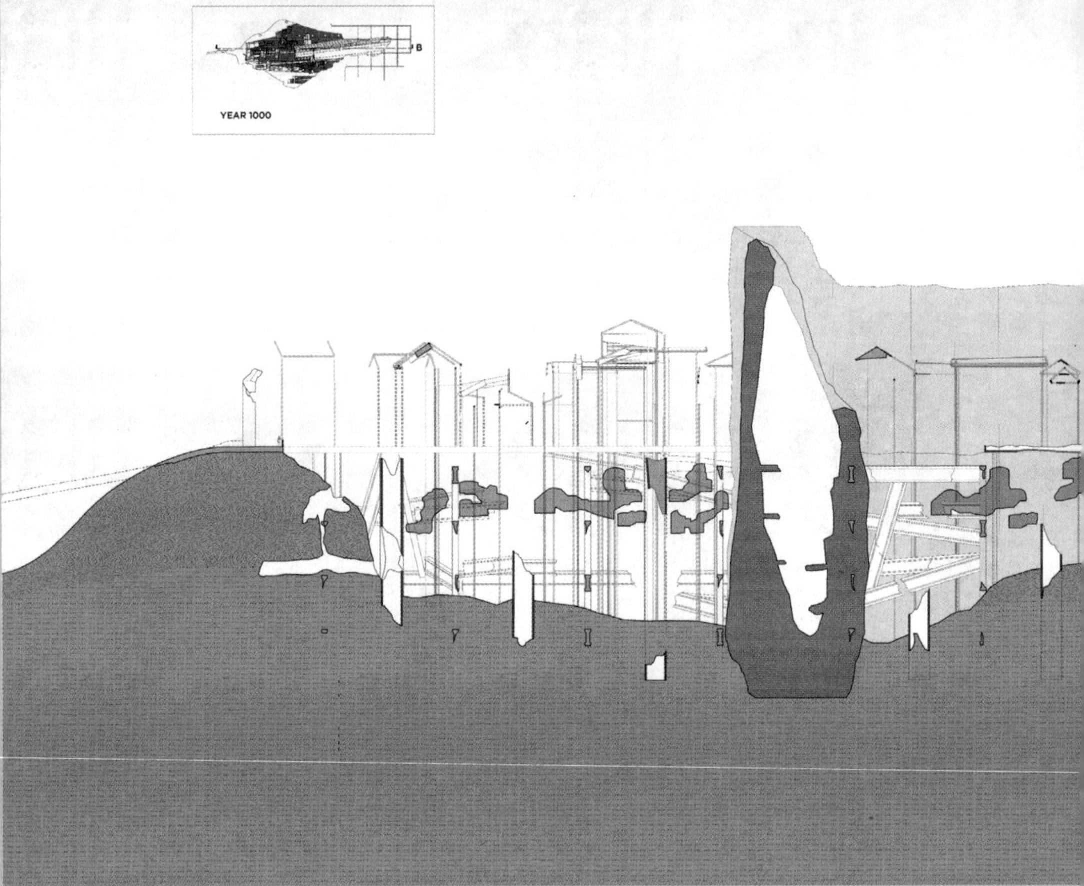
B
YEAR 1000

"The Constructed Ruin" explores the tension between the visual and physical construct, through the lens of historic preservation. In anticipation of gradual and catastrophic decay, the project translates the Italian hilltop town of Civita di Bagnoregio into an archived representation of itself: a future ruin that compresses history into material fragments.

Home to a dwindling population of twelve, Civita is visited by thousands of tourists each summer, attracted by the medieval town precariously perched on quickly eroding volcanic tuff. It can only be reached by a single footbridge, which has in turn created the iconic view of Civita: picturesquely framed from a fixed vantage point throughout its history. Today, a webcam sponsored by the town makes a live stop-motion film of the same view every five minutes, making Civita a life-sized stage set.

Drawing on Civita's history as a filming location—an alternate life where it becomes a place of magic, theatricality, and contested identity—this thesis asks, can we inhabit images? If so, it is the view from the inside that is most revealing. As the city decays, it is archived, translated, and condensed: its physical collapse caused by landslides and soil erosion is mirrored in a collapse into cataloged material. The construction of these parallel spaces for the preserved city revolves around the perspectival and historic construction of that single image of Civita; conversely, that image is fragmented into multiple versions of an imagined past and a reconstructed future.

All images by Charisse Foo, 2017. P.401: *Section A, 3000 AD*. Previous spread: *Section B, 3000 AD*. Opposite page top: *Section C, 3000 AD*. Bottom: *Section D, 3000 AD*.

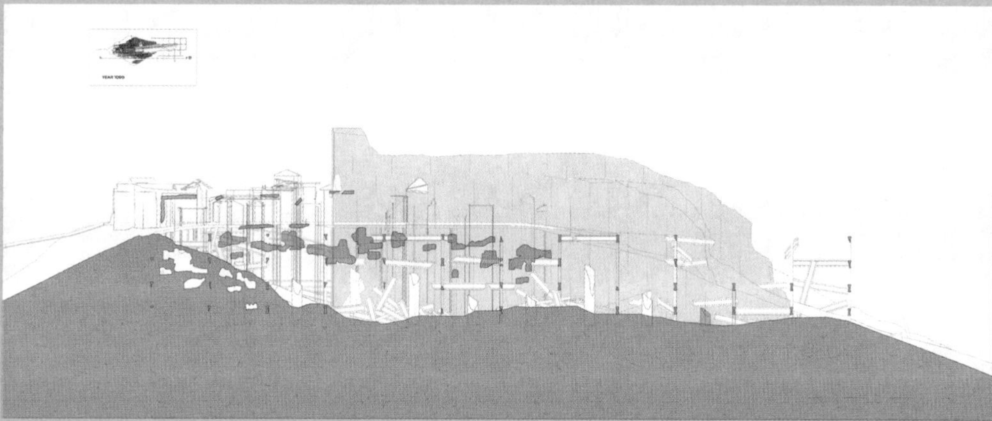

Previous spread and this spread: Perspectives of Civita di Bagnoregio.

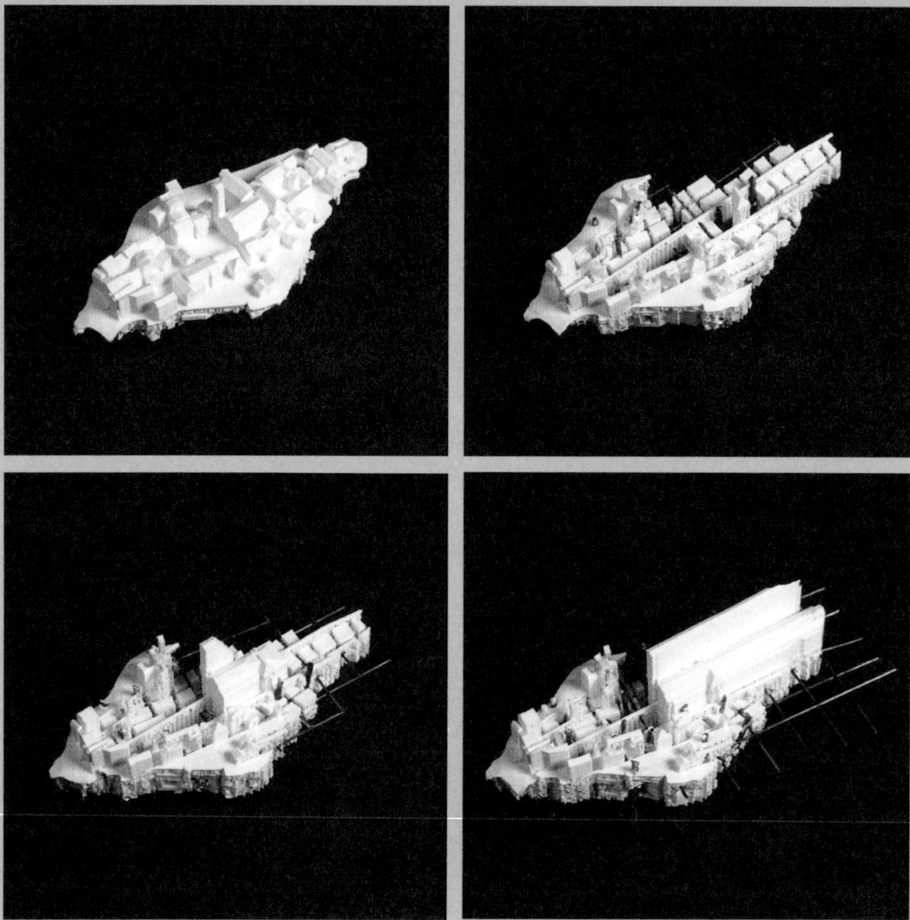

This spread: PLA models showing decay and development from 2000–3000 AD. (*6 Models, 6 Eras.*)

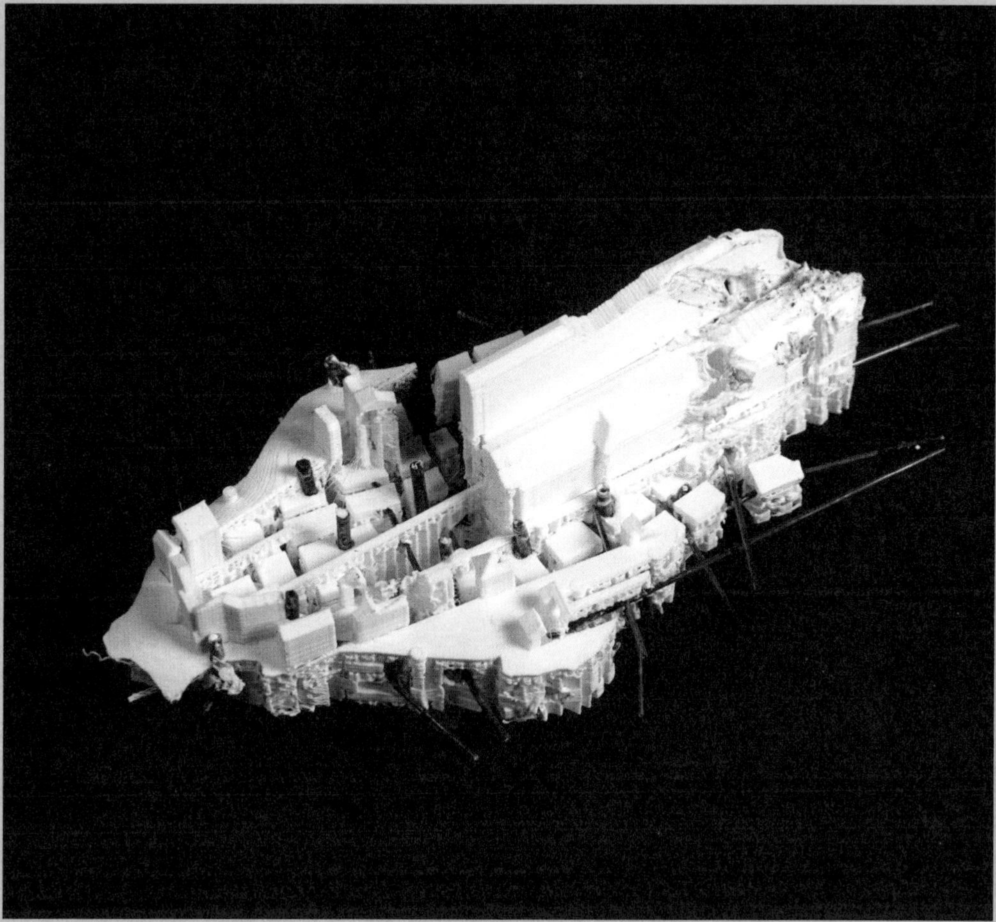

This page: Fifteen edited images of Civita from its live webcam, assembled in an interactive viewing device. (*Constructing A View.*)

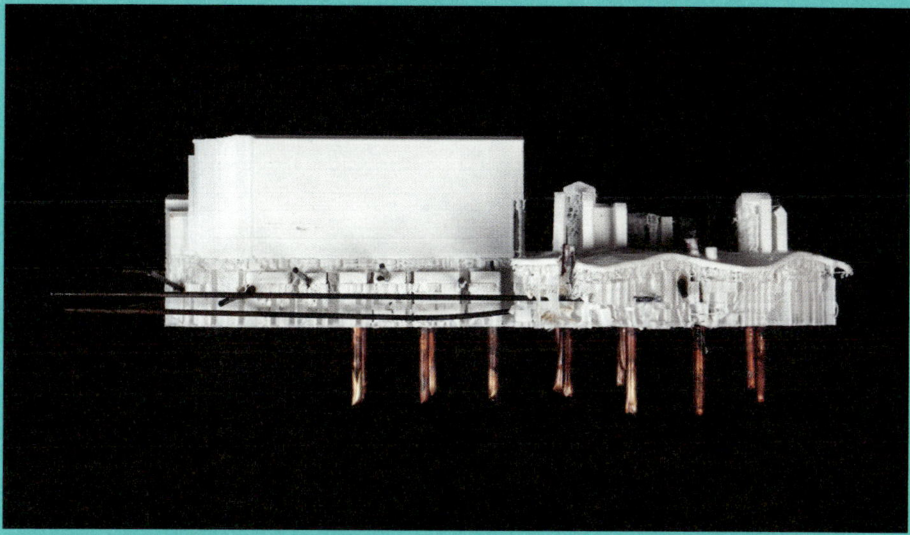

Top: *Civita di Bagnoregio, 2750 AD* (detail). Bottom: *Civita di Bagnoregio, 3000 AD* (detail).

Hansy Better Barraza is a Professor of Architecture at the Rhode Island School of Design, Founding Principal of Studio Luz Architects, and Co-Founder of BR+A+CE: Building Research + Architecture + Community Exchange, a 501(c)(3) nonprofit dedicated to creating new spaces through community partnerships. Barraza's research focuses on the intersection of design methods, social practices, and equity.

James Biber, FAIA LEED (Cornell AAP B. Arch. '76), practices in New York in his eponymous firm and has taught design at Cornell, Syracuse, and The New School. He believes that architecture is inseparable from issues of identity. Biber has applied this approach in projects as disparate as The Harley-Davidson Museum (Milwaukee, WI), the USA Pavilion at the 2015 Expo (Milan, Italy) and oceanside homes (Montauk, NY). At one point every single staff member in his firm was proudly a Cornell AAP grad. He is still waiting for his "Certificate of Appreciation" which he assumes is held up in the mail.

Hallie Black graduated from Cornell University in May of 2019 with a Bachelor of Architecture concentrating in visual representation and a minor in German studies. Her thesis, "Building Up in Flames," won the Charles Goodwin Sands Memorial Thesis Award for design and academic excellence and was nominated for the Michael Rapuano Memorial Award. She is the managing editor of the *Cornell Journal of Architecture* for issues 11 and 12 and completed a teaching associateship for the school's first-year program. Her work has been featured in exhibitions at Cornell and Yale University as well as printed in several publications. Currently, she is the research assistant to Thom Mayne at Morphosis Architects in Los Angeles, California.

Georgine Botha is a recent graduate from Cornell's B. Arch. program with a minor in Art History. Her interests include storytelling and visual representation in architecture. She grew up in Bahrain and is a dual citizen of the Netherlands and South Africa. Her professional experience includes offices in Dubai and New York City.

Gesa Büttner Dias is an architectural designer, writer, and educator whose projects and research investigate the intersection of architecture, landscape, and art. Currently a visiting critic at Cornell AAP, Büttner Dias has lived and worked in Los Angeles, Chongqing, Paris, and Berlin. She received her M. Arch. from the Technical University in Berlin and her postgraduate degree from SCI-Arc. Büttner Dias was cofounding principal of gabpa, a design studio based in Paris and Los Angeles. Gabpa's work was awarded several awards and their urban design proposal for Jakarta, Indonesia was exhibited at the Rotterdam Triennale of Architecture. In her research, Büttner Dias investigates Los Angeles as a case study for the role materiality, vernacular practice, and urban activism play in making a city. Büttner Dias worked for thirteen years at Gehry Partners, where she was the project architect for several award-winning projects, notably the Boulez Hall, the UTS Business School, the Battersea Power Station, and the Beekman Tower.

Kate Chen is an artist and architectural designer based in Berlin, Germany.

She received her B. Arch. from Cornell University in 2018. Kate is interested in entanglements between body, cybernetics and ecology, as well as the spatial-political dimension of these encounters. Kate has worked for Studio Olafur Eliasson, Yoko Seyama, m-a-u-s-e-r, and Storefront for Art & Architecture on artworks, installations, scenography, texts, and exhibitions.

Sam Chermayeff is an architect and cofounder of the office June14 Meyer-Grohbrügge and Chermayeff. He worked for SANAA in Tokyo for more than five years, leading projects such as the Serpentine Pavilion and the curation of the Venice Biennale. He has taught at the Dessau Institute of Architecture, Columbia University, and Cornell University. Chermayeff is a recipient of a Graham Foundation grant and has lectured and exhibited internationally. Both June14 and his private office are engaged in a wide range of projects including furniture and multiunit housing projects.

Ihwa Choi holds a Bachelor of Architecture from Cornell University ('20). Her undergraduate awards include the Charles Goodwin Sands Memorial Bronze Award for her undergraduate thesis exploring the potentials of indeterminacy and ambiguity as new methods of storytelling as well as the Clifton Beckwith Brown Memorial Medal.

Common Accounts, founded in 2015 by Igor Bragado and Miles Gertler at Princeton University, is an office for design inquiry that operates principally between Toronto and Madrid. Their work examines the intersections of the body with spaces both online and IRL, and considers extra-architectural material that often passes below the radar of the discipline. They are recognized for their work in self-design, death and the virtual afterlife, including "Three Ordinary Funerals" for the 2017 Seoul Biennial on Architecture and now a part of the permanent collection of the National Museum of Contemporary Art of Korea. Common Accounts has contributed to publications such as *e-flux*, PIN-UP, 032c, The Avery Review, and FRAME Magazine. Gertler and Bragado have variously taught at Cornell University, the University of Toronto, the University of Waterloo, The Cooper Union, and Instituto Empresa in Madrid, and they are recipients of the Suzanne K. Underwood Prize from Princeton University. Gertler is represented in Toronto by Corkin Gallery, and Bragado was awarded the 2019 Spanish Rome Prize and the 2017 writing prize by the Design History Society.

Brunno Douat is an architect and urban designer who graduated from Federal University of Paraná. Brunno currently works as the head of the architecture department at MUPA–Museu Paranaense and is the co-founder of BOMBUS, a young architecture and design practice based in Curitiba, Brazil.

Luke Douglas Erickson is currently a designer with Morris Adjmi Architects in New York City and Excursus in Brooklyn. His drawings have been exhibited in London and New York and he is frequently an invited guest critic at institutions across the United States. Luke is a Registered Architect in the state of New York.

Jacques Ferrier is an architect and urban planner. His work follows a clear philosophy aiming to create architecture and cities for creative and sustainable societies. Jacques Ferrier is the author of a number of articles and books and has been the subject of monographs, notably The Architecture of Jacques Ferrier (London: Thames & Hudson, 2016).

Charisse Foo graduated with a Bachelor of Architecture from Cornell University, where she was awarded the Charles Goodwin Sands Memorial Medal for excellence in her undergraduate thesis. She started her career as a CGI designer at DBOX in New York City and is now based in Singapore. Charisse is fascinated by the creation of literary and visual worlds, and the potential of fiction to examine the ethical and the critical realities of architecture. Her recent work explores the role of time in undermining notions of architectural permanence. She was once described as a poetic pragmatist, an expression she cherishes to this day.

Lior Galili is an Israeli architect, urban researcher, and educator based in New York City. Her research explores the intersection between architecture, media, and public space. She holds a master's degree in architecture from the Harvard Graduate School of Design and a B. Arch. from the Cooper Union School of Architecture.

Munjer Hashim is a Bangladeshi, multidisciplinary designer and artist based in New York City. He has exhibited at the AEDES ArchitekturForum in Berlin, Germany, the A+D Museum in Los Angeles, and a83 Gallery in Soho, New York. Munjer has also been published nationally and internationally, recently in Houston: Genetic City (Actar: 2020), PLAT, and Fresh Meat Journal XII. He was the 2020 Steven Myron Holl Foundation / 'T' Space Architectural Resident.

Felix Heisel is an architect and academic working towards the systematic redesign of our built environment as resource storage in an endless cycle of use and reconfiguration. He is an assistant professor in the Department of Architecture at Cornell University, where he directs the Circular Construction Lab. He is also partner at 2hs Architekten und Ingenieur PartGmbB in Germany, an office specialized on the development of circular prototypologies. Heisel received numerous awards for his work and published widely, including the books Addis Ababa: A Manifesto on African Progress with Hebel, Wisniewska, and Nash (Ruby Press, 2019), Cultivated Building Materials with Hebel (Birkhäuser, 2017), Lessons of Informality with Kifle (Birkhäuser, 2016), and Building from Waste with Hebel and Wisniewska (Birkhäuser, 2014).

Samia Henni is an architectural historian and Assistant Professor of History of Architecture and Urbanism at Cornell University's College of Architecture, Art and Planning. She is the author of the multi-award-winning Architecture of Counterrevolution: The French Army in Northern Algeria (gta Verlag, 2017; Éditions B42, 2019), the editor of War Zones: gta papers 2 (gta Verlag, 2018), and the maker of the exhibitions Housing Pharmacology / Right to Housing (Manifesta 13, Marseille, 2020) and Discreet Violence: Architecture and the French War in Algeria (Zurich,

Rotterdam, Berlin, Johannesburg, Paris, Prague, Ithaca, Philadelphia, 2017–19).

Valeria Rachel Herrera is an artist and designer who works in a variety of media including printmaking, sculpture, drawing, and architectural explorations. Valeria holds an MFA in Printmaking from the Rhode Island School of Design (RISD) and a Bachelor of Architecture professional degree from the Syracuse University School of Architecture, where she serves as a full-time Assistant Teaching Professor.

José Ibarra is Assistant Professor of Architecture at the University of Virginia and director of research and transformation of CODA. Ibarra received a B. Arch. from Cornell University and a Post-Professional M. Arch. from Princeton University. He is co-editor of the forthcoming book, Werewolf: The Architecture of Lunacy, Shapeshifting, and Material Metamorphosis.

Olalekan Jeyifous (b. 1977) is a Brooklyn-based visual artist who has exhibited at venues such as the Studio Museum in Harlem, the MoMA, and the Guggenheim Bilbao. In addition to his extensive exhibition history, he has spent over a decade creating large-scale artwork for a variety of public spaces.

Eleanor Krause (Cornell M. Arch. 2019, Middlebury College 2014) pursues architecture that leverages climate change to reconstitute the individual and the planetary: a proposition practical and theoretical, calculated and intuitive. Her graduate thesis received the Shreve Award and will be published in Archiworld's "Excellent Student Works from 20 Prestigious World's Top Universities."

LUCITO is a multidisciplinary art and design practice founded in Minneapolis by Andrew Lucia (M. Arch. UPENN, 2008) and Iroha Ito (M. Arch. Cornell AAP, 2015). Their work spans the visual arts, conceptual art, architecture, and land art. Lucia is currently a visiting faculty at the Weitzman School of Design, having formerly held positions at Cornell University and the University of Minnesota. Prior to LUCITO, Ito worked in award-winning architecture firms in New York and Japan.

Katie MacDonald is Cofounder of After Architecture and an Assistant Professor at the University of Virginia. She is a recipient of the Tennessee Architecture Fellowship, the Paul M. Heffernan Grant, the Arnold W. Brunner Grant, the AIA Upjohn Research Initiative, and was named a Next Progressive by Architect Magazine. She holds a B.Arch. from Cornell University and an M.Arch from Harvard University.

Akshay Mehra is a Neukom Postdoctoral Fellow at Dartmouth College, where he leverages the rock record to better understand the history of life on Earth. He earned a B. Arch. from Cornell University in 2011. In 2019, he received a PhD in Geosciences from Princeton University under the guidance of Adam Maloof.

Aleksandr Mergold, AIA, is a partner at Austin+Mergold, an architecture, landscape, and design practice, a testing ground for his inquiry into the contemporary interpretation of spolia, a form of radical reuse of materials, spaces, and ideas. This research continued at Cornell University where Mergold taught architecture. Prior to the practice and the teaching, Mergold worked at Pentagram in New York on a variety of architecture and design projects. A third-generation architect, Aleksandr was born in the ancient city of Tashkent, that contains simultaneous traces of the Great Silk Road, colonial conquests, and a socialist planned economy.

Isidoro Michan-Guindi (b. Mexico City, 1990) received his Master of Architecture from Princeton University in 2018 and a Bachelor of Architecture from Cornell University in 2015. He is Principal at Isidoro Michan-Guindi, based in Mexico City.

Meredith Miller is an architect, founding member of T+E+A+M, and Associate Professor of Architecture at the University of Michigan's Taubman College of Architecture and Urban Planning.

Michael Murphy is the Founding Principal and Executive Director of MASS Design Group, an interdisciplinary architecture and design collective. As a designer, writer, and teacher, his work investigates the social and political consequences of the built world. MASS's work has been published in over a thousand publications, from the New York Times, Domus, the Washington Post, to Log. MASS was awarded the 2017 Cooper Hewitt National Design Award, the 2018 Arts and Letters Award, and the 2020 WSJ. Magazine Architecture Innovator award. Michael has taught at the Harvard Graduate School of Design, the University of Michigan, Columbia University, MIT, and Cornell. Michael is from Poughkeepsie, NY, and holds a Master of Architecture from Harvard Graduate School of Design and a Bachelor of Arts from the University of Chicago.

Felipe Orensanz is a Mexico City-based architect and urbanist. His work has been published in journals such as Pidgin, CLOG, MONU, Displacements, Ground Up, Horizonte, Lunch, STUDIO, and Bracket. He has been a fellow at the HKW Berlin, The People's Forum, Institute for Critical Social Inquiry, and Art Omi.

Javier Pérez Puchalt is a Spanish architect and researcher educated internationally. He graduated in 2017 from the Federal School of Technology in Lausanne, Switzerland. He is currently carrying theoretical research as a PhD candidate on the architectural potential of the city at the University of Bologna and the UCL, Belgium.

Anthony J. Piermarini is an Associate Professor of Architecture at the Wentworth Institute of Technology, Founding Principal of Studio Luz Architects, and Co-Founder of BR+A+CE: Building Research + Architecture + Community Exchange, a 501(c)(3) nonprofit dedicated to creating new spaces through community partnerships. Piermarini's academic interests lie in the intersection of social justice, media of representation, design research, and built material expression at any scale.

David Salomon is the Coordinator of the Architectural Studies program at Ithaca College, where is an Associate Professor in Art History. He is the co-curator of the exhibition Ambiguous Territory: Architecture, Landscape, and the Postnatural.

Bob Schalkwijk was born in Rotterdam in 1933 and has lived in Mexico since 1958. His work as a photographer seeks to capture the essences—the amenable and universal aspects—of daily life. He published Mexico City (Paul Hamlyn, Spring Books) in 1965, the first of a long list of books and exhibition catalogues.

Kyle Schumann is Cofounder of After Architecture and an Assistant Professor at the University of Virginia. He is a recipient of the Tennessee Architecture Fellowship, the Robert A.M. Stern Architects Travel Fellowship, the Robert James Eidlitz Travel Fellowship, and was named a Next Progressive by Architect Magazine. He holds a B.Arch. from Cornell University and an M.Arch from Princeton University.

Duncan Steele is a Toronto-based architectural designer interested in narrative drawing and print ephemera. His thesis project, "Drawn to the Gutter," proposes sequential maps that represent a site's many AFTERs, AND SOs, BUT THENs, and SUDDENLYs. He received his B. Arch. from Cornell University in 2020 while in hiding.

T+E+A+M is an award-winning architecture practice led by Thom Moran + Ellie Abrons + Adam Fure + Meredith Miller and based in Ann Arbor, Michigan.

CoCo Tin is a multimedia architectural designer based between Hong Kong and New York City. Her work draws from art, theory, and activism in the public sphere, forming a bottom-up, interdisciplinary approach to architecture. She is currently working on a research publication, A Healthier Place: Sanatorium Lessons for Architecture Today, investigating architecture and health. She holds a Bachelor of Architecture with a minor in Art History from Cornell University, where her thesis was awarded the Charles Goodwin Sands Memorial Medal for exceptional merit.

Dan Torop is a photographer whose images examine how we shape and imagine the land. He is co-editor of ASMR4, a series of photography monographs. He contributes code to darktable, an open source tool for processing photographs. He is an Assistant Professor at Cornell University's Department of Art.

Jaret Vadera is a transdisciplinary artist whose work examines how imaging and translation colonize the ways that we see the worlds around and within us. Vadera hacks different visual systems, and rewires them to rupture, self-destruct, and open up parallel ways of seeing. His work is influenced by decolonial theory, science fiction, and the study of impossible objects. Vadera's prints, collages, sculptures, videos, and installations have been exhibited and screened internationally at venues such as the Queens Museum, MoMA, the Smithsonian APAC, Asia Society, Aga Khan Museum, Bhau Daji Lad Museum, and the Maraya Art Centre.

Peter van Assche began his career in science and experimental mathematics before transitioning into architecture. He is the founding principal of bureau SLA, an Amsterdam-based architecture firm. As an office, bureau SLA consists of a team of architects and builders, supported by architectural historians, landscape architects, and energy experts. The studio builds and develops in the city from their own initiatives and with their own manpower.

With this trial-and-error mentality, van Assche discovers the full potential of material use, energy, waste flows, smart living and working, and development processes. Van Assche is the chairman of the Committee for Architectural Review and Monuments in Utrecht, supervisor architecture for the Utrecht station area, and professor of Architecture and Circular Thinking at the Academy of Architecture Amsterdam. He received a Master of Information Technology (cum laude) from the Technical University Eindhoven and obtained his architecture degree from the Rotterdam Academy of Architecture.

Jha D Williams is a Senior Associate at MASS Design Group and Co-Director of the Public Memory and Memorials Lab. As a Project Manager, she has contributed to the Gun Violence Memorial Project, Franklin Park Action Plan, and Kendall School Division II Memorial. Before joining MASS, she worked as a Designer at Sasaki Associates for four years. She received her Bachelor of Science in Architecture from Northeastern University and her Master of Architecture I from the University of Pennsylvania. Prior to pursuing her graduate degree, she taught design studios at the Boston Architectural College. Outside of architecture, Jha D is a spoken word artist, event producer, and overall SpaceMaker for LGBTQ+ communities of color.

CORNELL JOURNAL
OF ARCHITECTURE

ISSUE 12
AFTER

Cover Studio Elana Schlenker.

Front End John Martin, *The Great Day of His Wrath*, 1851–53. Oil on canvas, 197 cm × 303 cm. Courtesy of Wikimedia Commons, public domain.

Back End John Martin, *The Plains of Heaven*, 1851. Oil on canvas, 199 cm × 307 cm. Courtesy of Wikimedia Commons, public domain.

16–23 Courtesy of Akshay Mehra.

26 Collection of the Wadsworth Atheneum Museum of Art, Hartford, CT, 1942.281. Photo by Allen Phillips.

30–32 Courtesy of José Ibarra.

33–34 Courtesy of Nick Middleton.

37–43 Courtesy of Isidoro Michan-Guindi.

46–48 Courtesy of the National Library of France, public domain.

49 Courtesy of the National Archives of the Netherlands / Anefo, public domain.

50 Courtesy of Edd Simons.

51 Courtesy of The Architects' Journal.

53–54 © René Burri / Magnum Photos.

56 Courtesy of bureau SLA and Overtreders W.

63–64 Courtesy of Felix Heisel.

65–66 Courtesy of 2hs Architekten und Ingenieur PartGmbB.

67 Courtesy of Felix Heisel.

67–68 Courtesy of 2hs Architekten und Ingenieur PartGmbB.

68 Courtesy of Felix Heisel.

69 Courtesy of 2hs Architekten und Ingenieur PartGmbB.

70–72 Courtesy of Werner Sobek with Dirk E. Hebel and Felix Heisel.

77 Courtesy of the US National Archives, 519835, public domain.

79 Courtesy of the US National Archives, 519833, public domain.

80 Courtesy of the US National Archives, 519836, public domain.

82 Courtesy of the US National Archives, 519831, public domain.

85–92 Courtesy of Duncan Steele.

96 Courtesy of John Horner.

97 Courtesy of Hansy Better Barraza.

98 Courtesy of John Horner.

100 Courtesy of Studio Luz Architects.

102 Courtesy of John Horner.

104 Courtesy of Studio Luz Architects.

106 Courtesy of John Horner.

110–118 Courtesy of LUCITO. All base images and data for this project have been sourced through the public domain from the US Geological Survey. Special thanks to Sean Burkholder for aiding in the sourcing of images, and to Jeffrey Oman for historic consultation and insight.

122–130 Courtesy of Katie MacDonald and Kyle Schumann.

136 Courtesy of La Mode En Images.

139 Courtesy of the National Library of France, public domain. © The Estate of R. Buckminster Fuller.

140 Courtesy of NASA, public domain.

143 © IMAXtree Group.

144 Courtesy of Balenciaga.

148 Collection of the Museum of the City of New York, 75.200.58.

149 Courtesy of Alexander Severin.

150 Courtesy of Lior Galili.

153 Reprinted by permission from Jill Steinberg.

154 Courtesy of the NYC Department of City Planning, public domain.

155 Reprinted by permission from Jill Steinberg.

156 Courtesy of Stillman Development International.

157 Courtesy of Elliot Kaufman.

158 Courtesy of Stillman Development International.

160 Collection of the Museum of the City of New York, 41.420.514. Courtesy of Stillman Development International.

165–179 Courtesy of Ihwa Choi.

181 Courtesy of the Library of Congress, LC-DIG-ppmsca-41913, public domain.

182 Courtesy of the Library of Congress, LC-DIG-stereo-1s06996, public domain.

184 Courtesy of the Library of Congress, LC-USZ62-89936, public domain.

185 Collection of the New-York Historical Society, 2013.12.

187 Image courtesy of James Biber.

191 Collection of the National Gallery of Art, Washington, DC, 1967.13.9.

193–200 Courtesy of Common Accounts.

204 Courtesy of Museu Paranaense (MUPA).

208 Reprinted by permission of Instituto Lina Bo e P. M. Bardi.

210 Courtesy of Museu Paranaense (MUPA). Courtesy of Instituto Lina Bo e P. M. Bardi. Courtesy of Hugo Segawa.

211 Courtesy of Hugo Segawa. Courtesy of Instituto Lina Bo e P. M. Bardi.

212 Courtesy of Rubem Rodrigues Nogueira Jr. Courtesy of Instituto Lina Bo e P. M. Bardi.

214 Courtesy of Museu de Arte de São Paulo (MASP) Research Center, image courtesy of Instituto Lina Bo e P. M. Bardi.

217–224 Courtesy of Marie N. Benaboud.

229–236 Courtesy of Dan Torop.

240–242 Courtesy of Gesa Büttner Dias.

248 Courtesy of Victoria Clarke, images courtesy of Gesa Büttner Dias.

249 Courtesy of Sam Gomez, image courtesy of Gesa Büttner Dias.

250 Courtesy of Nina Koscica, images courtesy of Gesa Büttner Dias.

257–261 Courtesy of Hallie Black.

263–272 Courtesy of Jaret Vadera.

277–283 Courtesy of Valeria Rachel Herrera.

290–299 Courtesy of Ferrier Marchetti Studio.

301–312 Courtesy of Eleanor Krause.

320–321 Courtesy of Eray Aydin, images courtesy of Sam Chermayeff.

324–328 Courtesy of Luke Douglas Erickson.

331–341 Courtesy of Georgine Botha.

343–351 Courtesy of Munjer Hashim.

353–363 Courtesy of Olalekan Jeyifous.

365–375 Courtesy of T+E+A+M.

378–381 Courtesy of MASS Design Group.

384–388 © Bob Schalkwijk, images courtesy of Felipe Orensanz.

392–398 Courtesy of CoCo Tin.

401–413 Courtesy of Charisse Foo.

IMAGE CREDITS

Cornell Journal of Architecture 12: After
Department of Architecture
College of Architecture, Art, and Planning
139 E. Sibley Hall
Ithaca, NY 14853
U.S.A.
Tel: (607) 255-5236
cornelljournalofarchitecture.cornell.edu
cjoa@cornell.edu

Chair, Department of Architecture
Andrea Simitch

Editor-in-Chief
Val Warke (B.Arch. '77)

Managing Editor
Hallie Black (B.Arch. '19)
Todd Petrie (B.Arch. '20)

Submission Editors
Rabei Javaid Bhatti (B.Arch. '22)
Auri Ford (B.Arch. '21)
Sam Gomez (B.Arch. '20)
Zeli Grey (B.Arch. '22)
Gracie Meek (B.Arch. '22)
Jonathan Plass (B.Arch. '22)
Aishwarya Sreenivas (B.Arch. '21)
Chloe Tsui (B.Arch. '22)
Jessie Xiang (B.Arch. '21)

Editorial Participants
Ottavia Boletto (B.Arch. '20)
Simón Campuzano (M.S.AAD '22)
Sean Gowin (M.S.AAD '20)
Claire Guffey (B.Arch. '20)
David Ni (B.Arch. '24)
Reuben Posada (M.Arch. '20)
Mitchie Qiao (B.Arch. '21)
Shruti Shah (B.Arch. '20)
Yolande Wen (B.Arch. '24)
Qian Xiao (M.S.AAD '20)
Haotian Zhang (M.S.AAD '20)
Peng Zhang (M.S.AAD '20)

Design
Studio Elana Schlenker

Printing
Ofset Yapımevi

Publishing
Cornell AAP Publications

ISBN: 978-0-9972602-5-0
ISSN: 0731-5384
Library of Congress
Control Number: 2021910789

Our appreciation to:

The students and special guests in the seminar "Architectural Publications: CJoA12," whose insights and perspectives were essential in the development of this journal.

The students and faculty of the Department of Architecture at Cornell and in the College of Architecture, Art, and Planning, whose advice and support motivates the substance of this effort.

All of those who contributed to this journal, for their commitment, efforts, and patience.

And especially, to the memory of Mrs. Ruth Thomas, whose belief in the importance of speaking, writing, and publishing architecture, and whose support in honor of her son, Preston Thomas, continues to provide the funding and inspiration without which this journal a nd its predecessors would never have been possible.

Cornell AAP
Architecture Art Planning

COLOPHON